THE
TIME
OF
THE
ASSASSINS

Also by **Claire Sterling**
THE MASARYK CASE
THE TERROR NETWORK

THE
TIME
OF
THE
ASSASSINS

Claire Sterling

A WILLIAM ABRAHAMS BOOK

HOLT, RINEHART AND WINSTON
NEW YORK

For my beloved Abby and Luke

First published in January 1984 by Holt, Rinehart
and Winston, 383 Madison Avenue,
New York, New York 10017.
Published simultaneously in Canada by Holt, Rinehart
and Winston of Canada, Limited.

Library of Congress Cataloging in Publication Data
Sterling, Claire.
The time of the assassins.
"A William Abrahams book."
Includes bibliographical references and index.
1. Criminal investigation—Italy—Rome. 2. Offenses
against heads of state—Italy—Rome. 3. John Paul II,
Pope, 1920–   . 4. Agca, Mehmet Ali. 5. Terrorists
—Turkey—Biography. I. Title.
HV8073.S733   1984   364.1'524'0945634   83–18382
ISBN: 0-03-063554-3

First Edition

Designer: Robert Bull

Printed in the United States of America
1 3 5 7 9 10 8 6 4 2

Grateful acknowledgment is made for use of excerpts
from *The Heroin Trail*, copyright © 1973, 1974 by
Newsday, Inc, based on *Newsday*'s Pulitzer
Prize–winning series. Reprinted by
permission of Newsday, Inc.

ISBN 0-03-063554-3

ACKNOWLEDGMENTS

While I was writing this book in Tuscany, Judy Harris was my lifeline in Rome. On special assignment for NBC to follow the story of the papal shooting, she went after it with skill, perception, and style.

She knew everybody, checked everything, talked herself into getting in everywhere, and had an all but infallible instinct for what to keep or discard.

We used to talk on the phone every night, turning the day's news around and around, matching it against what we knew and remembered, and looking for the giveaway signs of manipulation and misinformation—which got to be all too easy to spot after a while.

I don't know how I could have gotten through the book without her help, or how either of us could have gotten through some of the rougher days without counting on the other to hang on to what we both believed.

Thanks, Judy.

•   •

My husband, Tom, doesn't really need my written words to know how I feel about the help he gave me. He was patient, he understood, he had remarkable political antennae, and his infallible eye for the wrong word in the wrong place saved me more times than I could count. There was hardly a day when he didn't take time from his own writing to help grace mine.

—C.S
October 1983

CONTENTS

PROLOGUE **A WALL OF MIRRORS** 1

PART ONE **DISCOVERING THE PLOT** 15

PART TWO **PUBLISHING THE PLOT, DISTURBING THE PEACE** 97

PART THREE **ANSWERS AND ENIGMAS** 199

NOTES 236

INDEX 251

PROLOGUE

A WALL
OF
MIRRORS

1

The order of arrest for Mehmet Ali Agca signed last night by Attorney General Achille Gallucci accuses the Turkish terrorist of "an attempt on the life of a head of state . . . in concourse with other persons who remain unknown." This last "is not just a precaution; it is more than that," he said.

[Judge] Luciano Infelisi, the examining magistrate who signed the warrant, said more explicitly: "For us, there is documentary proof that Mehmet Ali Agca did not act alone."

LA STAMPA *of Turin, May 15, 1981 (datelined Rome)*

Police are convinced, according to government sources, that Mr. Agca acted alone.

THE NEW YORK TIMES, *May 15, 1981 (datelined Rome)*

He did not act alone. We know that now, since he has said so himself and the Italian judiciary has confirmed it. If not for Agca's testimony, no amount of fragmentary evidence would have convinced the world that the Bulgarian secret service, acting on behalf of the Soviet Union's KGB, conspired to murder the head of the Roman Catholic Church. Much of the world still refuses to believe it: because it seems unbelievable, and because the Western public, deliberately deceived by its own leaders, was led to conclude that there was never a conspiracy at all.

It took less than forty-eight hours to mount the deception. Pope John Paul II was shot and very nearly killed in St. Peter's Square on the afternoon of May 13, 1981. The first official falsehood showed up on the morning of May 15, in *The New York Times*, as cited above, and elsewhere in the international press.

There might have been no need for the cover-up if the Pope's would-be killer had been killed in turn, as planned, eliminating the crucial witness who might tell what he knew. Long afterward we would learn that he was meant to be murdered as soon as he got away from St. Peter's Square—if an enraged mob or a gun-happy cop didn't get him first.

He was saved by a fluke in the form of a sturdy little nun, who saw him fire his heavy Browning and hung onto his arm until the carabinieri got to him, before his treacherous companions could. ("Not me! Not me!" he kept shouting, struggling to fight free of Suor Letizia's clutching hands. "Yes, you! It was you!" she cried back.)

Alive and in prison, Mehmet Ali Agca was a time bomb, ticking away until the inevitable day when he would be induced to talk. So began a singular Western effort to discredit what Agca might say before he said it, suppress the supporting evidence, dismiss him as an incorrigible liar of unbalanced mind. Why the governments of free nations should have gone to such lengths to shield the Soviet Union is a long story, told only in part here, of ingenuous expectations and self-inflicted defeats. *How* they did it is easier for me to explain than why, because I saw it happening from the start, and went through the punishing experience of trying to get past the shield right up to the end.

I was lucky to have had the chance. It isn't every day that a reporter gets an offer like the one I had from the *Reader's Digest:* take as long as you like, go wherever you please, spend as much as you must to get as close to the truth as you can.

It took nine months before I published my first findings; and Agca was already talking in private to an Italian judge by then. When the first arrests were made on the strength of his confession, in late November 1982, his image was so effectively distorted that hardly anybody was prepared to believe him. Those who might have been willing to listen were discouraged by semiofficial leaks to the press. A spokesman for Whitehall in London warned against crediting "convicts who sing to get out of jail."[1] German and Israeli secret services were quoted in *The New York Times* as blaming the arrests on "doubtful information or downright disinformation."[2] The CIA's deputy director in Rome was quoted in the Italian press as telling the interior minister bluntly: "You have no proof"[3]—this last while rumors were spreading through Europe that Agca had been told what to say, secretly, in his prison cell, by the CIA itself.

Looking back, it seems amazing that the story could have been turned around so swiftly and smoothly, before the eyes of several hundred journalists gathered in Rome from the four corners of the globe to cover the papal shooting. The truth was close enough to touch for a fleeting instant, and then it was gone. At the first sign of a probable conspiracy, government and Church leaders instantly perceived the dangers of exposing it. A wall of refracting mirrors went up overnight, deflecting our vision at every turn.

By and large, this seemed to escape the attention of editors abroad, engrossed in the immediate drama. Scarcely half a dozen reporters stayed with the story, trying to look behind the wall from Rome to Ankara and Istanbul to Vienna, Zurich, Hamburg, Munich, Bonn. For this we were regarded with skeptical amusement by our colleagues, and with mounting irritation by a formidable array of Western politicians—of left, right, and center—and Western secret services, including the CIA. In time, we came to be seen as an international menace, threatening peace among nations if not the entire planetary order. These feelings would harden into astonishing hostility when our findings were substantiated by the Italian courts.

It was the crime of the century, the press had said, thereupon retiring from the field. Certainly no other in this century compared to it. Somebody had tried to murder the Pope of Rome, spiritual leader of three-quarters of a billion Catholics, nearly a sixth of the human race. Within two days, the Italian magistrates most closely concerned had found evidence of an organized plot. Yet not a single big newspaper or television network had sent a crack team of reporters to investigate the crime in all its enormity.

Those on the scene stuck resolutely to the daily news, grinding out column after column on the trajectory of the bullets, the nature of the papal wounds, the hospital's hourly bulletins. Their editors would keep them in Rome just so long as Pope John Paul hovered between life and death. When it was clear that he was going to live, they went home.

There was little to detain them by then, all visible trace of a so-called plot having disappeared. The seeming discrepancy between those early accounts in *La Stampa* and *The New York Times* had soon been ironed out. Dr. Infelisi's original warrant for Mehmet Ali Agca was revised, deleting the reference to "other persons who remain unknown"; and in a matter of days after signing it, Dr. Infelisi himself was off the case. "We have no proof, no hints, no clues, no evidence at all that there was an international plot," said Alfredo Lazzarini, head of Italy's DIGOS, the antiterrorist police.[4]

The world was left with a somewhat confusing yet somehow comforting image of the Pope's would-be assassin that would never quite fade. He was a Turk: that was something people would always remember. It made him truly a stranger in Western eyes, coming from an alien and indistinct Islamic land, stirring hazy visions of fierce mustachioed Ottomans, starving Armenians, and Ambleresque Byzantine intrigue. (Clearer visions of a Westernized, declericalized Turkey holding down NATO's easternmost flank did not appear to get in the way. For columnist Joseph Kraft, writing in the *Washington Post* that May, the attempt on the Pope's life was a lesson to us all about this "turbulent Islamic society, pregnant with nasty surprises."[5])

Personally and politically, Agca was held to be everything and its opposite. Planetwide headlines had made him out to be at once an unregenerate neo-Nazi and a Moslem fanatic consumed with hatred for the Christian West; a cold professional killer already convicted of murder at home—"a terrorist with a capital 'T,' " Dr. Lazzarini called him—and an irrational crackpot; a member of Turkey's right-wing Gray Wolves, who presumably travel in packs, and a loner—above all, a loner.

Dr. Infelisi's documentary proof to the contrary was not mentioned again. Agca, caught in the act with a smoking gun in his hand, remained the only guilty party on the scene. Official investigators shrugged off the question of his possible accomplices. Nobody raised the issue at his brisk three-day trial that July. Summing up for the State, Prosecutor Nicoló Amato pronounced this to have been an "isolated attack" by a "terrorist who came from nowhere." Agca was "an exalted paranoiac," he said, "a manic psychopath," and a man of "delirious fanaticism . . . who alone had planned and decided to carry out this act of terrifying obscenity."[6]

Allowing for Dr. Amato's ardent prose, that seemed to settle it. Agca, who refused to testify in court, was found guilty of firing the gun and sentenced to life imprisonment, the first year in solitary confinement. He did not appeal. His court-appointed lawyer withdrew. To all appearances, the case was closed.

That suited a great many people at topmost international levels who feared—indeed assumed—that the truth, if uncovered, would prove to be awkward, untimely, impolitic, inexpedient, and thus unacceptable.

Much the same reasoning had contributed greatly to the global expansion of international terrorism over the previous decade. The argument went that détente must not be endangered by exposing the Russians' peccadilloes, that scolding them in public would merely bring out the worst in them—in effect that the KGB would go away if we would only be nice to it.

The results could be measured year by year in the rising levels of terrorist equipment and proficiency, assured by the Russians directly or through their surrogates. By 1981, practically all Western governments had a lengthy record of denying in public what they knew in private to be the provenance of these terrorists' training and weapons. Bigger and bolder terrorist strikes, which they might be said to have brought upon themselves, did not deter them from this course. Judging by experience, the Pope's assailants might logically count on their continuing indulgence.

The operation was evidently planned to simulate the kind of mindless terrorist hit that has gradually been accorded a kind of numbed acceptance, a hit designed not so much to eliminate the victim as to frighten the audience. In this instance, however, the purpose was not to frighten the audience but to eliminate the victim. It was no terrorist hit at all. The setting was an elaborate ruse. The assassin had been hired, and paid. He had no passionate ideological commitments, nor did his employers, who were simply agents of a foreign state. Would Western governments—whatever their past performance—help to keep a secret of such magnitude?

They would, and did.

Faced with a crime of the highest international order, against the supreme leader of the largest organized church on earth, a crime committed on Vatican soil by a Turkish citizen whose trail crossed at least seven national frontiers, the Italians were essentially left to deal with it alone. Neither the six other countries implicated directly nor any of Italy's natural allies made an urgent point of gathering relevant information, still less of passing it on to Rome. The papal shooting was "not a matter of intense scrutiny" for the CIA, said one of its senior officials in Washington. "It is an Italian matter, and it would be inappropriate for us to intrude."[7] Yet, as we shall see, the CIA *would* intrude, unaccountably taking the Bulgarian line.

Vital leads were frequently ignored, knowledge infrequently shared, indispensable evidence withheld. An establishmentarian longing to keep the lid on was apparent wherever I went. "Come, now. Whatever makes you believe there was any such thing as an international plot? Our police in Germany really don't see the attack on the Pope as the big operation you seem to think it was," I was told with a tolerant smile by a ranking functionary of West Germany's Bundeskriminalamt.

In general, my interlocutors seemed to think, or hope, that the investigation in Rome wouldn't get anywhere anyway. Had Italy been the land of Keystone Kops it is so often mistaken for, they might have been right—in which event the conspirators' secret might still be intact.

The Vatican itself had seemed more than ready to preserve a discreet silence at the start. The implications of doing otherwise were decidedly alarming for worldwide Catholicism. Apparently, Pope John Paul was not quite of the same mind. He had been aware of who was planning to take his life and why, and even hinted at what was coming a week before it came. "Let us pray that the Lord will keep violence and fanaticism far from the Vatican's walls," he had said to his mystified Swiss Guards at an early mass. We know now that he had in fact been warned in advance by the French intelligence service, SDECE, possibly informed in turn by a Bulgarian defector in Paris.[8]

Once the attack was actually made, then, the Pope was obliged to choose between the Vatican's millennial habits of discretion and the dubious morality of covering up for such infamy. His decision was reflected subtly but discernibly. As he slowly recovered his strength, the Church gradually shifted its stance.

By midsummer, it expressed a first cautious doubt aloud. "Something keeps all this from adding up," commented the *Osservatore Romano* on the second day of Agca's trial. "The very fact of this trial could carry us past the confines of surrealism, because of the evident disparity between small questions that may perhaps never be answered and great ones that will assuredly never be answered. . . . Sentence will be passed, and the questions will remain. Was it madness or something else that guided that homicidal hand?"[9]

At the trial's end, the *Osservatore* ventured a bit further, speaking of "secret ties and conspiracies whose existence is sensed even if it often cannot be proved."[10]

The Papal Secretary of State was a shade more forthright shortly afterward. "A heart (or are they hearts?), a hostile heart, has armed the enemy hand to strike, through the Pope—and this Pope!—at the heart of the Church," said Cardinal Casaroli.[11] Forty-seven days after the attack, the Catholic hierarchy had explicitly discarded the theory of the lone, mad killer and implicitly acknowledged the plot.

A month later, the very court that had tried and convicted Agca went further. The presiding judge, Severino Santiapichi, was president of Rome's Court of Assizes, a jurist whose competence, integrity, and courage symbolized the finest traditions of Italy's independent magistracy. He had suffered vexing restraints imposed on the court in the Agca case, by the State's presentation and the defendant's refusal to take the witness stand. But nothing could keep Judge Santiapichi from speaking his mind when his court issued its formal Statement of Motivation explaining the reasons for Agca's life sentence. Drafted by his judge "in latere" Antonio Abate, filed in Chancery on September 24, 1981, it confirmed Agca's guilt but in every other way demolished the state prosecutor's prose, and case.[12]

Agca "did not come from nowhere," the court declared: "hidden minds" had sent him. He was no "delirious ideologue," felt "no personal hostility" toward the Pope, and "not a word of the proceedings" had shown him to be a religious crank. Far from being crazy, he had "*uncommon gifts of mental equilibrium.*" His "spirit of discipline, professional commitment, and skill in the use of lethal weapons" had made him an ideal instrument for the operation in St. Peter's Square—just that, and no more. In the court's opinion, Agca had "merely been used as a pawn."

The Statement went into considerable detail on the matter of Agca's sanity: "Numerous validated test results . . . have shown no sign in the subject of premonitory symptoms of pathological anomalies that might classify him as mentally retarded." It reported that the official police doctor had found him calm and self-possessed just a few hours after his arrest. "Dr. Giancarlo Cupperi was able to note his alertness and self-control, the normality of his behavior and reactions, his sensory perceptions of place and space. During the interrogation, he showed lucidity and prudence, care in his choice of answers, an ability of response whenever questions touched on difficult themes. . . . The qualities he demonstrated justify a diagnosis of full psychic maturity."[13]

He was, in fact, the Statement went on, "a singular figure of a negative hero, with a different dimension from other assassins of illustrious men." Behind him was "a story concealing a disquieting reality. . . . It is unthinkable that he could have undertaken this difficult project in absolute autonomy, or for his private reasons. We must ask ourselves how those forces who armed and trained Mehmet Ali Agca, who entrusted him with exacting tasks from the assault on Abdi Ipekci [Turkey's leading editor, murdered in 1979] to later terrorist acts, who took the trouble to arrange his escape from prison in Turkey and help him while in hiding, who more recently continued to provide him with conspicuous funds, could ever have allowed him then to take an extraordinary initiative on his own . . . watching impassively as he acted, doing nothing to stop him. . . .

"Grave questions arise concerning the possibility of material complicity in the crime and a plot at high levels. . . . Everything points to the conclusion that Agca was no more than the emerging point of a deep conspiracy, complex and threatening, orchestrated by secret forces, carefully planned and directed down to the smallest detail."

Neither then nor later did the public learn that the legend of the lone, mad killer had thus been destroyed as early as September 1981—wholly, and at the most authoritative level. The court's fifty-one-page Statement of Motivation, representing the sum of knowledge available even then to Italy's outstanding legal minds, might have turned the prevailing international view of the case right back around again. But the Statement, though available for the asking, was never published anywhere in full. The legend of the mad loner continued meanwhile to be artfully cultivated, and skillfully revived whenever fresh evidence should by rights have finished it off for good.

It was rescued *in extremis* as late as the winter of 1983, by which time Italian judicial authorities had formally accused seven people—three in prison already, another four sought by international warrant—of "direct complicity" with Agca in the plot. Some months after these sensational developments, an unnamed CIA spokesman told the *Los Angeles Times* unofficially that Agca was "a known crazy . . . too unstable to be included in an assassination plot, let alone be trusted to do the shooting."[14] The story was promptly picked up and flashed around the world, where it was taken to mean that in the CIA's opinion the Italian authorities were either dunces or dupes.

In reality, the judges in charge by the winter of 1983 had worked with infinite patience and care, against singularly obstinate resistance at home and abroad, to solve what had looked like an impenetrable mystery. The fact that many Western leaders might have preferred to leave it unsolved was no fault of theirs.

Not even their own government had really expected them to solve it in the first place. Those who mattered in Italy's upper echelons took it for granted, with relief or regret, that a conspiracy whose parentage they also took for granted must necessarily have been perfectly planned and executed. The judges might try, for appearance's sake, but it looked like a hopeless case.

Yet the leads were there from the beginning. Summarized in the court's Statement of Motivation, buried in a thick mass of documents attached to the trial proceedings, unread in court and also largely unpublished in the press—though these too became available for the asking—were dozens of Italian police and secret-service reports; telexed exchanges with their opposite numbers in West Germany, Switzerland, Austria, Turkey, Tunisia; communications to and from Interpol; texts of Agca's earliest interrogations; and a first handwritten confession. These last in particular showed that the mystery of Mehmet Ali Agca was at once more and less daunting than the public imagined.

His refusal to testify in court had led to the widespread assumption that he did not talk at all before his trial. But he did. Practiced liar though he was, he told his questioners quite a lot that turned out to be true. Indeed, he offered some tantalizing clues that the police might otherwise never have found. In this and other ways, he was full of surprises.

The two-dimensional picture drawn of him in newspaper headlines—the deranged killer and cheap Fascist thug—had not prepared the Italians for the baffling character of their prisoner. From the moment he was brought to police headquarters, Agca's distinctive personality was manifest. Tall, gaunt, his deep-set dark eyes framed by austerely cropped hair and dramatic high cheekbones, he displayed exceptional self-command and a quick intelligence. No sign of nerves, guilt, or fear marred his confident arrogance.

At twenty-three, all but four years of his life passed in a poor peasant home deep in Turkey's Anatolian plains, he had moved with apparent ease for the better part of a year around a score of sophisticated European capitals, sported camel's-hair coats and a gold Rolex watch, shopped at Yves St. Laurent boutiques, consumed champagne and smoked salmon with Milan's opera buffs at Biffi's, wintered at elegant resorts in Tunisia's Hammamet and Spain's Palma de Majorca—all this with no foreign language save a halting and harshly accented English. If he was closely chaperoned—and authorities came to suspect that he was rarely out of somebody's sight— that would still take some doing.

Fresh from an attempted assassination of breathtaking audacity, he faced down his interrogators with cool professional skill. This too was at least partly his personal style, though examining magistrates had little doubt that he had been coached by experts.

After days of close questioning, they did not really know what to make of Agca. Whether or not he was the hardened killer he boasted of being, he was too complex and contorted a figure to be anything like Turkey's run-of-the-mill terrorists, rightist or leftist. Clever, imperious, vain, ambitious, alternately secretive and oddly talkative, he fit into none of the conventional slots: messianic nut case, Moslem fanatic, nationalist zealot, Fascist hood, mere hired mercenary, even underground Communist agent. If some foreign power was running him, which seemed more and more likely as his story unfolded, he would still have to be manipulated and flattered into believing he was working for more than just money—or so it seemed. What else?

Terrorism for its own sake was what he cared most about, he said. While insisting that he alone had dreamed up the idea of shooting the Pope, he bragged of getting help from both rightist and leftist terrorists abroad: "Bulgarians, English, and Iranians" were those he singled out, dropping a hint that would long be overlooked. Ideologically, he declared himself to be on neither side, and both. "I make no distinction between Fascist and Communist terrorists," he said. "My terrorism is not red or black; it is red *and* black."[15] He styled himself "an international terrorist" pure and simple, the prototype of a new breed emerging after a decade of planetwide terrorist warfare.

The account he gave of himself at the time—we are still in May 1981—appeared to bear this out. Laced with random falsehoods, enticing half-truths, and what turned out to be a surprising amount of useful information, the account was summed up in the court's Statement of Motivation that September. However widely unread by the public, the Statement could not be ignored by the Italian Establishment. In effect, Judge Santiapichi's court had shifted the wall of mirrors just enough to reveal an irresistibly mysterious interior landscape waiting to be explored. In doing so, the court also exposed the subterfuge and cowardice that had gone into closing the case.

The case was reopened on November 6, 1981, six weeks after the court Statement was filed in Chancery. A cautious, unassuming judge in pebbled glasses named Ilario Martella, known for keeping his head down, eyes open, and mouth shut, was appointed as the new examining magistrate. His mandate was to investigate Agca's possible international connections.

An amazing time of discovery began, of false starts and dead ends, unaccountable bottlenecks and inexplicable contradictions, lost and found documents, halting advances and disheartening retreats. Then came a sudden glare of light, and rolls of political thunder so deafening as to spread the belief that the truth had brought us to the verge of World War III. It was a grinding but ultimately victorious period for Judge Martella, and the story of a lifetime for me.

PART ONE

·

DISCOVERING THE PLOT

·

2

My efforts to find out who wanted to kill the Pope, and why, began in the autumn of 1981. The Italian court's Statement of Motivation was my first and unexpectedly rich source of information. It went like this:

On the 14th of May, the day after Mehmet Ali Agca's arrest, Turkish functionaries arrived in Italy to provide DIGOS, the anti-terror police, with detailed information on Agca's life, student career, political affiliations, and possible connections. Other foreign police reports reached Rome over the next week or two, while still others were submitted by DIGOS and Italy's military intelligence service, SISMI. From all this and Agca's own declarations, the court attempted to reconstruct the would-be assassin's short adult life, recent past, likely motivations, and final movements in the months before he reached St. Peter's Square.

In his early youth, the Statement said, Agca had "begun to show open sympathy for nationalist positions tinged with fanaticism . . . frequenting young anti-Communists with a vein of racism who called themselves Gray Wolves." Starting in 1976, however, he went through "a disconcerting change."[1]

"Always moving in the shadows, remaining unknown to the Turkish police, Agca approached various underground guerrilla organizations of opposite tendencies." In a handwritten statement prepared spontaneously for his interrogators, he had confessed to having "secret relations" with Turkish extremists of both the right and left from 1976 to 1980.[2]

In the spring of 1977, he had decided to go to Palestine for guerrilla training. A school chum from his hometown of Malatya, Sedat Sirri Kadem, took him as far as Gaziantep, near the Syrian border. Slipping across by night, he reached Damascus, where he was met by another "comrade" from Malatya, a man whose name, he learned later, was Teslim Tore.

Tore then took him by taxi to Lebanon, where he received forty days of guerrilla training in a Palestinian camp south of Beirut. Many of his countrymen were in camp with him, coming from "the most disparate of Turkey's subversive groups." Upon returning to Turkey, Agca claimed to have "established clandestine relations with six underground organizations": AKINCILAR, ÜLKÜCÜLER, EMEGIN BIRLIGI, HALKIN KURTULUSU, THKO, and THKPC. Two of these groups were on the far right, the rest on the far left.[3]

"AKINCILAR was a religious-fanatic group proposing the Koranization of the Turkish constitution. Legal until 1978, when the imposition of martial law suspended all extremist activity, it continued to work clandestinely, with propaganda and sporadic acts of aggression.

"ÜLKÜCÜLER was the largest legal group on the right until 1978, made up of young anti-Communists and nationalists veined with racism. Its official symbol is the Gray Wolf. After martial law was declared, its members were responsible for murdering Communists and attacking their headquarters.

"EMEGIN BIRLIGI was an underground group of the extreme Marxist-Leninist left, active in the factories above all, dedicated to violence, the murder of rightists and law-enforcement officers, and extortion for self-financing.

"HALKIN KURTULUSU was another Marxist-Leninist organization analogous to the preceding one.

"The THKPC (Turkish People's Liberation Army) was an organization parallel to the THKO (Turkish People's Liberation Movement), an armed resistance group of the extreme Leninist left, outstanding for its attacks against right-wing objectives and against police officers and installations."

The Turk who had allegedly escorted Agca from Damascus to the Palestinian camp near Beirut was the THKO's leader, Teslim Toro.

From the time he completed his guerrilla training and returned to Turkey, Agca said—the autumn of 1977, when he was just nineteen—he had "benefited from secret sources of financing."[4]

Whoever was paying him (this he would not say), he "continued to weave his intrigues, waiting for the propitious occasion to leap into the limelight and prove his fidelity to his avowed ideals of destruction." The occasion appeared to have come along on February 1, 1979, with the murder in Istanbul of Turkey's foremost editor, Abdi Ipekci. Whether as a rightist or a leftist or both, it was reportedly Agca who pumped five bullets into Ipekci, shooting his way from oblivion to stardom as the nation's most notorious terrorist killer.

He was arrested nearly five months later, on June 25. In another five months to the day, he managed "with outside help" to escape from the Kartal-Maltepe military prison, "after promising sensational revelations about the complicity of others, unleashing a congeries of hints, suspicions, and accusations."

The day after his prison breakout, Agca sent a letter to the late Abdi Ipekci's paper, *Milliyet,* threatening the life of Pope John Paul on the latter's impending visit to Istanbul:

> Western imperialists, fearful that Turkey and her sister Islamic nations might become a political, military, and economic power in the Middle East, are sending to Turkey in this delicate moment the Commander of the Crusades, John Paul, disguised as a religious chief.
>
> If this visit . . . is not canceled, I will without doubt kill the Pope-Chief.
>
> This is the sole motive for my escape from prison.
>
> Furthermore, the responsibility for the attack on Mecca [the armed seizure of Islam's holiest Mosque in 1979], of American and Israeli origin, will not go unpunished.
>
> Mehmet Ali Agca[5]

The court's Statement, having previously underlined Agca's lack of religious fanaticism or personal rancor toward the Roman Catholic Pope, noted the somewhat more plausible explanation Agca had offered his Italian interrogators for this curious letter. He had sent it "to agitate the Turkish police" and "concentrate their forces on the person of the Pope," distracting them from his own person so that he could slip away without hindrance and go abroad.

Once on the loose, Agca "sheltered in underground hideouts, covered by a network of friends who assured him substantial financing." During that December, he was said by the Turkish police to have murdered the man he thought had informed on him, Haydar Serangah.[6] Eventually, "notwithstanding a death sentence pronounced by the Istanbul Military Tribunal *in absentia,* he made his way tranquilly to Iran, with a false Indian passport and a considerable sum of money." Indeed, he claimed to have left Turkey with 40,000 Deutschmarks (around $17,000) supplied by "persons I do not intend to name who were supporting me."

From there on, the Statement traces Agca's bewildering itinerary as he crisscrossed Eastern and Western Europe.

It starts with a black hole, an entire spring when Agca's movements were utterly unknown: from his three-month visit to Iran— for what purpose no one has discovered—to the summer of 1980. Then, in early July, he went to Bulgaria and stayed for fifty days.

It was in the Bulgarian capital of Sofia, he said, that he bought the Browning 9-mm automatic for his use in Rome ten months later. A Syrian "student" named Ahmed supplied it, he claimed. There, too, in the deluxe Hotel Vitosha, he met a fellow Turk by the name of Omer Mersan, who lived in Munich. At one meeting, he declared, Mersan had offered to procure the counterfeit passport, bearing the name Faruk Ozgun, that had been found on Agca in Rome. On another occasion, in Room 911 of the Hotel Vitosha, Mersan had introduced him to a Bulgarian named Mustafaeff. That was early in July, Agca said, adding that Mersan had arranged another meeting with Mustafaeff in Tunis the following December.[7]

What else he did and who else he met in Bulgaria, Agca did not say.

Taking off for points west at the end of that August, Agca was forever on the move; his seemingly aimless zigzag journeys were described by the court as "the incessant pilgrimage of a nomad anxious to cover his tracks." As he told it, he visited Yugoslavia, France, Great Britain, Belgium, Switzerland, Denmark, Austria, Hungary, Tunisia, Spain, and Italy—this last again and again.

He had spent much more time in Italy than might be expected of a desperate fugitive on the run, traveling "from Milan to Rome to Palermo to Naples, again to Rome, to Milan, to Rome, to Perugia, to Genoa, to Milan . . . ," interspersing these hops with brief visits to Budapest, Vienna, Zurich, Lucerne, and a two-week package tour to Palma de Majorca. He had stayed in Perugia four days (April 8–12, 1981) to register at the university, and so procure a three-month student residence permit for Italy. And he had stayed in Rome on and off for at least thirty-four days:

December 15–19	Pensione Hiberia
December 26, 1980– January 11, 1981	Hotel Archimede
January 18–19	Pensione Isa
January 28–30	Pensione Isa
April 13–15	Hotel Torino
May 9–10	YMCA
May 11–13	Pensione Isa[8]

During just these months, a nationwide terrorist roundup was at its height in Italy, landing some 1,500 fellow practitioners of violence in jail. The police checkposts, the house-to-house searches, the meticulous screening of hotel registers, did not appear to bother Agca. "It's easy to be a terrorist in Italy," he said.

His tales about these wanderings in Western Europe were often improbable and occasionally preposterous. He had vehemently denied ever setting foot in West Germany, for instance, "because there were too many Turkish terrorists there" (as indeed there were). Yet dozens of Turkish immigrant workers (*Gastarbeiter*) had signaled Agca's presence in one or another West German city. The court cited West German and Italian secret-service reports saying he had been in the country "for some months, with false documents, traveling continuously from city to city, forming a close net of contacts with Turkish citizens wanted by the police in Ankara for subversive activities."[9]

He maintained also that he had studied the possibilities of assassinating Queen Elizabeth in London, but had given it up because she was a woman. The same scruple had kept him from knocking off the Council of Europe's president in Strasbourg, Simone Weil.

On top of this, he offered a bizarre story about going to Tunis on the telephoned instructions of the Turk he had met in Sofia's Hotel Vitosha, Omer Mersan, to meet again with Mustafaeff. The mysterious Bulgarian had come to his room secretly at the Hotel du Lac at noon on November 29, 1980, he declared. He had asked how Agca felt about assassinating Tunisian President Bourguiba and the Maltese premier, Dom Mintoff, expected momentarily in Tunis on an unannounced visit. Agca felt it was too dangerous, because of unusually heavy security arrangements. "The motive for this double homicide was political," the court reported Agca as saying. "But he refused to go into particulars."[10]

It was too early on to know how much of all this Agca was making up as he went along. But the court by no means dismissed it as a bunch of lies. His "spontaneous confession" was "believable in many ways," the court stated, and several parts had been confirmed. For instance, the Tunisian police had reported that Agca did spend the night of November 28, 1980, at the Hotel du Lac in Tunis, proceeding some hours after noon the next day to the fashionable beach resort of Hammamet. Whether any "Mustafaeff" slipped into Tunis or Agca's hotel room at the time, they couldn't say.

More important was Agca's deliberate and successful effort to prove that he really did spend the summer of 1980 in Bulgaria. The Omer Mersan he claimed to have met in Sofia early that July, in Room 911 of the Hotel Vitosha, existed. He was found in Munich, through two telephone numbers Agca had furnished: 89-530489 and 531070. The numbers belonged to a Vardar Export-Import Company, as Agca said they would.[11]

Picked up, questioned, and released in twenty-four hours, Mersan agreed that he had run into Agca in Sofia, and had occupied Room 911 of the Hotel Vitosha, early in July 1980. He conceded also that Agca, known to him only as "Metin," had phoned him several times at the Vardar Company after leaving Bulgaria. "But he did not want to specify the nature of the relations established between them," the court said.[12]

Its reference to Mersan, though brief, caught the eye. Throughout Agca's interrogation, he had identified nobody else precisely enough to be found and questioned. In this instance, he supplied Mersan's authentic name, his city of residence, and his company's name and telephone numbers, making sure the police could not miss him. Thus, Agca had steered his questioners straight to a prime piece of evidence they had no way of finding on their own—the first key that would one day unlock the case. Why?

That was just one of the many intriguing questions raised by the court's Statement of Motivation:

- Was it true that Agca had worked clandestinely in Turkey with underground groups of both the extreme right and left?
- Had he actually been put on a secret payroll at the age of nineteen?
- Who got him out of prison in Istanbul, took care of his hideouts and false passports, and plied him with "conspicuous funds"— around $50,000, police thought—for his European travels?[13]
- What did he do in Bulgaria for fifty days?
- What did he do in Rome for thirty-four days, come to that?
- Was there a "Mustafaeff"?
- Who guided him safely through the vast enemy territory of Western Europe—Agca, Turkey's most notorious terrorist fugitive, confessed and convicted murderer of Abdi Ipekci?
- Who taught him to use the Browning 9-mm automatic, the professional assassin's perfect weapon, to aim it in regulation style, with both hands, over the heads of the crowd, at a moving target whose vital organs he missed by only a hair?
- Why, if he was not an "exalted paranoiac," or a "manic psychopath," or a "delirious ideologue," or a religious fanatic, did he shoot the Pope?
- If he was not "a terrorist who came from nowhere," where did he come from? What "hidden minds" sent him?

Judge Santiapichi's court did not know, and said so. "The elements gathered so far are not such as to confirm a definitive truth," it stated. There was no doubt that Agca "had shown himself to possess an adequate knowledge of a composite phenomenon, of specific facts and intimate mechanisms, which he could not have had without somehow being involved in a criminal undertaking . . . on closely familiar terms with the interested parties." Nevertheless, the nature of this undertaking was still no more than "conjecture."

The judges therefore "had no alternative but to recommend a continuing investigation, leading to deeper examination of all the circumstances that could give a face to those who were jointly responsible for this most grave misdeed."

Entrusted with that continuing investigation in November 1981, Judge Martella would have the answers to nearly all these questions by the end of 1983.

3

"We'll give you Mustafaeff," said one of the three police commissioners walking me to the door, as if to atone for having given me next to nothing else. "We can agree on the existence of a Mustafaeff."

The conversation had gone on for hours, in the drab dun-colored offices of Rome's DIGOS, whose specialized antiterror squad handled the policework on the Agca case. It was the autumn of 1981, some weeks after Judge Santiapichi's court had filed its Statement of Motivation, which I seemed to be alone in having read. In fact, I had read it carefully more than once, remembering how Western governments had dealt with other cases seen as a threat to the normal course of international politics and diplomacy. Should the Western governments concerned here pursue the leads in this Statement to the end, they might well uncover a conspiracy whose international impact could be shattering. Therefore, I thought, the leads were unlikely to be pursued to the end.

The three DIGOS commissioners would be the first test of my suspicions, I decided, climbing the marble stairs of the Questura, the police headquarters, to their offices. Not that I expected much. All three were very good cops, but they were still not required to behave like friendly neighborhood policemen. The case was too big, too highly charged, too heavily under wraps for companionable confidences. I imagined they would tell me as little as they could decently get away with, and I was right. It would be months before I had the bargaining power to ask for more.

The talk started off smoothly, as we sank into the sprung brown armchairs treacherously set out for visitors in Rome's government offices. The three commissioners were at ease, doubtless because I was so transparently innocent of the facts.

I cannot identify these men, even with their correct initials. Here, as everywhere else, police detectives engaged in such sensitive work would never consent to being named. A reporter who breaks this unwritten rule would be given the lie and get no more out of them.

The three commissioners agreed from the start that Agca did have exceptional qualities. He was more than usually intelligent and remarkably self-disciplined, they said, with an "extraordinary capacity for concentration and resistance" under questioning. He could put himself to sleep sitting in a chair, and wake up refreshed for another round with his interrogators. But they had never come across so baffling a prisoner. What his politics and motives were, who his patrons—if any—might be, what secret furies drove him, they could not say.

He had "a whiff of the *santone*" about him—the saintly hypocrite, one suggested. "He likes to say he's a 'pure' terrorist, whereas he may just want to be a superman, like Nietzsche," observed another. He had begun by calling himself a Communist and friend of the Palestinian Marxist George Habash, then waved that away as irrelevant. He was said by Turkish reporters to be a member of the right-wing Gray Wolves, but there was no such proof in his Turkish police record.

"We might know more about these ties if we could trace Agca's movements in West Germany," said Commissioner S., that being where Turkey's Gray Wolves generally congregate in Europe. "But he and the West Germans both deny he was ever there." Rumors persisted, they said, that he had married there, killed a man there, and nearly been killed there himself, when these same Gray Wolves planted a bomb under his car: all unconfirmed rumors from a country in which he had officially never set foot.

"As far as we know, he probably told the truth about his itinerary," Commissioner S. went on. Nevertheless, there were "big lapses": a good three months were missing after Agca left Bulgaria at the end of August 1980, and large chunks of the rest had yet to be established. No entrance or exit records had been found so far for visits he claimed to have made to France, Belgium, Britain, Denmark, Hungary. Of course, he might not have been using the "Faruk Ozgun" passport found on him in Rome. Other sets of the beautifully faked papers he carried could have gotten him anywhere.

"The Faruk Ozgun passport was perfect, you know," said Commissioner N. (I didn't know). Issued by a Turkish passport office, with Agca's picture affixed under the name of a living Turkish citizen—the real Faruk Ozgun—it could never be detected abroad as counterfeit because, in effect, it was authentic. Not even Italy's Red Brigades had attained such heights of sophisticated forgery.

That sounded to me like collusion in high places, I said. Surely the Turkish authorities would have looked into the provenance of such a passport, traced it perhaps to some former top ministerial functionary or ranking security officer. Had DIGOS received a report from Ankara on that? The commissioners looked blank. A clerk in the Turkish passport office was said to have been fired or suspended, they responded vaguely. DIGOS did not hear much about what went on in Turkey.

I wondered how much Turkey might be hearing about what went on in DIGOS. What I'd learned so far didn't say much for the virtuous claims of close collaboration coming from every side. Still, it was hard to believe that Turkish authorities would withhold such important evidence if they had it; and I was willing to bet they had it. I began to feel that my three commissioners were being less than altogether forthright.

The feeling grew as the commissioners continued amiably to cover yard upon yard of sterile ground. Yes, Agca had told a lot of lies. No, he could not account for the money he threw around. Yes, he had spent around $50,000 on planes, deluxe hotels, clothes, holidays in Palma de Majorca. No, there was no evidence of his ever meeting anyone by appointment. In Tunisia, for instance, police had confirmed Agca's stay in the country, but not his meeting with the phantom Mustafaeff. "He traveled more like a fellow who had won a lottery than like a tourist trying to see the world," said Commissioner S.

I felt it was time to get to the point. Agca had to have help, accomplices, somebody who was running him, I ventured: anybody familiar with the case was bound to see that. Well, now, said the commissioners. A reporter was free to speculate, but a policeman could not go on guesswork; and that was pretty much all they had to go on.

Witnesses had sworn to hearing two, three, and four shots in St. Peter's Square. But only two spent cartridges were found, and Agca said he fired twice. Any number of reports about others in the Square with him had dissolved into thin air. Guesswork again. I protested that this last must be more substantial than that. Half a dozen magazines in Europe had published two memorable photographs, one taken an instant before Agca fired, the other seconds later. The latter showed a young man with his back turned, racing out of the Square. Lowell Newton, the ABC cameraman who took the picture, had seen him sprinting away with a gun in his hand, breaking out of the crowd just a few feet from where Agca had stood. The other snapshot showed Agca himself aiming his Browning with both hands over the heads in front of him. At his left side was a half-hidden face strongly resembling a Turkish friend of Agca's named Omer Ay. His identity had been confirmed at least tentatively by the Turkish police, on the last day of Agca's trial.

Nobody could prove who that second man was, said Commissioner N. When DIGOS technicians had blown the picture up to fifteen times its size, there was still just half a blurred face to see, with dark holes for eyes. As for the sprinter, the quarter-profile of a man glancing over his shoulder in flight was no use to anyone.

Then what was the documentary proof mentioned by Judge Infelisi—the first examining magistrate to interrogate Agca—within forty-eight hours of the shooting? And on what had Judge Santiapichi's court based its strong assertion of an organized conspiracy? The commissioners were firmly on both sides of this question. "Naturally we don't rule out a conspiracy," said Commissioner N. "On the other hand, we have nothing to prove it. Every clue we've followed so far has led nowhere. We're hardly any farther now than we were when we started. When and if the investigation turns up something solid . . ."

Judging from our conversation, the investigation looked as good as dead. Certainly the press appeared to think so. Scarcely a word had been printed on the papal shooting in or out of Italy since the end of that summer, when Julian Manyan of Thames Television in London produced a pioneering documentary. Put together quickly, it had sting enough to make one-day headlines and was then forgotten. Few remembered, a year later, how surprisingly intuitive it had been.[1]

It was hard to tell whether these three smart cops merely wanted me to think they were giving up on the case, or actually meant it. How could they give up now? The signs of conspiracy were a matter of public record. Somebody with a lot of money must have staked Mehmet Ali Agca to his $50,000 spending spree on the Continent. Somebody with a network of contacts must have passed him from hand to hand in Europe. Somebody with the right connections must have gotten the Browning automatic for him from its last known owner, a shady Viennese gun dealer named Horst Grillmayer, who had disappeared right after the Pope was shot and was said by the court to be hiding out "in some country of Eastern Europe."[2]

Furthermore, somebody with plenty of clout must have arranged for the Faruk Ozgun passport; and this, at least, was a lead that ought to be going somewhere. Agca himself had named a Turk who supposedly acted as middleman in procuring the passport. Omer Mersan, said to have performed that service in Bulgaria, was alive and well and living in Munich. He was the sole witness who had admitted to meeting Agca during the latter's travels, in Bulgaria of all places. How closely had the German authorities questioned Mersan, in the twenty-four hours they held him? Had they put him under surveillance after letting him go? Did the Italian examining magistrate ask to see him?

The DIGOS commissioners could not answer for Germany. As for the Italian judge, the answer was no.

There seemed to be something about Mersan that caused authorities involved in this case to look everywhere but at him. Perhaps it was indifference or apathy, inertia, bureaucratic bumbling? To my mind, though, it had more to do with the fact that Mersan was the first tangible link between the man who shot the Pope and the People's Republic of Bulgaria. In time, when other links were added, this would come to be known as the Bulgarian Connection.

•   •

I put it to the commissioners that Mersan was, at any rate, the only link they had to Agca's summer in Sofia. There were good reasons to consider this the heart of the matter.

To have stayed in the Bulgarian capital for fifty days, as Agca did from early July to the end of August 1980, was enough in itself to make his future actions suspect. The most inflexible of Eastern Europe's Communist police states, Bulgaria has long been Moscow's most reliable and useful surrogate in matters of terrorism and subversion. On behalf of the Soviet KGB, it has serviced terrorists from all over Western Europe since the early seventies, providing weapons, training, a privileged sanctuary, rest and recreation facilities.[3]

More particularly, the Bulgarians have serviced both left- and right-wing terrorists in neighboring Turkey, providing much of the wherewithal there—until the Turkish army takeover in September 1980—for the most raging case of terrorist warfare on earth. I had seen the proof of Bulgaria's work when I was in Turkey during its worst moments, gathering material for my book *The Terror Network*. The evidence was incomparably more damning by the time I returned for the Agca story.

I knew, then, as any reporter covering this part of the world would, that Bulgaria's secret police had an intimate knowledge of Turkish affairs. Not much could escape them in regard to the comings and goings of Turkish citizens crossing the frontier, legally or otherwise. Even if a foreigner could loiter in Sofia for a while unobserved, a Turk would still find that out of the question, especially a Turk with Agca's record, a convicted terrorist murderer—*and a Fascist murderer, at that*—who had made a spectacular prison break, and whose picture had been featured on Turkey's front pages for weeks on end.

We could take it as a working hypothesis, therefore, that the Bulgarians had to know all about Agca in Sofia. I suggested this to the three commissioners, who were inclined to agree. Indeed, they seemed disposed to credit much or most of the Bulgarian interlude in Agca's story: they did give me Mustafaeff, after all. That was safe enough to say, within the privacy of four walls, since they evidently didn't think anything could be done about it. Bulgaria was unlikely to volunteer information on the subject, or leave much usable evidence lying around.

That was that. The three commissioners plainly considered Bulgaria to be the inaccessible key to what thus became an unsolvable mystery. If the Bulgarian secret services were somehow involved in the plot to kill the Pope, the West would never be able to prove it, they concluded. Never? Never.

We extracted ourselves from the sprung brown armchairs, more cross-grained than amiable now, and shook hands all around. Angry little pinpricks jabbed at my mind as I came out into Rome's soft mauve twilight.

It wasn't long before I began to see how much the three commissioners had left out. I had only to drop in at the Records Room in the central courthouse, and ask for copies of assorted documents attached to the Agca trial proceedings—in the nick of time. They were mine by sheer luck. Until the end of that trial, they had been a closely guarded secret. A few weeks after I dropped in at the Records Room, they became secret again, when Judge Martella was appointed to head a fresh investigation. Nothing could dislodge them after that.

Italian law is inflexible in imposing secrecy on every written and spoken word in a case under judicial investigation: the *segreto istruttorio,* as Italians call it, is comparable to an American grand jury investigation. The law is honored in the breach more often than not, since court reporters have to make their living. Nevertheless, a leak, however small, can mean prison, if the judge in charge is tough enough. As I would learn soon after safely making off with my documents, the rigidly upright Judge Martella was as tough as they come.

The documents I'd brought home were picked more or less at random, extracted from a bored clerk impatient for her lunch. "But which ones do you *want?*" she had demanded. "There must be hundreds. You can't just walk in here and ask for them all!" I took what I could get and fled.

It wasn't a bad haul, I found, on looking the papers over: a couple of notes in Turkish discovered on Agca's person; two or three reports by SISMI, Italy's military intelligence service; a few more by DIGOS; some exchanges of telexed police messages abroad; the testimony of a prostitute Agca had slept with in Genoa (which, if nothing else, seemed to rule out Italian movie director Bernardo Bertolucci's theory that Agca had fired in a paroxysm of homosexual rage); summaries of Agca's interrogations day by day; his first handwritten confession.

Here at last was firsthand information known to the authorities and largely ignored by the press. It was raw, unprocessed material, mostly in disconnected scraps. Pieced together, however, it gave me some idea of where to start looking—in the murky international underworld of terrorists, gangsters, dope pushers, gunrunners, bent politicians, spies, secret agents, and devious "information analysts" working a curious kind of diplomatic protection racket. They were all in the cast, would all have their uses, as we learned when the plot was laid bare at last: a deliberately intricate plot, exploiting popular prejudice and political folklore, requiring layer upon layer of deception. For the point was not merely to kill the Pope—it isn't all that hard to kill so vulnerable a target—but to plant broad killer's tracks pointing in exactly the wrong direction.

I would like to think I was prescient enough, as I read through those documents, to see the whole grand design emerging. But all I could see was how thoroughly my three police commissioners had misled me. The signs of conspiracy were based on a lot more than guesswork, as they must have been among the first to know.

One of the papers in my batch, for instance, was a note found in Agca's pocket, jotted down in Turkish. The examining magistrates themselves had concluded that it was a list of last-minute instructions:

Friday between 7 and 8 P.M. *telephone.*
May 13, Wednesday, appearance in the Square.
May 17, Sunday, perhaps appearance on the balcony.
May 20, Wednesday, Square *without fail.*
Choose a shoulder bag carefully.
Hair dye is essential.
If necessary, wear a cross. Short jeans, tennis shoes, Montgomery jacket.
After Wednesday, round trip to Florence or nearby station.
Be careful not to be seen around Vatican or places where might attract attention.
Necessary *tear up postcards.*
Finances: 500,000 lire (180,000 hotel, 20,000 telephone, 200,000 daily expenses, 100,000 reserve for emergencies).
Tomorrow, money for three days in hotel.
Necessary: trip to Naples, purchase bag and hair dye. Check if train ticket valid.
Be very careful about food.
Breakfast *here* at 9:00.[4]

"Here" was the Pensione Isa in Rome, where, according to the court's Statement, Agca's room had been reserved by somebody speaking fluent Italian. Agca's Italian at the time was limited to saying "*Avére caméra*," using an infinitive and a noun with the accent in the wrong place.

The bottle of hair dye for his getaway disguise was found in his room, and little else. He had dutifully torn up picture postcards of the Pope riding around St. Peter's Square in an open jeep, or so he said. The shoulder bag, carefully chosen to contain his bulky Browning, was with him at the Vatican. He had changed his mind, or been advised to, about the tennis shoes and short jeans and the military jacket, opting for a neat gray summer suit instead. He had only 300,000 lire on him when captured—less than $300, scarcely enough to keep him long on the run.

The DIGOS reports in my collection revealed how much more than guesswork the three commissioners had to go on. Two weeks after the papal shooting, on May 27, 1981, Chief Commissioner Lidano Marchionne of DIGOS had sent out a list of seventeen names for international circulation.[5] All were Turks said to have had some contact with Mehmet Ali Agca in the past. Four would eventually be fingered by Agca himself as having something to do with the plot. Judge Martella would issue international warrants of arrest for two of these, Oral Celik and Musa Cerdar Celebi, on charges of "direct complicity." Celik was never caught. Celebi was arrested in Frankfurt and extradited to Italy—he is still in prison as I write.

In a second report dated June 24, 1981, Commissioner Marchionne had written of "the Omer Ay in the photograph" as a possible "second accomplice." Omer Ay was "*known to Agca, and helped him to get his false passport* [my italics]," the commissioner stated, betraying the fact that he must have received a report from Turkey to that effect. The half-hidden man to the left of Agca in the photograph taken an instant before the shooting "does resemble Omer Ay," he added.[6]

Here, then, was a prime suspect who not only might have been present physically at the scene of the crime, but appeared to have had a hand in logistical preparations. The incriminating evidence was strengthened in another DIGOS communication: a composite drawing circulated internationally through Interpol, over the caption "Presumed accomplice of the Pope's would-be assassin."[7] Several witnesses had described this man, carrying a black dispatch case, seen running for a bus just beyond the colonnades of St. Peter's Square within seconds of the shooting. The witnesses had taken particular notice of him because, after trying so hard to get on the bus, he got off again at the next stop. When the composite drawing was placed side by side with the half-hidden face in the photo and a picture of the real Ömer Ay, the resemblance was striking.

Another possible accomplice turned up in a police report from Tunis. Five foreign workers employed by the Milanese firm Saipem in Belli, Tunisia, had been seen in Agca's company while he was there. The most interesting was a Turk called Youssef Dag, traveling on a Turkish passport (number 696187) issued October 8, 1980. Dag, who had been seen around quite a lot with Agca in Hammamet, had left Tunisia on April 24, 1981—three weeks before the papal shooting. He had boarded a Tunis Air flight to Rome (TU/782), landed at Fiumicino Airport, and vanished.[8]

A SISMI report signed by its director at the time, General Giuseppe Santovito, referred to a single meeting his agents had in Vienna with the local president of the Turkish Gray Wolves there, Gihat Turkkoglu (passport number 206285). The Turk had asked for the meeting, saying he had important information on the Pope's assailant. But after a brief preliminary contact, he vanished too.[9]

A report from Rome's Hotel Torino, where Agca had stayed a few weeks before the shooting, revealed that he had made a 15,000-lire, twenty-minute phone call through the hotel switchboard, to a number in Hannover, West Germany. The number was listed for yet another Turkish Gray Wolf leader, Hasan Taskin, who denied all knowledge of the call. The German police had questioned him, believed his denials, and so let him go.[10]

On May 25, 1981, SISMI had also submitted an alluring report on the Viennese gun dealer Horst Grillmayer, last known possessor of Agca's gun—still another witness who had vanished. Inexplicably (though I thought I had the answer when it was all over), Agca had used the Browning without filing off its factory number. Thus it was easily traced to Belgium's Fabrique Nationale Herstal, which had made it. From there, it had passed legally to a clean gun dealer in Liège, who sold it to another in Zurich, who sold it legally in turn on July 9, 1980, to an Otto Tintner, who used a license of purchase from Horst Grillmayer's Austrian firm. Though acquired legitimately in Switzerland, the Browning and twenty-one other guns were smuggled undeclared into Austria, where they went underground.

According to SISMI, the forty-two-year-old Grillmayer came from "a family of fervent Nazis" and had been investigated "several times" by the Austrian police for possessing unlicensed weapons. He also had a record of selling used cars—presumed to be stolen—to Turkish workers and spoke "excellent" Turkish. A "frequent visitor" to West Germany and Italy, he also "traveled often to Syria, East Germany, and other countries of Eastern Europe." He had long been suspected of furnishing contraband weapons to terrorist organizations, and maintained "an extremely high standard of living."[11]

Agca's account of how and where he got the Browning, continued SISMI, seemed credible on several counts. The Hotel Vitosha and other hotels Agca claimed to have stayed at as well in Sofia—the Sofia Grand Hotel and Novo Hotel Europa—were receiving centers for contraband weapons and stolen cars. During the summer, the stolen-car trade boomed between Sofia and Turkey, Syria, and Lebanon, the cars moving in caravans of ten or fifteen at a time.[12]

The SISMI report closed on an intriguing note. Until the Turkish army takeover in 1980, "arms smuggling into Turkey from Sofia went on with no particular secrecy. The arms smugglers habitually lodged at the same hotels frequented by Agca."

The shade of a thought came to me, reading the SISMI report. What if Agca had some connection to the smugglers who seemed so at home in Sofia? Did he have any dealings with them when he was there? Might anything tie that to his mission in St. Peter's Square?

It was the merest hunch, too thin to be worth anything, were it not for another DIGOS document I had. This one was a telex from DIGOS in Rome to West Germany's Bundeskriminalamt in Wiesbaden, asking about Omer Mersan.

Dated May 21, 1981, the telex stated: "Mehmet Ali Agca affirms that he met an Omer Mersal or some similar name in Bulgaria. *Omer Mersal was engaged in smuggling cigarettes, liquor, and, on occasion, arms* [my italics]. Omer Mersal occupied Room 911 of the Hotel Vitosha in Sofia. He offered to procure a Turkish passport for 60,000 Turkish lire. He received four passport photos from Agca and sent them to friends in Turkey to falsify a passport there. The falsified passport was delivered to Agca in about a month. The delivery was presumably between August 27, when a Turkish bank stamped the passport for export of currency, and August 31, 1980, date of the Bulgarian exit stamp."[13]

If Agca was telling the truth—still a big "if"—we now had a

Turkish *smuggler* in Sofia serving as middleman to procure the perfect Faruk Ozgun passport, through "friends in Turkey" evidently including Agca's "possible second accomplice," Omer Ay (quotes from the DIGOS report of June 24, cited earlier). Not a hint of all this had been dropped at my lengthy DIGOS briefing. The figure of Omer Mersan began to look decidedly promising.

The telex to Wiesbaden went on to report Omer Mersan's alleged introduction to Agca of a Bulgarian named Mustafaeff, and the subsequent arrangement of a meeting between the two in Tunisia. It noted Agca's claim to have called Mersan at the Vardar Company in Munich (phone numbers 89-530489 and 89-531070) shortly before November 28, 1980, the day Agca flew to Tunis from Rome.

The Bundeskriminalamt's reply on May 22 was also among my batch of papers. Omer Mersan had been found through the Vardar telephone numbers, it said. He admitted to having met Agca as "Metin" in Sofia, at the Park Hotel or Hotel Vitosha–New Otani. Only after seeing Agca's picture in the papers following the papal attack had he recognized Agca as Metin. Earlier that winter, Agca had called him at the Vardar Company "to inquire after his health." Mersan denied the passport episode and the whole "Mustafaeff" story.[14]

The West Germans' message said nothing about Rome's reference to Mersan's alleged smuggling activities. Nor did it speak of Mersan's occupation, the circles he moved in, the nature of the Vardar Company, or Mersan's business in Sofia.

So uninquisitive a view of Omer Mersan by the German police seemed all the odder to me after reading what Agca actually had to say about him. On May 18, before the whole Rome-Wiesbaden telexed exchange, Agca had declared in his handwritten confession that Mersan was not only a smuggler, but *"a friend of people involved in the black market on a vast scale in Turkey* [my italics]." He had made it a point to look up Mersan in Sofia because "his name was given to me in Turkey by a comrade." Mersan "told me he could deliver the new passport to me in Bulgaria," Agca went on. "He said it was easy for him to get to the Bulgarian-Turkish frontier." Once the money and photos were handed over, Mersan had sent them into Turkey from the border, promising that the Faruk Ozgun passport would be back in a month. And it *was* back in a month, delivered as promised. Whether or not Mersan handed it over in person, Agca did not say.[15]

Going on to describe the Tunisian episode, Agca stated that Mersan had instructed him by phone to go to the Hotel du Lac in Tunis on November 28, 1980, because "Mustafaeff needed to see me, and would meet me there at noon. The meeting took place as planned. Mustafaeff told me that the Maltese premier, Dom Mintoff, was coming to visit Tunisian President Bourguiba, and asked if I was disposed to kill them both. I said no, because there was too much security laid on: it was Mustafaeff himself who showed me where the security would be deployed. . . . He made the proposition because he knew all about my past in Turkey. . . . The motive for this double homicide was political. You ask me what political ideal (which I evidently shared with Mustafaeff) could induce me to kill the Maltese and Tunisian leaders. I refuse to answer. I refuse to explain my refusal. . . ."

The Tunisian visit was one of only three episodes recounted with any precision in Agca's rambling tale. Another was his visit to the Palestinian training camp, in which he described his underground route, his fellow Malatyan sponsors Sedat Sirri Kadem and Teslim Tore, and the nature of the camp. There was a forty-day military course, he said, given in a building some thirty-five to forty kilometers south of Beirut. Since the camp "was under the surveillance of the Turkish secret service [MIT], I did not see any documents of identity there, or have any particular contacts." Trainees were forbidden to speak to each other anyway, "on pain of grave sanctions," he went on. He was not paid, or given a gun when he left for home. "In reality, that wasn't necessary, because my Turkish friends had a plentiful supply of guns," he said.

Apart from that account, Agca had gone into detail only about his visit to Bulgaria. There was nothing else of interest in the papers I had. That was the sum of my information in the fall of 1981.

Puzzling over what I had learned, I kept coming back to the same perplexing point. Why did Agca go to such lengths to make sure the Italian police would know about his Bulgarian summer—and stop right there? Doubtless he was sending out a signal; but to whom? To whoever would see an urgent need to get him out of jail before he really started talking, was the obvious answer. He had as much as said so publicly at the close of his trial in Rome, announcing that he meant to go on a hunger strike in exactly five months. It had been five months to the day after Agca's imprisonment for the murder of Abdi Ipekci that, after threatening to talk, somebody got him out of jail in Istanbul.

But as I prepared to double back over Agca's trail, the five months were nearly up, and nobody had gotten him out yet. Nor was there much chance that anyone would. Upon sentencing him to life imprisonment, Judge Santiapichi had also decreed a year of solitary confinement. Agca was under twenty-four-hour surveillance, his own cell surrounded by empty cells, wholly cut off from his fellow prisoners and the outside world. At twenty-three, he could be reasonably sure now of facing a lifetime in captivity—or, once his year under special protection was over, of being murdered in prison to ensure his silence.

After reading his interrogation, I felt that he was neither tough enough nor stupid enough to withstand such strains forever. Someday, I thought, Agca will tell his secrets to a sympathetic judge. In due course, we would know what to accept and discard from the story he had told so far: how much was made up of casual lies, or calculated falsehoods, or the truth insofar as Agca himself might know it. For that too was part of the mystery—how much Agca actually knew, had been allowed to know, as he acted out a scenario written, staged, and directed by others.

But it might be years before Agca decided to talk—if he did— while the trail grew colder, the evidence moldier, the inclination of Western governments stronger than ever to bury the case. Judge Martella, a man of seemingly limitless patience, might be prepared to wait. I wasn't.

4

Ankara, huddled in cold and shrouded in smog, its massive brick governmental compounds unrelieved even by softening snow, was at its midwinter worst when I flew in from Rome that December. But it hadn't looked so relaxed and cheerful in years. The pervading, paralyzing fear of a city under relentless terrorist siege was gone.

On my last visit two winters before, Turkey's nationwide terrorist kill-rate was nearing a corpse an hour. Shops and cinemas were empty, the streets were deserted by nightfall, armed policemen sat in classrooms to protect eight- or nine-year-old children. In those days, nearly everyone I knew in Turkey carried a gun—newspapermen, members of Parliament, university professors—and they locked themselves in at home after dark.

Now the sidewalks of Ataturk Boulevard were crowded with shoppers, moviegoers, and young men in and out of uniform, bundled up to the ears, but arm in arm with their girls. Tables were filled in the steamy little cafés serving *doner kebabs* and numberless glasses of hot tea. My friends had put their guns away and stopped looking over their shoulders, went out to dinner, took off on weekends to ski.

In *The Terror Network,* I had tried to explain Turkey's calamity to an often uncomprehending Western audience. The country was too far beyond the realm of the familiar for West Europeans and Americans to grasp the dimensions of its tragedy. Had they done so in time, and given a hand, there might have been no need for the Turkish army to take over, wounding the democratic sensibilities of its NATO partners; and Mehmet Ali Agca might never have made his way from a remote Turkish province to an isolation cell in an Italian maximum-security prison.

.   .

Agca was a true child of his time. He was ten when the terror began, and would be immersed for the rest of his youth in an ungovernably wild and bloody scene.

Born in 1958, he grew up on the outskirts of Malatya, a provincial seat in an ancient Hittite land, deep in the Anatolian plains. An attractive and normally prosperous city of some 300,000, Malatya was noted mostly for its apricots, until terrorism added to its fame. The bloodletting there was "prodigious even for Turkey in those days," I was told by Brigadier General Mustafa Türker, the local garrison commander. Machine-gunned, strangled, beaten, bombed, burned, stabbed, and hacked to death, Malatya's victims made up an inordinate share of the nation's terrorist kill-rate; and some of the toughest terrorist leaders in the country were born there. Several of these leaders have a part in this story: Oral Celik, Sedat Sirri Kadem, Teslim Tore.

For over a decade, left-wing mobsters held the city, while rightists held the outlying shantytowns such as Yesiltepe, where the Agcas lived. If mindless adolescents did most of the killing, the direction behind them was grimly political, well heeled, and abundantly supplied with logistic necessities. Religious friction suddenly flared, between right-leaning Sunnites and left-leaning Alawites, fanned by calculated provocation on both sides. While doctrinal differences between these two Moslem sects were old and deep, they had nevertheless managed to live peaceably together for centuries. Now they were cutting each other's throats daily—two or three a day, sometimes.

The Agcas were Sunnites. But that is neither here nor there in Mehmet Ali's case, since he never went out to slit Alawi throats. Religion played no decisive part in the destiny of this silent, sober child.

For all the furor in the world press over Agca the cold, hardened killer, few reporters had ventured out to see where he came from. By December 1981, when I did, hardly any still cared. I was already getting those politely quizzical looks—less polite and more quizzical as time went by—for poking in the ashes of a dead story.

To avoid a freezing, seven-hour bus ride from Ankara, I flew with an interpreter to Elazig, some hundred kilometers from Malatya, completing the trip by vintage taxi. It was austere country: bald beige hills humped against taller snow-covered mountains, scattered mud-brick homesteads in treeless valleys, the homes visible for miles in the clear wintry light. Malatya itself was by no means the backwater I had imagined, with its governor's mansion, pleasant squares, bookshops, an opera house. Still, I could see how boredom might drive a restless young Malatyan to desperation.

The message from Ankara's military authorities had been mislaid when we arrived at Malatya's Martial Law Command. An obliging young captain sat us down before a red-hot iron stove, ordered tea, and phoned through to the capital for our clearance. Reassured, he offered to be our guide for the day, running through Agca's dossier as we went along.

The instant image we foreign reporters had been given at once began to crack. Mehmet Ali had no police record whatever in Malatya: not for the rightist-leftist massacres, not for the Sunni-Alawi blood feuds, not even for the petty hooliganism popular among his peers. He certainly kept the wrong company at school. Old photographs showed him mostly with right-wingers, the so-called Idealists or Gray Wolves, who took the school over during his last two years there. Nevertheless, he did not join in their vicious extramural sports, still less join their movement. He was too self-absorbed, perhaps, too inwardly troubled and weighed down by family problems.

He was born poor, the captain said, of a long-suffering mother and brute of a father. The father, Ahmed, was an alcoholic—"an enormous drinker," the governor of Malatya told me later—who beat his wife regularly until he walked out on her and their three small children. He died of "a traffic accident," said to be cirrhosis, when Mehmet Ali was eight. His widow, Muzeyyen, was left with a tiny pension and nobody to count on but her eldest, her favorite son. Mehmet Ali was a good son to her, the captain had heard.

We stopped off first at the Yesiltepe *Lisesi*, Mehmet Ali's old high school. Set back from a rough dirt road traveled by loaded donkeys and peasants on foot, it was a small but cheerful and immaculate schoolhouse, decked in shiny green plants and full of sunshine. The principal, gravely courteous, remembered Agca as a model student. "Mehmet Ali was very bright and conscientious," he said, opening a huge ledger to read out Agca's grades (8 out of 10 each in Social Science, Agriculture, and the Turkish language, 10 in English). "His English was not perfect," said his sweet-faced language teacher, whose English was not perfect either.

"He was very kind, very quiet and thoughtful," said another of his teachers, "always thinking about his personal problems," and indifferent to politics. They recalled him as a lonely boy, without close attachments, uninterested in games, or girls, never one of the crowd. "But he always said he'd be famous someday," noted the sweet-faced language teacher. (He'd also said he would never be a poor slave of a schoolteacher, which I hadn't the heart to tell her.)

Agca had said much the same about himself, in an earlier handwritten confession after his arrest for Abdi Ipekci's murder. "I did everything alone, went to the movies, to the football games, to the theater, sometimes to the opera or the public library, always alone. That made me look interesting, in the circles I moved in. . . ."

We went on to his home, a ramshackle cottage and courtyard back to back with others like it, opening onto a narrow unpaved street. The woman who came to the door, Muzeyyen Agca, was slight and taut, wearing the traditional baggy flowered pants of the region. A long white headscarf—the bas örtüsü—covered her face up to the eyes, one of them markedly crossed.

She received me with dignity in her low-ceilinged, two-room house. It was chilly, with the small potbellied stove unlit, sparsely furnished but remorselessly neat. Sharing pride of place with Mehmet Ali's photograph set high on the thin plastered wall was a large television set covered in patterned cotton cloth. He had sent the money for it from Istanbul, where he'd evidently had money to burn, though his mother refused to admit it. (In fact, she would flatly deny even the photocopied evidence of a local bank account he had opened in her name.)

Adnan, at eighteen a startling image of his older brother, came in to join us, watchful and wary. His sister, Fatma, tall as all three siblings were and painfully timid, came along later with the ritual cups of Turkish coffee, expensive enough to have cost the Agcas their dinner.

There was a mystery about Mehmet Ali's birth, Muzeyyen began. He had fainted a week afterward, his lips turning black, then recovered ten minutes later. The fainting spells recurred until he was ten, she said, not knowing that these were mild epileptic fits: the "petit mal." He was inclined to be rather nervous after that.

All the same, he took good care of his mother. The family was "no poorer than others, not too poor, not too rich, anyway not in need," Adnan put in with a touch of defiance. Still, Mehmet Ali had been obliged to work after school since early childhood, peddling water at the railroad station, hauling bricks and cement (as Adnan did too). A solitary child and introspective teenager, he seemed to take no interest in politics, Muzeyyen told me.

The family's accepted leader, he had even forbidden any political talk in the household. "All he cared about was reading. He would stay up to read until three in the morning. The house was full of books," she said. "What kind?" I asked. "Every kind, whatever he could get his hands on, rightist, leftist, poetry, newspapers, comic books. . . . The police have taken it all away," she answered.

What about religious works, I inquired. Did he study the Koran? Was he an ardent believer? "A believer, of course; we're all good Moslems here. But he never had a grudge against the Alawis, whatever the papers say—none of us did," Muzeyyen replied. "He went to the Mosque—sometimes," Adnan added, meaning none too often. (He drank alcohol too, unthinkable for a devout Moslem.)

I asked Adnan who Mehmet Ali had been close to at school. Nobody special, he replied with a shrug. Adnan himself had been very close to his brother, hadn't he? Yes, very. Did he know anything about Mehmet Ali's visit to a Palestinian training camp in the summer of 1977? Not a thing. Adnan remembered that Mehmet Ali had come home from Ankara University sometime that year, but he wasn't sure just when. What about Sedat Sirri Kadem, named in Agca's confession as the friend who had sponsored his Palestinian trip? Yes, Mehmet Ali had spoken of him "once in a while" when the two were attending Malatya's Teachers' College, but he did not frequent the house. Was Sedat Sirri Kadem rightist or leftist? Adnan wouldn't know.

I hesitated, trying to reconcile the picture they were giving me with the calloused killer Mehmet Ali had become. What could have turned this quiet, obedient son into a murderer, I asked, finding no way to put it more kindly. Muzeyyen would never understand it.

"Whatever I'd say, I'd be biased. But he was just a kid, like other kids. He was so loyal, so respectful. . . ." The whole family would feel "very sorry" if the Pope were killed, she went on, though Adnan looked more impatient than sorry. "The world is so big, everybody has a right to live in it. . . ."

There was nothing wrong with Mehmet Ali until he went away in 1976, she continued. It was during his years at the university in Ankara and Istanbul that "those villains got him."

The sadness of this ruined family stayed with me when I left: the pale, neurotically repressed sister; the closed, distrustful brother undoubtedly trying to protect Mehmet Ali's secrets; the worn, fiercely defensive mother. "Life was pressing too hard on them all, especially on Mehmet Ali," said the governor of Malatya that afternoon. That was how the villains got him.

The governor, a cultivated and courtly man who had lived through Malatya's long terrorist nightmare, felt that even if Mehmet Ali took no active part in the seething violence around him, he was doomed to be caught up in it. Troubled youths like Agca were just the kind likely to be spotted and used eventually by professionals, the governor said. "From our observations during the terror, the professionals deliberately chose people with tormented family backgrounds."

"Professionals like Teslim Tore?" I asked, still trying to check back on Agca's alleged Palestinian adventure. Yes, of course, Teslim Tore was the biggest professional of them all in Malatya, on the Marxist-Leninist side. The governor had heard that Tore was teaching in a Palestinian camp now, in Beirut or Damascus. He had no idea whether Agca did or did not go to such a camp; there was no evidence either way. If he did, though, it probably wouldn't have mattered to him whether Teslim Tore, or Sedat Sirri Kadem, were leftists or rightists. "Agca's personality was vulnerable. He was easily influenced by the *display* of violence, before he had a political idea in his head."

Leaving Malatya, I wondered just when Agca did get a political idea in his head—and what it was, for that matter. While left-wing Turks insisted that he'd been an unregenerate Fascist from earliest youth, I had seen for myself that this wasn't true. Nor was there any sign of his leaning toward the other side. Most of the judges and lawyers who had dealt with him, in Istanbul and Rome, would tell me as I moved along that Agca probably had no strong political convictions at all. "Frankly, I don't think he gives a damn one way or the other," said an Italian judge who got to know him well. If his right-wing credentials were a help—indeed, a necessity—for the professionals who did spot and use him, he didn't actually have to *believe* in anything for the work they had in mind.

Whatever they had made of him, he was no ordinary Turkish terrorist. That much I could be sure of, soon after returning to Ankara. I learned it from a policeman, superior in more than mere rank, who gave me a first glimpse of the strange anomalies in Agca's record as a terrorist. It was enough to convince me that his role in the papal plot must somehow be linked to the mysterious origins of his terrorist career.

The Ankara policeman was sufficiently senior to know a lot, and wise enough in the world's ways to understand that much of what he was telling me was unlikely to reach Rome through official channels. Since I cannot use his name, for obvious reasons, I'll call him "Selim Bey."

He wasted no time on small talk, after we settled down to our glasses of tea in his anonymous gray-walled office thick with tobacco smoke. He started out with a piece of news that made me long for another word with my three police commissioners in Rome. Omer Ay, the "presumed second accomplice" about whom Rome's DIGOS had professed to know nothing, was wanted officially by the Turkish martial-law court for collusion with Agca. The collusion went far beyond merely "helping to procure" Agca's Faruk Ozgun passport. *Two* such perfectly faked passports were issued by a provincial passport office in the town of Nevsehir, on the same day (August 11, 1980), with consecutive numbers (136635 and 136636), carrying the photographs of Mehmet Ali Agca and Omer Ay, and bearing the names of two other living Nevsehir residents, Faruk Ozgun and Galip Yilmaz.

The Turkish General Staff had announced this publicly on July 4, 1981.[1] A warrant for Omer Ay's arrest had been issued through Interpol Ankara *a month earlier,* on June 4—only twenty-two days after the papal shooting. It was an all-countries "Red Bulletin," number 511-23-7693, requesting arrest on sight and extradition. Describing Omer Ay as a "rightist" (he was a local Gray Wolf leader), the warrant charged him with "instigating two murders" in Nevsehir on June 11, 1980, and "procuring a counterfeit passport in the name of Faruk Ozgun" for Agca two months later.

Here was hard, documented proof that Agca did not get to St. Peter's Square on his own, and a strong indication that Omer Ay not only helped him on his way but joined him. Unaccountably—incredibly—the existence of this international arrest warrant would be ignored and even denied in Western Europe from June 1981 until February of the following year.[2]

Selim Bey did not know how Omer Ay had worked the fiddle in the Nevsehir passport office. The director of security there, a religious right-winger named Haydar Tek, was arrested when the fraud was discovered. But Selim Bey could hardly see him as the brains of an important clandestine operation. Nor did he know how Omer Ay might be connected to Omer Mersan, said by Agca to have served as middleman in the transaction. Mersan had no police record in Turkey, where he was wanted only as an army deserter. Whoever was running this operation must be much bigger than these two—a man to be reckoned with, said Selim Bey.

The mystery of Agca himself began in Ankara, he continued. The young man from Malatya was said to have spent two years there, from 1976 to 1978, enrolled as a geography student at the university. Those were the years of uncontrollable terrorist ascendancy on the campus, when anybody with a vocation for violence could have made a name for himself. But Agca apparently took no part in the whole frenetic business: never pulled a gun, tossed a Molotov cocktail, cracked the skull of a Red, joined a riot. He also appeared not to have taken a single exam, was unremembered in classes he should have attended, and was unrecognized by students majoring in his subject. The police in Ankara were unaware of his existence until long after he was gone.

It was the same story after Agca transferred to Istanbul University, in the autumn of 1978. The Istanbul police had never heard of him either, until he was arrested for Abdi Ipekci's murder the following summer, five months after the event.

"Ipekci's murder: that's where you have to look," said Selim Bey, tapping a bulky folder on his cluttered desk. The answer to my enigma in Rome, he declared, lay in the riddles within riddles of Agca's arrest, confession, trial, and conviction for that murder in Istanbul. "Mehmet Ali Agca may not be the real murderer of Abdi Ipekci. *There was no evidence.* The only thing they had on him was a composite drawing that looked something like Agca and any number of other people. There were no witnesses, before he confessed.

The pistol was never found. Read the file. They had no case." (He did not offer me the file, however.)

Here, continued Selim Bey, was one of the "dark areas" on the Turkish scene before the army took over a country in collapse. In his private opinion, the left-wing government in power at the time would have gone to almost any lengths to pin the guilt for Ipekci's death on the right. In fact, leftist groups had offered the police a list of fifteen Gray Wolves resembling that composite drawing. One of them might even have been guilty; some rightist group probably was. But the government was so anxious to prove it that any trumped-up case would do. Agca's trial and conviction were no proof of anything.

"You mean he was framed?" I asked. "Not at all. Somebody paid him to take the fall, so he took it." "Who did?" "Ah! There I can't help you. Ask the people who saw it all firsthand: the presiding judge, the military prosecutor, the lawyers, the local police. See Hasan Fehmi Gunes, who was minister of the interior in those days. He was there when they interrogated Agca; the whole case was in his charge. . . ."

Neither of us thought I was going to break the case on my own, and I didn't. But I made some smashing finds in Istanbul all the same.

As always in that splendid city, I checked into the Pera Palas Hotel. The height of glamour half a century ago, it had been the favorite haunt of those Continental aristocrats, crooks, and spies eternally weaving their webs of intrigue in such books as Agatha Christie's *Murder on the Orient Express.* She was supposed to have written this most celebrated of her thrillers on the second floor of the Pera Palas. The great Kemal Ataturk, father of modern Turkey, was fond of dining there. It was down on its luck now, with its faded velvet drapes, tottering elevator, and rusty water gushing from cracked bathroom taps. But I knew I was in Istanbul when I woke up there in the morning—I couldn't always be sure in a Sheraton or Hilton— and there was a glorious view of the Bosporus from my window.

I had a lot to do in Turkey then and later, but only one thought in my mind right now. I meant to home in on the Ipekci case.

Almost any foreign correspondent visiting the country was bound to have met Abdi Ipekci at some time, as I had shortly before he died. I knew what he stood for—genuine social democracy, personal liberty, firm friendship with the West—and what his assassination could mean for a democratic nation going under.

His murder on February 1, 1979, marked the start of the Big Fright in Turkey: the chilling sense that terrorism had finally skidded out of control. Editor of the moderately left daily *Milliyet,* he was the nation's most influential commentator and nearly its last voice of reason. Toward the last, he was calling urgently on the perpetually warring major parties—Bulent Ecevit's Socialist Republican Party and Suleyman Demirel's conservative Justice Party—to join forces against terrorists of both extremes. But Premier Ecevit's party, then in power, had always been open-ended leftward, and Demirel's rightward. Not once in ten disastrous years had either party cracked down on its own extremist fringe. Each had made resolute efforts to blame all the ravages of terrorism on the other.

Each had also made use of sinister secret forces for that purpose. Right-wing and left-wing infiltrators had penetrated deep into the nation's police force, intelligence services, and sensitive military posts. Police unions of the far left and right (the Pol-Der and Pol-Bir) would habitually cover up for terrorists on their own side, and frame the other side's. When police were sent out in pairs to make terrorist arrests, a Pol-Der cop might kill his Pol-Bir partner before reaching the scene, or the other way round. The MIT, Turkey's CIA, was torn apart by such factional rivalry. In fact, it was up to its neck in the frame-up business, on behalf of one or the other side, if not both.

Against that background, Selim Bey's suspicions on the Ipekci case were more than plausible, and widely shared. Hardly anybody I met in Istanbul could be sure of which side had ordered that hit, directly or through an *agent provocateur.* "Either the right or left might have killed Ipekci. Both had their hit lists of VIPs," I was told by Saim Cotur, Istanbul's deputy governor. "At first, Agca seemed to us right-wing. But during the trial we could not prove any criminal links," said Ilderen Turkmen, who headed the Justice Ministry's Criminal Division. "We still don't know what Agca's ideology is. Others have a cause, but not Agca," said Istanbul's chief military prosecutor, Judge-Colonel Suleyman Takkeci. "Which side could gain the most by plunging Turkey into blind panic? Right or left? I think left," said Nahir Erman, the Ipekci family's lawyer.

It was through Nahir Erman that I stumbled on my first real find. I'd spent a few frustrating days before getting around to him. The presiding judge in Agca's trial was away and could not be reached. The prosecutor at his trial would see me only in the presence of his boss, who, in my presence, forbade him to answer any questions (I marched out in a rage). Judge-Colonel Takkeci had reared up and fled the room at my first awkward demand, promising to be right back (he never returned).

But Nahir Erman, a big, comfortable man of unimpeachable reputation, was full of the story and happy to talk. One of Istanbul's outstanding lawyers, he had been asked by Ipekci's widow, Sybil, to represent the family, halfway through the trial. The verdict was a foregone conclusion by then. Nevertheless, Erman had tried to jolt the court with fresh evidence, which was brushed aside.

Ipekci was shot around seven in the evening, Erman said, shortly after returning to Istanbul from an interview with Premier Ecevit in the capital. He had driven home alone, turning slowly into his narrow, uphill street. It was snowing and dark, and the corner was unlit. Passersby could barely make out the shadows of two men running toward a getaway car. A composite drawing was made of one, whose face had shown up for an instant in the glare of Ipekci's headlights. The drawing resembled Agca. That was all the police had on him when he was arrested.

The police had been tipped off five months after the murder, by an anonymous caller who told them to pick up "Ali" at the Marmara Coffeehouse, a right-wing student hangout. Agca went along peacefully, and confessed at once, invoking an automatic death sentence for homicide under Turkish law. "I did it, I killed Ipekci," he told a nationwide television audience later, as if discussing the weather.

Agca had come directly to that press conference from an underground cell, where he'd been interrogated secretly for eleven days. Looking jaunty and fit, he had joked with reporters. He showed no sign of the police brutality customary under whatever political regime in Turkey. Indeed, he may have been the first murder suspect in years to come out of an Istanbul interrogation cell without a mark on him.

Once he had confessed, a fabulous prize awaited whoever turned him in. Though Ipekci's paper, *Milliyet,* and the Turkish Journalists' Union had offered a reward of 6 million Turkish lire to catch the killer—well over $200,000 at the time*, a princely sum there or anywhere—the anonymous caller never showed up to collect it.[3]

The story kept getting fishier, Erman went on. While two gunmen had undoubtedly been on the scene, Agca insisted to the last that

---

*In 1977 the Turkish lire was 17.5 to the dollar. In 1978, it was 25 to the dollar.

he had acted alone (this began to sound familiar). He had offered three versions of the killing, "each giving the police their only proof of his guilt," observed Erman. First he named the driver of the getaway car, a right-winger from his hometown (who admitted driving the car, but said he didn't know what it was for). Next, Agca said he got the gun from a notorious Gray Wolf, Mehmet Sener (who then skipped the country with suspicious speed). Finally, he claimed to have returned the gun to Sener at the National Action Party offices of Colonel Alpaslan Türkes, whose Nazi-style paramilitary Gray Wolves literally howl—I have heard them—in the presence of their leader.[4] (The gun could not be found, then or since.)

All this appeared to satisfy the court, but not Nahir Erman. Agca's "spontaneous confession" had to be hogwash, he said. Nobody would ask to be hanged when not a thing could be pinned on him. And how come Agca wasn't tortured to get the name of the second gunman out of him? And why didn't anybody ask who was paying him?

For he was certainly being paid, *had in fact been on some secret patron's payroll long before the murder,* and Erman had the evidence to prove it.

Setting out to trace Agca's possible backers, the Ipekcis' lawyer had turned up *half a dozen accounts, in different banks, in different cities, opened in Mehmet Ali Agca's name by somebody forging his signature.* The discrepancy in signatures was obvious, Erman assured me. Amounting in all to some 300,000 Turkish lire, around $18,000, the funds had been paid in over a period of twelve months, deposited in one city and invariably withdrawn in another by the real Mehmet Ali Agca.

The last deposit, for 200,000 lire, was paid in to the Yapi ve Kredi Bankasi on December 29, 1978—a month before Ipekci's murder. The first one, for 40,000 lire, was made in the Turkiye Is Bankasi on December 13, 1977—a full year before Ipekci died, when Agca was still an obscure student in Ankara.

For the penniless student he was also presumed to be, $18,000 was a fortune. It could hardly be explained away by the murder of Ipekci. Any number of willing students could have been found to take that on for much less. The whole arrangement was outside the familiar pattern of Turkish terrorism. Prodigal payrolls like this simply did not exist in a country whose many thousand terrorists normally lived on petty holdups or on pin money doled out by their political backers.

What could Agca have done to earn so much money in twelve months? Nothing, according to the Turkish police. During those months, he had been not only inactive but practically invisible. The explanation seemed to me to lie in the date of that first deposit. By Agca's own account, he had spent the summer of 1977 in a Palestinian training camp. "From that time on, Agca claimed to have 'benefited from secret sources of financing,' " the Italian court had said. So he did, we knew now.

The opening of his first bank account that December followed his return from the camp by just two or three months. It seemed logical to assume that he had indeed been spotted by a professional while he was there or shortly thereafter. Evidently he had looked cool-headed, tough, and intelligent enough to be singled out for particular attention. In professional parlance, he had all the marks of a sleeper, carefully groomed and kept on ice for very special assignments.

The amateur detective in me mourned that lost opportunity. What a lead the bank accounts might have been! Pursued to the end, they could have led to Agca's first secret paymaster, pointing in turn toward those who took over the fugitive Agca in 1979 and sent him on to Rome. In the event, however, the lead had never been pursued at all.

"I brought photocopies of the bank accounts and signatures into court. I proved that others were involved in the Ipekci killing. But the Istanbul court was not interested," Nahir Erman told me. Judge-Colonel Takkeci, the chief martial-law prosecutor who had taken fright at the very sight of me, made the point more neatly when I went back to ask. "The judges couldn't see the connection," he said. "They were satisfied with the evidence they had."

Agca did not wait around to hear the court's predictable verdict. Imprisoned in July 1979, he waited in what appeared to be the obvious expectation of getting sprung. On the witness stand that autumn, he sent out a first cryptic signal. On October 12, he told the court: "After I was captured, the minister of interior, Hasan Fehmi Gunes, came to Istanbul and talked with me. His proposal was that if I would say a high official of the National Action Party ordered me to kill Ipekci, or state that I was a member of that party, Gunes would rescue me."[5]

There was no saying how much of this statement might have been bluff or blackmail. But if Agca was laying a false trail the first time, his blackmailing intent was unmistakable when he took the stand again. "I did not kill Ipekci, but I know who did," he told the court on October 24, adding that he would reveal the true assassin's name at the court's next sitting.[6]

When the court next sat, Agca was gone.

On November 25, 1979, he had donned an army uniform and walked out of the Kartal-Maltepe prison, an impregnable military fortress, passing through *eight* successive doors, each heavily guarded. His escape would have been impossible without help from high quarters.

The next day he sent that curious letter to *Milliyet,* threatening to kill Pope John Paul, who was expected in Istanbul within forty-eight hours. It was the letter of an exalted Islamic zealot, which this champagne-drinking youth seldom seen in a Mosque evidently was not. Did he make it up simply to divert police attention from himself to the Pope, as he claimed later? Or was he advised to write it, for future use?

The answer would be stunning when it came, but I wouldn't have believed it at the time. Either way, I thought then, the letter was a grand exit line. Agca's escape from prison had clearly ended the first stage of his singular terrorist career. Everything up to that point had been entangled in domestic Turkish politics. Everything afterward suggested that he had been handed over the border and up the line, to patrons with broader international concerns.

Bulgaria was the place to ask about that, but frank and forthcoming Bulgarians were likely to be thin on the ground. I stood a better chance of following up from Turkey, where I'd already learned more than I could have hoped for.

Over my last Turkish coffee and *raki* at the Pera Palas before going home for Christmas, I tried to piece together what I had learned. I jotted down some notes to myself.

1. Agca's accomplices in papal assault: proof of Omer Ay's collusion on fake passport, possible presence in Rome. *Press on this.*
2. Agca's motives for shooting Pope: not a nut case, religion and politics out. Must be in it for money. *Whose?*
3. Agca's terrorist career: abnormal. *With* Gray Wolves but not *of* them. *Persona* created deliberately as right-wing terrorist killer? Maybe, since somebody running him from age of nineteen. (The Faceless Paymaster. *Spook?*)
4. Agca's Palestinian training: knew Sedat Sirri Kadem, as

claimed. No confirmation Teslim Tore. But Tore big professional left-wing terrorist and teacher Palestinian camps. Could have spotted Agca there, view timing of first payola. *Get more on Tore and Kadem.*

5. Agca's role in Ipekci murder: could have been there, but confession phony. This the giveaway he was being managed. Who set stage, coached him, turned him in? *Ask man who should know best* (Interior Minister Gunes).

6. Agca's disembodied Turkish friend (accomplice?) in Tunisia, Youssef Dag: zero.

7. Agca's Bulgarian summer: zilch.

8. Omer Mersan: army deserter. Nothing yet on links to Omer Ay in passport deal. No hint his ties to "people involved in black market on vast scale in Turkey," as Agca said. *Just what is this vast black market?*

That was enough to leave on and come back to.

5

"No, madame, we have no evidence that any Turk in Germany, apart from Omer Mersan, ever met or had any contact with Agca, for any reason, or that Agca was ever here himself. We are in close collaboration with the Italians, and we have told them this. According to Agca, he did not enter Germany, and the passport he carried showed that he didn't. So there is no proof, you see."

This was a nonconversation I was having with two senior officers of West Germany's famed Criminal Police in Wiesbaden, the Bundeskriminalamt, said to be among the most efficient in the world. The BKA's policy is to refuse official interviews and deny reports of anything said in unofficial interviews, as my interlocutors were careful to point out. That was the mutual risk we were running: that I would write this, and they would deny it.

I would visit them twice to be sure of my ground—naturally without a tape recorder, but taking copious notes.[1]

They were the first of the stolid, gray men I would meet as I traveled around Germany in the raw gray weather of the early new year—cautious, anonymous, and deliberately dull, methodically diminishing the import of a sinister historic event, reducing high drama to a monotonous recital of selected and minor half-truths. If Germany was by no means the only place where such policemen abounded, these were particularly good at their work.

I was privileged to be received by these two ranking BKA officers, who greeted me cordially in a pleasant cretonne-curtained conference room tucked off the far side of labyrinthine carpeted corridors. Having read my book on international terrorism (doubtless the reason they let me in), that was plainly what they preferred to talk about. But I had come to talk about Mehmet Ali Agca, and in time we got around to him.

Their emphatic denial of Agca's presence in Germany seemed to make no sense. I had the Italian court's Statement of Motivation in my briefcase. On page 15, it spoke of reports by "DIGOS and SISMI in collaboration with the German police" to the effect that Agca had been in Germany "for some months, with false documents, traveling continuously from city to city, forming a close net of contacts with Turkish citizens wanted by the police in Ankara for subversive activities."

Furthermore, at least two Turks in Germany must have had contact with Agca: the Taskin brothers, Hasan and Pehlnel. A DIGOS report in my possession had established that Agca made a 15,000-lire phone call from the Hotel Torino in Rome to the Taskins' number in West Germany's Hannover district (5066/62216) on April 13, 1981—a month before he shot the Pope. The Taskins were well known in Germany's huge Turkish community. Hasan was one of the top ten Gray Wolves in the country, newly elected to the executive board of their Turkish Federation. What did the Taskin brothers have to say about Agca?

Nothing, apparently. The BKA had no proof of the Taskins' Gray Wolf ties, for a start, said Herr A., the more authoritative of the two BKA officers. As for Agca's phone call, I might as well forget it. Both brothers were taken in for questioning about that, and soon released. "They denied ever speaking to Agca," said Herr A. "They claimed it must have been a wrong number. So there was no proof." Surely the length of the call was proof of a kind, I insisted: living in Rome myself, I happened to know that a 15,000-lire phone call to Hannover would have lasted around twenty minutes. "Oh, I don't think so," said Herr A.

I shifted to Omer Ay. The Turkish police, I said, had told me about the two false passports with consecutive numbers from Nevsehir, procured by Ay; and I had seen the international arrest warrant accusing him specifically of procuring the one as Faruk Ozgun for Agca. Ay himself would presumably be traveling as the other, Galip Yilmaz. Had the BKA found any trace of his presence in Germany, under that name if not his own?

"Lots of false passports come from Nevsehir," replied Herr C., the second officer, with a dismissive shrug. "We have nothing on this Omer Ay. Nobody of that name has entered Germany." But what about Galip Yilmaz? Wasn't Ay more likely to have shown that counterfeit passport, if he did slip into the country? Herr C.'s bland expression did not change. "Galip Yilmaz is not a wanted person. Therefore it is not possible to make a passport check in that name," he declared.

The triumph of bureaucracy over reason was too much for me here. Nothing could be clearer than the fact that the genuine Galip Yilmaz was not a wanted person. But Omer Ay was. He had borrowed the name for a false passport that he was suspected of using as an accomplice in an attempt to assassinate the head of the Roman Catholic Church. I imagined most West Germans would want to see that possible accomplice found. Surely the Roman Catholics among them—27 million, almost half the population—would expect the police to move heaven and earth in search of those who had tried to murder their spiritual leader. I wanted to get this straight. Did Herr C. mean to say that routine rules on a passport check should apply in a case like this? He did.

Herr A. intervened. Why should I care so much about Omer Ay, anyway? As usual, we reporters were making a fuss over nothing. Nobody could prove that Ay had been with Agca in Rome. The photographs in St. Peter's Square were useless. Riffling through a folder on the conference table, he pulled one out to prove his point. It showed the unidentifiable man in quarter-profile, running away from the Square with his back turned. "But that's the wrong picture! It's the other one that's supposed to be Omer Ay—the half-hidden face next to Agca's!" I protested, struggling to suppress the thought that these two dignified gentlemen were pulling my leg. The BKA had not seen the photograph I referred to, they said. Nor did they recall the composite drawing resembling Omer Ay, which Rome's DIGOS had circulated internationally through Interpol. I displayed both. The two men shook their heads doubtfully.

We moved on to Omer Mersan. I was not alone in wondering how a key witness like this could have been released with a clean bill of health in twenty-four hours. According to Agca's account, Mersan had a lot to explain: the nature of his meeting with the Pope's would-be assassin in Bulgaria; the counterfeit passport he was said to have procured for Agca; the introduction of a mysterious Bulgarian named Mustafaeff; and Mersan's own alleged ties to, in Agca's words, "a vast band of smugglers operating in Turkey." Such matters could hardly be investigated thoroughly by the German police overnight. Or could they?

Herr C. answered at some length. Omer Mersan was picked up around 11:00 P.M. on May 21, he said, directly after the telexed message from DIGOS reached Wiesbaden. "Mersan admitted that he'd met Agca in Sofia, around the date Agca mentioned, at the Hotel Vitosha," he said. "The Vitosha is frequented by many Turks, of course. Mersan met him under a false name, and didn't know who he was. We could not confirm that he got the false passport for Agca, or introduced him to a Mustafaeff.

"Mersan was very cooperative," continued Herr C. "He answered all questions readily. All the indications were that this had been a chance encounter. We cannot prove the contrary: everything he said sounded plausible. While he was detained, his house, car, and shop were searched—all negative. The only thing against him was Agca's statement. He was released in twenty-four hours under German law, because of insufficient evidence to hold him. We have no Third Degree here, you know. . . ." I joined in the good-humored laughter.

Still, it wasn't much of an answer. Although I'd never met Mersan, his version of the Sofia meeting didn't sound so true and reliable to me. Judging from what I'd learned in Turkey, it was next to impossible that he could have failed to recognize Agca, whose notoriety as the confessed murderer of Abdi Ipekci had made his face as familiar as a movie star's to Turks nearly everywhere. Turkey's two largest dailies, *Milliyet* and *Hurriyet,* published special editions in Germany for some million and a half Turkish immigrant workers there. Living in Munich, Mersan was bound to read one of these Turkish papers. Both had splashed Agca's picture over their front pages time and again.

Apart from that dent in his credibility, there was Agca's charge that Mersan was a smuggler. I could see for myself by now that Agca had a certain credibility of his own, especially in those parts of his interrogation where he went into detail. He had told in detail about meeting Mersan. It was only reasonable to question the wisdom of taking Mersan's word against Agca's without looking further.

If the BKA had in fact looked further, it would not tell me so. Mersan had committed no crime in Germany, Herr A. said firmly. To all appearances he was a respectable businessman, free to do as he pleased and entitled to his privacy. No, the BKA had no address for him in Munich. He was still there at his old job, though.

We parted with affable smiles, and Herr A.'s assurance that I was welcome to come again anytime. But he wasn't sure there was much more to say. "To tell you the truth, madame, we don't understand this obsession of yours with the idea of an international plot. Come, now. Whatever makes you believe there was any such thing? Our police in Germany really don't see the attack on the Pope as the big operation you seem to think it was. There is no proof of a plot on the police side. Have you found a single piece of solid evidence down there in Rome?"

There was no profit in arguing the matter with this fatherly BKA officer who had stonewalled me for two solid hours. The morning had been profitless enough.

It wouldn't do to be irreverent about the Bundeskriminalamt, I thought, looking back at the squat, clinical building neatly hemmed in evergreen hedge and sealed in bulletproof glass trimmed with steel. There were men of imposing reputation in there, not to mention a computerized data bank storing ten million items of information on the international terrorist and criminal underworld. To believe they actually knew less than I did about a case of such worldwide importance would be impossibly arrogant. To assume they knew more would be natural enough: I certainly didn't expect them to share their every thought with me.

Coming from a lowlier source, however, some of their statements would have sounded distinctly uninformed. Had my interlocutors been anybody but Herr A. and Herr C., I would have concluded that they either did not *want* to know the ascertainable and verifiable facts about the papal shooting, or were covering up what they did know.

One or the other could have applied to my discovery that same afternoon. Omer Mersan was not still there at his old job. A phone call from the Wiesbaden railroad station to the Vardar Company in Munich (at the number furnished by Agca) left no room for doubt about that. Mersan did not work there, had never worked there, would never work there, was the burden of the message. He could have stopped by and picked up a business card or something, to pretend he did; but he was not known to the proprietors of the Vardar Export-Import Company. "But the police found him through your number," I began, whereupon my party hung up.

By the following day, I knew that Mersan was indeed connected to a vast smuggling ring operating in Turkey. The evidence was dropped in my lap, by a Turkish reporter as obsessed with the case as I was. Orsan Oymen was *Milliyet*'s correspondent in Bonn, a youngish, rumpled-looking, sleepy-eyed man, likable, generous, and competent.

An old friend of Abdi Ipekci's, Orsan had started to build up a dossier on Mehmet Ali Agca since the latter's arrest for Ipekci's murder. Making the most of a sharp mind, diffident manner, and wonderfully ingenuous, open face, he had collected what is probably the most complete file on Agca in existence. I have never seen him without his bulging leather dispatch case, crammed with unavailable documents from five or six countries.

We talked through the morning at Orsan's home in Bad Godesberg, where his pretty German wife served coffee, then kept at it as we walked through a blustering January wind to lunch at a restaurant, and went back to his home for documents to be photocopied. We differed politically in general, he tilting toward the East and I toward the West, and so were bound to disagree about this case. Orsan felt that the Gray Wolves had to be the prime movers, since we kept tripping over them at every turn. But that was too simple, I thought. Apart from lack of motive—neither of us could imagine what good it would do the Gray Wolves in Turkey to kill the Pope in Rome—there was the whole mystery of Agca himself.

His years as a sleeper in Ankara and Istanbul, his mysterious bank accounts, his strange behavior in the Ipekci affair all suggested a level of sophistication and duplicity far above the Gray Wolves' habitually crude performance. The Gray Wolves plainly had to be part of it. But I could not see how to reconcile that with Agca's summer in Bulgaria. What could a gang of Turkish neo-Nazis have to do with the most orthodox Communist regime in Eastern Europe?

The clue to the answer was in the handful of typewritten pages Orsan gave me (mostly in Turkish), whose full significance I would not grasp for months.

Omer Mersan was the clue. What Orsan had learned about him wasn't really much. It was the proof of his connections that mattered.

The smuggling ring he worked for was known as the Turkish Mafia, and its home base was Bulgaria. The Hotel Vitosha was its big meeting place in Sofia, which was why Mersan often stayed there (Horst Grillmayer, the shady Viennese gun dealer, was a frequent guest too). Orsan had gotten the tip on Mersan's connections from an oldtimer in the Turkish Mafia, Suleyman Necati Topuz, imprisoned in West Germany for smuggling dope.

Topuz was in Sofia when Omer Mersan first showed up there in 1977. An army deserter on the run, Mersan was taken under the Mafia's wing, Topuz said. Eventually, he rose to be an assistant to a top Mafia boss, Abuzer Ugurlu—a man whose menacing shadow would loom large as the plot unfolded. There were four other Ugurlu brothers in the trade, all men of immense power in Istanbul. But Abuzer was the Godfather, the kingpin of their contraband ring in Sofia, where he lived on and off, and had once kept a villa (the address was Arh Milanov, 18; later, in the 1970s, he settled in another villa in the port of Varna, his to this day).[2] From Sofia and Varna, he was said to direct a colossal traffic in and out of Turkey: drugs, out; cigarettes, liquor, electronic goods, and weapons, in.

Orsan had no firm facts on the dimensions of Ugurlu's two-way traffic. "Big. Very big," was all he knew. He did have a document or two on Mersan's tie-in, however.

Topuz, who repented after his capture, had been running dope into Western Europe for and with Abuzer Ugurlu. (Both their names were on the Interpol warrant that landed Topuz in jail in 1979, I discovered in Turkey later.)[3] Waging a one-man war from his Bayreuth prison cell, he had tried to expose Omer Mersan's connections well before the papal shooting.

In one letter dated December 2, 1980, he had written to remind the Counselor of the Turkish Embassy in Sofia: "Omer Mersan, a Turkish citizen, applied to your consular office to have his passport renewed in 1977. The consulate rejected his request because of information received. . . . Omer Mersan is the lieutenant of Fikri Koçakerim, who works for the Ugurlu family, which works together with the Bulgarian secret service. . . ."[4]

How the German police could have missed this was beyond me. Agca had actually told them that Mersan was a smuggler (reported in the DIGOS telex). If Mersan was in Sofia on business when the two met there, it was in all likelihood the Turkish Mafia's business. Since he gave Agca the Vardar Company's phone number, and was found through the same number ten months later, the Vardar Company appeared to be in the same business. Whether he was working alone or with Vardar for the Godfather, it was a safe bet that the Godfather was working for or with the Bulgarian secret services. I didn't need the letter from Topuz to recognize that no Turk could run a colossal contraband traffic out of Sofia without their knowledge and consent.

This was the man—the Godfather's man—to whom Agca claimed to have been sent in Bulgaria by "a comrade in Turkey."

One more link and I'd have it, I thought. I was beginning to see how it all might have worked. From the comrade in Turkey to Mersan the middleman in Sofia, to the Godfather and his Turkish Mafia, to the Bulgarian secret police, several degrees removed: that was how Agca would have been passed on and up the line after his big prison break. If most of this would need confirmation, it had just enough substance to be a plausible working theory. But I couldn't see where the Gray Wolves fit in. "Is Omer Mersan a Gray Wolf?" I asked Orsan, who looked startled. "Mersan? No, no. He's just in business . . . ," he replied. There must be some other explanation, then, I told myself. The Gray Wolf link had to be there—it was— but at the time, I couldn't find it.

What bothered me was that I was at least looking for such possible connections, whereas the German police apparently were not. It was hard to believe that they could have failed to inquire into the nature of Mersan's business in Sofia, not to mention the Vardar Company's, during the twenty-four hours they held him. Even after releasing him, they had superb facilities for tracking such things down. Thinking back to my morning with the Bundeskriminalamt, and the information said to be stored in its data bank, I didn't know what to believe. Orsan, who had been in Bonn long enough to know more about these matters, rolled his eyes heavenward when I asked. He couldn't help me there.

Moving on around West Germany—from Wiesbaden and Bonn to Hamburg, Berlin, Frankfurt, Munich—I could see why West German authorities might hate to get entangled in even the outermost fringes of the Agca case. The very presence of a million and a half Turks was an intractable police problem. It was impossible to watch over the doings of so many foreigners speaking an incomprehensible language, flocking to a land of legendary affluence by hook or crook, clustered in ethnic ghettos from Cologne and Frankfurt to West Berlin: "Turkey's fourth largest city," Herr A. of the BKA had observed.

Having no way to sort out a small criminal contingent of hoods, smugglers, and con men from the overwhelming majority of honest Turkish immigrant workers, the German police tended by and large to leave them alone. Unfortunately, that also applied to thousands of Turkish terrorists. No other West European state offered so safe a harbor for Turkey's terrorist fugitives of the right and left, both groups able to melt into the Turkish community background and enjoy the benevolent protection of one or another side in German politics.

From a steady trickle during the early seventies, the terrorist influx swelled to a flood after the Turkish army took power in September 1980. By the time I got to Bonn in the winter of 1982, the Federal German Interior Ministry had reported the presence of 56,000 Turkish extremists, split half and half between rightists and leftists.[5] The hard-core left-wingers, though divided into forty factions, tended to gather around the pro-Moscow formation called FIDEF. The other half buzzed mostly around the Gray Wolves' Turkish Federation, with 120 branches on German soil.

They were one big floating mine. Nestled in among the 56,000 extremists were some 7,000 terrorists wanted by the Turkish courts for acts of shocking violence, 125 of them for multiple murder (these were the Turkish ministry's figures, not Federal Germany's).[6] Accustomed to living by their wits and their guns, untrained for legitimate work and forever short of money, they might be bent to any criminal purpose, from gunrunning and dope pushing to hiring out as hit men (exactly the role some played in the papal plot). Keeping track of them would have occupied much or most of Germany's national police force. To put it baldly, the Germans didn't bother.

What had started as mere neglect became a matter of political principle after the Turkish army took over. The new military regime was anathema to Chancellor Schmidt's Social Democratic constituents, few of whom had the smallest notion of the intolerable terrorist provocation that had left the Turkish army no choice. Almost any Turk who could make it from Ankara or Istanbul to Frankfurt or Cologne was accepted on sight as a freedom fighter and political exile, fleeing persecution at home. How that affected German police inquiries into the Agca case would soon become scandalously plain.

Above and beyond all this was an apparently widespread conviction in German governing circles that, in an investigation that could end only as this one finally did, invincible ignorance was their safest course. The everlasting problem of a divided Germany, the anxiety for more livable relations with its eastern wing by way of more indulgent relations with the Soviet Union, had made *Ostpolitik* a political imperative for many years. There would be no confrontation with the Russians over the shooting of the Pope if Bonn's Social Democratic government could help it.

Considerations like these might explain why Agca's presence could never be ascertained in West Germany during his year or so on the loose in Europe: this despite four formal notes from the Turkish Embassy in Bonn indicating his whereabouts there, another five communications directly from Ankara, and an Interpol "Red Bulletin" warrant for his arrest going back to the summer of 1980 (after Agca was sentenced to death *in absentia* for the Ipekci killing).[7] Omer Mersan could go about his business unimpeded for the same reasons, demanding—and getting—judicial and police protection from harassment.[8] Others turned out to be doing better still, as their names came to light one by one.

I was back in Rome, getting ready to leave for Turkey again, when Omer Ay's face suddenly appeared on the evening television news. He had been picked up for driving without lights in Hamburg's red-light district. A ripple of excitement emanated from the studio as the announcer flashed the famous photograph of the half-hidden face, side by side with the real Omer Ay's, on the screen. This was as near as any country had come yet to producing a possible live accomplice of Agca's, still less arresting one. I rushed out, muttering something unintelligible to my husband, Tom, and headed for DIGOS headquarters.

Police Commissioner N. was less on his guard and a shade more informative now. I had not betrayed his confidences so far, meager as they were; and, having been to Turkey and West Germany, I was no longer a hopeless innocent. (To mark the change in my status, I was spared the sprung brown armchair in an antechamber, and offered a straightbacked armless one in his own box of an office.) Unflappable as always, the commissioner tried not to look surprised when I mentioned Omer Ay's arrest. "Is that so?" was all he said, from which I gathered that he had not yet been informed by the BKA.

I asked if he might have something more on Omer Ay's double passport dealings. Looking a little shamefaced—we both remembered the yawning gaps in his original account—he said there was nothing new. Evidently, Omer Ay did procure the two counterfeit passports in Nevsehir on August 11, 1980, after which there was a blank till the end of the month. Agca had received the one in Faruk Ozgun's name on August 31, when he used it to cross over the Bulgarian border into Yugoslavia on a Turkish tourist bus.

I was curious about the blank. How could the commissioner be sure that Agca got the passport on August 31? Mightn't it have been delivered anytime after August 11? Not likely, said Commissioner N.

Pulling a well-stuffed cardboard file from his desk drawer, he read out three dates that made my day. The Faruk Ozgun passport was stamped for currency export (540 Deutschmarks) by the Osmanli Bank in Istanbul on August 27. It was stamped for exit from the Turkish border town of Edirne on August 30. *Then it was stamped for entry into Bulgaria at Kapitan Andreevo, the opposite border post, on August 31, and for exit from Bulgaria on the same day at Kalotina, on the Yugoslav border.*

We were onto something here. Where was the courier who carried the passport on the night between August 30 and 31? Assuredly not encamped on a strip of no-man's land between the two frontiers. How to explain the Bulgarian entry and exit stamps on the same day? If the stamps were authentic, somebody would have had to rush the fake passport from Kapitan Andreevo straight across Bulgaria to the Yugoslav frontier—a grueling five-hundred-mile drive—between morning and evening. There was no obvious need for such haste, after Agca's leisurely summer in Sofia.

Not until I was putting the whole story together did I stumble on the explanation.

I underlined the dates heavily in my notebook as Commissioner N. talked on, starred them, then added a row of question marks: a reminder to look into this on my next visit to Turkey.

We chatted a while longer. I told the commissioner about Agca's strange terrorist career in Turkey, the secret payroll, the Ipekci affair, the information I'd gotten on Omer Mersan's ties to the Turkish Mafia and the Godfather. He listened impassively. An occasional glint of interest filtering through his tinted glasses revealed that at least some of this was news to him. For once, we discussed the case with a degree of candor. Commissioner N. agreed that we could write off the lone, mad gunman, or any conventional terrorist band. "This was *not* an ordinary terrorist hit, meant to spread blind panic," he said. "It was a deliberate, high-level political hit, to create pandemonium among states of the Mediterranean and Europe."

There was reason to believe that Agca did have two accomplices in St. Peter's Square, he added. Instead of creating a diversion so that the gunman could slip away, they appeared to have abandoned him, leaving him to be caught and identified as a right-wing Turkish killer. Right-wing and Turkish . . . That would fit into the intricate design beginning to emerge.

The next morning, I canceled my flight for Ankara and booked for Hamburg, where Omer Ay was being held. Before leaving, I dropped in on Judge Martella. Checking in to see the judge was standard operating procedure, if only to find out what mood he was in. He didn't usually give away anything else.

At this stage—mid-February 1982—the general public was no more than dimly aware of Judge Martella. Those who had heard of him at all were inclined to take him for a plodding, unimaginative fellow, unlikely to get very far, if anywhere, on the Agca case. Whether he knew this or minded, he did nothing to correct the impression. Time would take care of it.

Judge Martella's office was one of a dreary row on a poorly lit floor of the singularly depressing jerry-built warren of purplish granite buildings known as the Tribunale, Rome's central courthouse. He was in a rather good mood this time, as he settled back in his chair to listen. (He was a very good listener, I had noticed.) I gave him much the same account I'd given the DIGOS commissioner. He nodded occasionally, jotted down a note or two, asked me to spell Abuzer Ugurlu's name. (He was plainly not onto the Turkish Mafia yet.) Then he sent me off with a wryly apologetic smile. He knew I would not want him to violate the *segreto istruttorio* and so endanger the whole investigation, he explained unnecessarily for the tenth time. Of course not, I answered insincerely. Might he just give me a hint of how he felt about Omer Ay's arrest? He was interested, naturally.

After a day in Hamburg, I was riveted. Omer Ay had been sitting pretty there, even as the BKA was assuring me that he had never been in the country. According to official German records, he'd been there all along.

Omer Ay, it turned out, had shown up at a government office in Hamburg on May 27, 1981—two weeks after the attack on the Pope—to ask for political asylum. Flanked by two lawyers, he gave his own name and claimed to have lost his passport. Friends had smuggled him into West Germany in a sealed Transports Internationaux Routiers (TIR) truck the previous April 16, he said.[9] He presented himself as a "schoolteacher and intellectual" from Nevsehir, forced to flee Turkey because of his sympathy for the former left-wing Social Democratic premier Bulent Ecevit. Both the Gray Wolves and the military regime were hunting him in Turkey, because of his own "social and democratic views," he declared.[10]

By November, West German authorities had granted him provisional asylum, traveling papers, and a welfare allowance of 714 Deutschmarks a month (around $350). His wife and child, who joined him in Hamburg the next January, were granted similar status. Her brand-new passport from Nevsehir bore no exit stamp from Turkey or visa for West Germany.

My information this time was coming from two members of Hamburg's Special Branch, plainclothes detectives who admitted they could not make head or tail of the Ay case. They were less gray and dampening than most of the others I'd met, and more willing than any to tell me how things stood.

Captain L., who did most of the talking, confessed to telling the press a harmless fib about Ay's arrest. He was not picked up by chance, for a traffic violation. The police were after him because of a message from Turkey ten days earlier, on February 4. Transmitted to Hamburg by the BKA, the message said that Omer Ay was wanted by the Turkish authorities, and a warrant would follow shortly. No sooner did the warrant arrive than the Hamburg police promptly hauled him in. "We knew him here, but not as a wanted person," said Captain L. "He was known to us as one of the Gray Wolves."

If he was known to the German police, it seemed incredible that he hadn't been arrested long ago. I had seen the text of Turkey's request to Interpol for an international "Red Bulletin" arrest warrant for Omer Ay: it was dated June 4, 1981, twenty-two days after the Pope was shot. Omer Ay was already in Hamburg then—had in fact gone to register with the authorities there as a political refugee. Why didn't the police go after him?

Captain L. looked mystified. The first official notice of an Interpol arrest warrant had reached Wiesbaden on February 13, 1982; he was sure of that. Nevertheless, the German police did know about Omer Ay and his forged Galip Yilmaz passport long before. Turkish authorities had sent a message "several days after the attack on the Pope," he declared, concerning Omer Ay and the two counterfeit passports with consecutive numbers from Nevsehir. The message had specified that "a" Galip Yilmaz would probably be found in West Germany.

Sure enough, "a" Galip Yilmaz *was* found. He had actually enrolled at the university in Frankfurt before anybody in Europe had heard of Agca and Omer Ay, in January 1981. A Xerox copy of his passport photo was on file there. The trouble was that *it did not really look like the real Galip Yilmaz, or Omer Ay either.* "The picture is of a younger man, without a beard. It *could* be Ay when he was younger, but . . . ," said the baffled Captain L.

Before I could digest this amazing news, the captain had dismissed it. If Omer Ay was not the fellow in the passport picture, he was off the hook. The two counterfeit passports from Nevsehir were his only connection to the Agca case, and the Turks must have gotten that story wrong. Ay denied ever setting eyes on Agca anyway, and had an alibi besides: on the day the Pope was shot in Rome, Ay was supposedly visiting "a distant relative" in Bochum, West Germany.

The captain was giving up too easily, to my mind. Several authoritative Turkish officials had told me about the Nevsehir passports, including the redoubtable Ankara policeman Selim Bey. A martial-law court in the region had investigated thoroughly before ordering Ay's arrest. Evidently Turkey and West Germany were not communicating too well, on this and other matters. Apart from the passport mix-up, furthermore, there was still the matter of that half-hidden face next to Agca's in the celebrated photograph, and the composite drawing resembling Omer Ay. Captain L. and his colleague had never heard of either one.

On my request, the captain sent a messenger for a back copy of the popular German weekly *Der Spiegel*, where Orsan Oymen had published an article on Omer Ay with pictures, in the summer of 1981. Then I produced my own copy of the composite drawing. The physical description under it tallied almost exactly with the Special Branch description of Omer Ay: "from 30 to 33 years old" (Ay was 30); "about 1.7 meters tall" (he was 1.69); "slender, dark hair slightly balding at the temples, dark olive skin, flattened nose, small black eyes" (Omer Ay's features, word for word).

The whole thing was too much for us. It was up to the Hamburg court to straighten it out in extradition hearings, Captain L. concluded, and the best of luck to the presiding judge.

He had one thing more to tell me, a "clear indication" of the peculiarities surrounding the Ay-Agca case. A number of Turks were interrogated after Omer Ay's arrest—"the same Turks who were questioned about Agca." They all turned out to have no stamps or visas in their passports. To a man they claimed to have been smuggled into West Germany from Turkey by TIR truck. "They said they were never checked by the Eastern Europe border police," the captain exclaimed. "Fantastic! Straight out of *A Thousand and One Nights!*"

Three months would pass before Ay's case came before the Hamburg Supreme Court. The Turkish court responsible for his original arrest order had now cleared up the tangled passport mystery. Omer Ay had borrowed the real Galip Yilmaz's identity card, and *substituted the photograph with that of yet another Nevsehir resident named Hyseyin Fidan*, closely resembling Ay and Yilmaz both.[11] Using the doctored ID card, he procured the counterfeit passport and lit out of Turkey, heading for Germany as Galip Yilmaz.

That settled, the Hamburg judge ruled in favor of Ay's extradition to Turkey.

The postscript to this story would be funny, if it did not reflect a striking indifference to the attempt on the life of Pope John Paul II and a political state of mind in painful disarray.

Shocked by the extradition ruling, Omer Ay's defense attorney appealed for help to the president of the Social Democratic Party, Willy Brandt. His letter was published by Orsan Oymen in *Milliyet* with a certain glee:

Dear Comrade Willy:
I have been a party member for eighteen years, and have worked for you and Helmut Schmidt. Today I would like you to do me a favor that is quite urgent.

I am the attorney for a Turkish exile in asylum here named Omer Ay, who is to be extradited as the alleged would-be murderer of the Pope. On May 4, the Hamburg Supreme Court ruled that he should be returned to the military dictatorship of Turkey and its hangmen. I have presented a petition to the Constitutional Court today, to stop the return proceedings. For reasons of eminent political importance, however, I fear the court will be timid.

In his application as a political refugee, Omer Ay stated that he is a Social Democrat. But he is accused of being a Gray Wolf. . . .

Whatever he is, I believe that we are in need of solidarity. . . . An attempted assassination of a Pope is just about a textbook example of a political deed. An attempted assassination of a statesman is a political deed under German law. . . . The extradition would be unlawful because Mr. Ay has asked for political asylum. In this application, he certified . . . that he is a democratic-thinking human being.

Mathias Scheer[12]

To add a postscript to the postscript: Omer Ay did not call himself a Social Democrat. He said he had "social" and "democratic" views. In point of fact, he was listed as a Gray Wolf in the Ankara police register, and known as such to the Hamburg Special Branch. He was also under indictment for instigating a murder in his own right, of a political leader in his hometown of Nevsehir—a Social Democrat, at that.

6

Sayin Basbugum:
First, I kiss your hands with my deep respects, and I want to express my debt of infinite thanks for your paternal interest. I am in no difficulties, with help of all kinds from brother Idealists who have taken me into their hearts. I find myself in the happy condition of doing my duty with honor, with the pride of being a Turk . . . the duty of grand Ideals.

May God protect the Turks and make them Great.

Mehmet Ali Agca

Sayin Basbugum means "Illustrious *Duce*," or *Führer,* or "Leader" in Turkish. The *Basbugum* addressed here was Colonel Alpaslan Türkes, patron of Turkey's neo-Nazi paramilitary Idealists—the Gray Wolves.

A photocopy of this letter, undated, was sent to *Milliyet* in Istanbul along with a torn envelope postmarked Munich, dated July 20, 1981: two days before Agca's trial in Rome. An anonymous caller had telephoned the editors to say that his dog had dug up the letter under a tree at the State Farm Ataturk Orman Çiftiliği near Ankara. The dog had gone on digging and unearthed the envelope too.

Agca had been in jail for two months in Rome, and Colonel Türkes for nine months in Ankara, when this letter was purportedly mailed in Munich. Had Agca been silly enough to write it, his prison guards would have been bound to intercept it. Colonel Türkes, imprisoned with 219 fellow party members directly after the army took over, would surely have torn it up in the unlikely event of his having received it. He was already accused of instigating 674 terrorist murders in the preceding nine years. A Pope-slayer's thank-you note was the last thing he needed.

For a laughably clumsy forgery, though, the letter was a big success. The military prosecutor in Ankara actually introduced the photocopy as evidence in the Türkes trial, where it was accepted as authentic and reported as such in the international press. (I had read the wire-service item in Italy and been taken in myself.)[1] Thus, two villains were framed for something that could not otherwise be pinned on either one. Though Agca had long moved in right-wing circles, all the evidence showed him to be a minor figure on the fringes of that movement. Nobody had yet come up with proof that he was a card-carrying Gray Wolf, still less that Colonel Türkes had ever met him, let alone taken a fatherly interest in his mission to Rome. Now the Gray Wolves' *Basbugum* became Agca's protector, and Agca his self-confessed ward—just what the public had been wrongly led to expect all along. That is how a persona is made.

It was *Milliyet*'s editor, Cihan Aytul, who showed me the letter, told me the tale of the purposeful dog and his unidentified master, and pointed out the dubious signature and improbable dates. He thought it was a joke, but I didn't.

The fact that a military prosecutor would use this crude piece of disinformation to hang yet another rap on an extremist leader— whether of the right or left made no difference—was a disheartening example of what I was up against in Turkey. While the army had quickly restored internal peace, it could not so easily restore the nation's sense of political balance after a decade of terrorism verging on civil war. Where the generals in power were understandably anxious to go after both extremes, much of the population continued to see only one as The Enemy—either one. Nearly everybody I'd met here had wound up siding with the left or right during the murderous seventies, when the middle dropped out of Turkish politics. Most were still trying to exonerate their side and incriminate the other for the worst of the savagery that had forced the country to its knees.

Not many could judge a case like Agca's dispassionately. One side had him ticketed and labeled as a rightist, the other as a secret agent of the leftists. The thought that he might have been both would scarcely cross their minds.

Accordingly, people who could tell me something about him were generally inclined to leave out something else. His story simply would not fit into the neat contours of a political world divided between Good Guys and Bad Guys. The idea that the two might see eye to eye about demolishing Turkish democracy, that the barrier between them was therefore not impassable, that in addition to infiltrating and manipulating each other they might actually work together, did not bear thinking about. Yet I was beginning to see that this was just the point. Whether Agca was at the outer edge or inner core of the Gray Wolf movement, his exact whereabouts on the right were of little importance. The central fact was that his mysterious connections led to the right and left alike.

Back in Turkey that February, I was trying to discover where and how these lines converged. The rain, suitably, would not let up while I went about this. Mostly, it was like trying to walk underwater.

I started with Agca's claim to have been trained in Lebanon. Could a right-wing Turkish student have gone to a left-wing Palestinian guerrilla camp? Certainly not, said Tayyar Sever, heading the Political Section of the Istanbul police. Certainly, said General M. of the Turkish General Staff in Ankara. I had no way of measuring their sincerity ("There's no such thing as a sincerometer," Lenin once said). But Tayyar Sever had a past to defend, whereas General M. had the facts in hand.

Istanbul's Political Police Chief had been holding down the same job in 1979—the year of Ipekci's murder in that city, of Agca's suspect arrest and confession there for the murder, of the disclosures in court about the bank accounts in Agca's name (these last never followed up by the Istanbul police). I could hardly expect more or less than the answers Tayyar Sever gave me.

Agca was a rightist from start to finish, he said from behind untidy peaks of papers in his pocket-sized, smoke-wreathed office; and "no right-wing Turkish militant ever went to a Palestinian training camp." Not a shred of evidence had been found in support of Agca's claim, while at least one key witness had denied it flatly. Sedat Sirri Kadem, said to have sent Agca on his way to Beirut, had been arrested in August 1981—I tried to look unconcerned at this casual announcement—and turned out to be an activist in the extreme left-wing terrorist band, Dev-Sol. Kadem had admitted to being a friend of Agca's during their Malatyan schooldays, and the two had apparently renewed their friendship at the University of Istanbul, continued Tayyar Sever. But Kadem insisted that "our hearts and minds were not the same," and said he knew nothing of Agca's pilgrimage to Palestine.

"We found Sedat Sirri Kadem's testimony very logical," Tayyar Sever went on. "Because if Agca had gone to a PLO camp, he would have been shot."

Perhaps he was trying to tell me that no self-respecting leftist would touch an unregenerate rightist with a barge-pole—or that any damn fool rightist would have sense enough to steer clear of sinister leftists. Whatever the case, he had to be wrong. Assorted PLO formations were on record as having taken in rightists from other countries. Among these were German neo-Nazis in the Karl Hoffman band, responsible for the dreadful 1980 Oktoberfest bombing in Munich. The German minister of interior, Gerhard Baum, had announced that publicly the following summer.[2]

Furthermore, Tayyar Sever's key witness didn't sound too reliable, once I'd learned where he came from. Sedat Sirri Kadem's underground group, Dev-Sol ("Revolutionary Youth"), was a hardcore Leninist band, among the deadliest on the terrorist left. The military wing of Teslim Tore's Turkish People's Liberation Movement, it was also the most closely bound to the Palestine Rejection Front (PFLP) leader, George Habash.

Habash's PFLP, also Leninist, had signed a formal aid pact with Dev-Sol in March 1980. I had the text, one of countless documents seized during the army's terrorist roundup in Turkey.[3] Apart from special guerrilla training courses for Dev-Sol, the PFLP undertook to provide 1,000 Brownings, 300 Kalashnikovs, 300 automatics for urban warfare, 500 hand grenades, 20 smoke bombs, 20 silencers, and 10 RPG-7 rocket launchers, for that single year alone. Hundreds of Dev-Sol cadres had passed through the Habash camps in Lebanon, before and after the pact. If Sedat Sirri Kadem did arrange for Agca to join them, he was hardly likely to endanger Dev-Sol's profitable relationship with Habash by admitting it.

General M. could not tell me whether or not Agca actually went to such a camp. No firm evidence on that had come his way. But this quiet, frail, silver-haired career officer, widely respected by honest Turks of left, right, and center for his straitlaced sense of justice, had a prodigious amount of information on the subject as a whole. Of all the high-ranking Turkish military officers attempting to set things straight after the takeover, General M. was probably the best informed and surely the most meticulous on the whole history of "The Anarchy." Some 43,000 Turks had been detained and interrogated about right- and left-wing terrorism, after the army came in.[4] Their testimony was available to him. By early 1982, when I met him, more than 400 prisoners had described their Palestinian training courses in detail.

Their confessions dovetailed with Agca's almost word for word, and left no doubt about the Palestinians' indiscriminate hospitality where Turkish terrorists were concerned. "The Palestinians gave training, aid, ammunition, and arms to leftists, rightists, Kurdish separatists, and Armenians," declared the general without any ifs, ands, or buts.

I had seen and heard one such confession, at a screening of television documentaries on "The Anarchy" at the State TRT/TV studios. A Kurdish Communist Party militant named Mehmet Girgin described his own Palestinian training experience like this:

From a Turkish border town where "everything was organized" and "railroad officials were greased," Girgin was smuggled to Damascus by train, then accompanied to Beirut. For the next three months, he was trained in "arms, bombing, attack, types of defense, some action patterns of a regular army, even bayonet fighting."

Afterward, "a lady came to the camp and took us to the Armenian Secret Liberation Organization. There they gave us special courses on bomb types with electronic parts, and along with this they gave us some things [sic]. *Later, they brought us to a meeting with other Turks. There were fifty or sixty from the Kurdish Democratic Front whom we knew were trained in Habash's camps. And also there were Idealists from ÜLKÜCÜLER [Gray Wolves] and those of AKIN-CILAR [religious right] who were being trained in the Ketai Region by the pro-Israeli Falangists [sic]. Those who were being trained there are being trained by the Kurdish Communist Party and Democratic Front too* [my italics]."

The end of Mehmet Girgin's Palestinian adventure had also caught my attention. "They were sending us home in groups of two or three," he said. "We waited about fifteen days to cross the border into Turkey. They arranged to get us across with the smugglers, who guided us through the mine fields. . . ."

The reliance on smugglers was no surprise: terrorists do that everywhere. The intriguing point here was a matter of scale. In a country with the highest terrorist kill-rate in the world (until the army takeover in September 1980), the proportion of smugglers involved with terrorists was likely to be high in any case. In Turkey, though, it began to look so excessively high that I felt I was onto something.

General M. had let me in because I had already written at length about "The Anarchy," as I had witnessed it in early 1979. Evidently, he thought I should be brought up to date. Dryly, precisely, referring to orderly stacks of single-spaced typewritten documents, he gave me an exemplary briefing on the methodical destruction of a democratic state. Piece after piece of the puzzle fell into place as he talked.

Between them, Turkish terrorists of the right and left had amassed an arsenal of staggering size. A million weapons had been confiscated since the army took over, said General M. Counting ammunition, walkie-talkies, electronic equipment, and explosives, the estimated value of this military equipment was around three-quarters of a billion dollars. There was no way the terrorists could have collected all that by raiding Turkish armories, still less raised the money to pay for it. Jewel robberies and bank heists covered a mere fraction of the cost, for all the country's terrorist bands combined.

Apart from a modest portion made secretly on Turkey's Black Sea Coast, the weapons had been manufactured all over the place: Soviet Russia, the United States, Czechoslovakia, Belgium, France, Spain, Italy, the two Germanys. What mattered, however, was not who produced them but who had seen to their delivery. A sizable quantity came from Palestinian sources, smuggled in from the south through Syria. Practically all the rest had arrived through "organized smuggling by Eastern-bloc states and certain established companies formed with the absolute knowledge of a certain state," the general declared. "We have captured certain people who explained how they got their arms from foreign countries, and found certain documents completely bearing them out."

The "certain state" he did not name, but meant, was Bulgaria: staging area for this organized smuggling, and the smugglers' home base. I was finally on the track of the contraband ring Agca had described as "operating on a vast scale in Turkey"—the Turkish Mafia.

It would take a while to grasp the ring's full importance in the papal plot, but at least Agca's baffling political ambivalence was starting to make sense. If Turkey's far right and left had a language in common, it was gunspeak. And if there was a place where that language could bring them together to meet and mingle freely, it was in Communist Bulgaria, under the auspices of a criminal confraternity whose benevolent purpose was to furnish both with a prodigal stock of weapons.

Where could I turn to find out how it all worked? General M. was politely evasive, with his "certain" people, companies, states. I could see, from the way opened doors would shut all over official Ankara when the subject came up, that Turkey's military regime did not intend to collide head-on with the Russians and their Bulgarian surrogates over it. (This exercise in restraint seemed remarkable, as I discovered the facts for myself.) The American Embassy was the last place to look for help: I had yet to find a political officer there who would admit to being aware of the Turkish Mafia's existence. And the local papers seemed too long on flashy headlines and skimpy on contents. I decided to try my luck with the Interior Ministry's director-general for security.

Fahri Görgülü was not easily gotten to, and not one to welcome an abuse of the privilege. He had received me before: a trim little man with a watchful eye and gravely attentive manner, whose large hushed office discouraged any hint of frivolity. The first time, he had talked mostly about Agca's background in Turkey. The press might say what it pleased, but the Interior Ministry, he'd told me then, had found no record anywhere of Agca's actual membership in the Gray Wolves. At home, nothing distinguished this common criminal from hundreds like him. Once abroad, Agca had evidently been "manipulated by international terrorism," which was something else again. Agca's freedom of movement in Europe plainly rankled. "We advised other countries through Interpol that he was a dangerous criminal, but some of our friends abroad were very silent on this," he had observed. "We advised the Germans *nine times* that he was in Germany, and submitted proof. But it didn't work. . . ."

Though willing to see me again now, Fahri Görgülü assured me that he had little to add. "We really don't know much about Agca after he left Turkey," he said. But one small thing he did know— the one he chose to tell me about, that is—made me forget the frustrations of a weeklong hunt, the driving rain outside, my sodden shoes.

Before getting to the Turkish Mafia, I had asked if he could help me reconstruct the passage of Agca's Faruk Ozgun passport from Turkey to Bulgaria. According to DIGOS in Rome, I explained, the passport bore the following stamps:

August 30   Exit from Edirne, Turkey
August 31   Entry at Kapitan Andreevo, Bulgaria
August 31   Exit from Kalotina, Bulgaria, into Yugoslavia

The exit stamp from Bulgaria was authentic; Agca's border crossing into Yugoslavia was confirmed. Could the director-general explain the twenty-four-hour gap between the exit from Turkey and entry into Bulgaria? Yes, he could. The Turkish exit stamp was forged. "No Faruk Ozgun crossed the Turkish border at Edirne or anywhere else, on August 30 or any other day," said Fahri Görgülü.

A short silence followed, while I tried to figure this out. Somebody must have smuggled the Ozgun passport with Agca's photograph into Bulgaria from Turkey, inserting a false exit stamp at leisure (if not at random). The Bulgarians had accepted the passport, from a courier who did not match the photograph and had unmistakably gotten his dates wrong. In other words, an illegitimate document had been legitimized by the Bulgarian border police. In this of all Eastern European states, only the secret service could have arranged that.

Having chased after that scrap of detail across half a continent, I felt pretty good about my find.

The director-general was waiting. I gave him a warm smile he could not account for, and got back to business. There ought to be some connection between this and other known bits and pieces of the Faruk Ozgun passport's history, I ventured. How might it fit in with Omer Ay, say, whose warrant of arrest charged him with procuring the passport in Nevsehir? Or with Omer Mersan, who supposedly acted as middleman in procuring it? Or with the Godfather, his boss in the Turkish Mafia? But Fahri Görgülü was not to be drawn on this last.

"We have no information on Omer Ay procuring the Ozgun passport," he said blandly (though the text of the arrest warrant was in my notebook). "The passport issue is just a claim; it hasn't been proved." Omer Mersan was not known as a smuggler in Turkey, but only as an army deserter. "We asked the Germans to have him here, for interrogation on his ties to Agca. But they refused.

As far as we know, they aren't even keeping him under surveillance." As for the Godfather, the whole matter was out of his hands. Abuzer Ugurlu had been arrested and was now facing trial in Turkey. Until the court was done with him, the director-general for security was not free to discuss it.

Who else? Somebody else must surely be in a position to know and talk about the Mafia, I thought, walking down the severely angled steps of the somber brick mass that housed Turkey's Interior Ministry. The obvious answer was already on my urgent checklist of people to see in Ankara. Who, if not the very interior minister in office throughout the Agca-Ipekci affair?

Former Interior Minister Hasan Fehmi Gunes was in deep trouble. I had gathered that from the Ankara press corps, and he told me as much himself. "I am under investigation. So is my brother. So are my two sons. So I must be careful what I say," he began, as soon as we sat down to our glasses of tea in the rather cramped and gloomy office where he had resumed his lawyer's practice. I suggested that he bring in a tape recorder for his own protection, and he did.

Soft-featured and just going plump in his youngish middle age, his mild gaze through rimless glasses at odds with an air of coiled tension, he was plainly ill at ease in describing the Gunes family's plight. His brother, Nizamettin, was mayor of Sakarya near Istanbul when arrested, shortly after the army takeover, allegedly for heading the local underground Communist Party there (the TKP). Two sons, Kutlan and Utkan, had been arrested for a jewel robbery meant to finance Teslim Tore's ultra-left strike force, Dev-Sol. Hasan Fehmi's personal trouble besides had to do with his seemingly equivocal role in the Ipekci case, among other things.

A Marxist since youth, Gunes had listed heavily toward the radical left as a member of Premier Ecevit's Socialist cabinet in 1979. That naturally made him fair game for the far right, which accused him of having "created" Agca when he was officially in charge of the Ipekci investigation. One of the defendants in the Türkes trial, an informer for the secret service (MIT) in 1979, had sworn that he was present when Gunes paid Agca to take the blame for Ipekci's murder and link it to the Gray Wolves.[5] "Did you?" I asked Gunes. "If everything he said about me was true, I'd be hanged by now," was his somewhat oblique reply.

As the cabinet minister who had directed Agca's interrogation personally at the time, Gunes was among the first to tell the world press what to think of the Pope's would-be assassin two years later. "Agca was helped by German and Italian right-wing extremists," he was prompt to declare. "He's tough. He'll never talk."[6]

If Agca was all that tough, I asked now, why did he confess so readily to killing Ipekci? "Maybe he knew that he'd be beaten and tortured into confessing anyway, so why not talk at once?" suggested the ex-minister accountable to a socialist government for the behavior of his police force.

I settled back to enjoy a conversation that promised a refreshing departure from the standard right-left script. What Gunes had to say from then on was still more unexpected. While he "firmly believed" in Agca's guilt, he was also convinced that "somebody else" was on the scene when Ipekci was killed. While he was sure that the Gray Wolves gave the order—"We got the feeling that Agca himself did not choose Ipekci as the target"—he admitted that "Agca never said a word about which organization he belonged to."

To keep the prisoner from knowing that the interior minister was in the interrogation room, Gunes had ordered Agca to be blindfolded, and had written questions on slips of paper. "Were you put under any pressure to confess?" he wrote on one such slip. "If they put pressure on me, I'll escape from prison and kill a minister," was Agca's answer, Gunes said. "But I don't see how Agca could have known I was there," he added. "Then, when I asked why he killed Ipekci, I think he answered 'Because he was not a Moslem.' But Agca drank, you know, and didn't behave like a religious crackpot. He really didn't seem like a fanatic Moslem."

He didn't seem much like an ordinary rightist, either—or leftist, for that matter, Gunes went on. Indeed, Agca had appeared to be "acting all the time" during his eleven days of secret interrogation. "When I asked him to describe how he actually killed Ipekci, Agca talked about it very coolly, very coldbloodedly. He would jump up and act out the scene: 'As Ipekci's car slowed to turn left, I approached, like this. . . . Then I fired through the window five times, like this. . . . Then a Mercedes drew in behind and I threw up my hands to cover my face in the headlights, like this. . . .' "

I inquired about the $18,000 deposited in various bank accounts for Agca, starting long before Ipekci's murder. Did Gunes ever find out who was putting up all that money? He was surprised to hear it was so much. True, Agca did spend money freely before his arrest and had stayed at some of Istanbul's most expensive hotels. But Gunes had never heard about the bank accounts. "Anyway, I doubt that he did this just for money," he said.

Like the Italians dealing with Agca, Gunes seemed unable to make him out. "Healthy and athletic," "strong-willed and supremely self-confident," the young man from Malatya had boasted of being called "Emperor" at school. For all his arrogance, though, Gunes said, Agca unquestionably stood out among his peers. Intellectually he was a cut above the average university student, spoke very good Turkish, seemed "more politically educated." He was also psychically sound, "not mentally unbalanced" at all. "He did not give the impression of being a tormented young man. All his psychological tests were very positive."

Though Agca "kept changing his story," furthermore, Gunes felt that "he did not like to tell lies. And he hated to be called a hired killer. . . . I think that if he was led to believe in something, he would throw himself into it and do it very courageously. . . ."

It was when we moved on to the attack on the Pope that Gunes really left the script behind. Where he had assured the international press that this was a simple right-wing plot, he acknowledged now that it was not quite so simple. "I am not sure of Agca's motives," he admitted. "And I cannot fairly put the emphasis on either the right or the Communists for trying to kill the Pope. I see no advantage for either side, in Turkey."

Of course, Agca "was no independent terrorist," so he must have been working for either the right or left abroad—by which Gunes meant the West or East. "The East might have done it to get the Poles under control," he went on, taking it for granted that the rise of Solidarity (*Solidarnosc*) in Poland was directly related to the enormous authority of a Polish Pope. "Or—as I believe—the West did it to provoke a Polish revolt, and pull Poland out of the Warsaw Pact." Either way, he concluded, Agca's mission to Rome was outside the context of Turkish politics.

That brought us at last to the question of Agca's possible sponsors abroad, and contacts with the Turkish Mafia in Bulgaria. As interior minister at the time, Gunes had to deal with gunrunning and other smuggling too. What could he tell me about Abuzer Ugurlu? "Ugurlu! Why, he's famous! The biggest! He's the Godfather!" Gunes exclaimed. He himself had launched the first serious police drive to round up the whole Ugurlu clan, in 1979. But such were Abuzer's powers of corruption that he was out of jail again in a matter of weeks.

Yes, the Godfather "had many contacts in Bulgaria," Gunes agreed: "He even used to carry a Bulgarian passport." He had been up to his eyes in running guns from Bulgaria, on a colossal scale. The SS *Vassoula,* flying a Cypriot flag but loaded in the Bulgarian port of Burgas, was carrying a huge load of weapons when Turkish security forces intercepted it in the Bosporus, in June 1977. (In fact, it was carrying 495 RPG-7 rocket launchers and 10,755 rockets, to be divided between Greek Cypriots and Turkish terrorists. Gunes did not mention these figures.[7]

Even so, Gunes was not overly critical of Bulgaria for indulging in such malicious mischief. If "many guns" had made their way into Turkey from there, the fact remained that "most of the rightists' and leftists' weapons were Western-made." While leftists had Russian Kalashnikovs, "the Kurdish Communist Party also had American M-16 rifles, which you can't get on the black market. That doesn't necessarily mean the U.S. supports the Kurdish separatists the most, but still, you know . . . ," he finished, recovering his more familiar political stance.

For an hour or two, we had been two normal people engrossed in a mystery. Now he was again a former cabinet minister under close surveillance, taut and wary, perhaps regretting that he had let down his guard. He had never heard of any Turkish Mafia connection with Agca, he concluded shortly, looking relieved when I refused a fourth glass of tea and got up to go.

One of his young sons, out on bail until his trial for the Dev-Sol theft, came to the door with us, his father's affectionate arm around his shoulder. I felt a pang of sympathy for the two of them, and for all the other Turkish fathers and sons whose lives had been blighted by that decade of terrorist madness. As a reporter, though, my opinion of the former interior minister was less indulgent.

His very honesty with me about his personal view of Agca underlined how deceptive he had been with the public. He knew that Agca was not the stick-figure caricature of a Fascist hood whose image he himself had helped to project. He knew that Agca's confession to the Ipekci murder was full of holes, holes he had not only ignored but had used his high office to paper over. He knew the papal plot was nothing so politically convenient as the one he had advised the world so authoritatively to look for, among "Italian and

German right-wing extremists." Whether or not he had ever heard of Agca's relations with the Turkish Mafia, furthermore, he certainly knew more than he was letting on about the Turkish Mafia's relations with the Bulgarian state.

He had to know more about this last, if only because a Mafia gunrunner's riveting account of that had enabled Gunes himself to arrest the whole Ugurlu clan.

I discovered this just before ending my second visit to Turkey. A freezing rain had driven me to my room at the Büyük Ankara. Soaked and chilled, my temper unimproved for having been trapped between floors in the elevator again—a daily occurrence in this otherwise comfortable hotel—I wrapped myself in a blanket and started to read through a bundle of translations from the Turkish press. And there it was, in the strident left-wing daily *Cumhuriyet* of all places: a personal account written by an old repentant sinner, letters from another adding rich details, the first inside story of a vast and versatile criminal ring unique in the world for its dependence on the secret services of a Communist state.

7

"For seven or eight years, I have been involved in arms smuggling, and now I don't know how to get out of it," wrote Ibrahim Telemen of the Turkish Mafia, in 1979.[1] "I have refused to go on with the smuggling for the past one or two months, and for this reason I am under pressure and threats. But I am still going to fight this arms traffic. . . .

"The smuggling of arms into Turkey is handled by Abuzer Ugurlu, and by his brothers Mustafa, Sabri, and Ahmet [along with a chief aide, named Celehattin Güvensoy, and some fifteen other "intimate friends" of Ugurlu's, named as well]. Abuzer works through cells, which often don't know each other. He has good relations at every level of the police and customs. The customs posts at Edirne, Kapikule, Ipsala, Hadarpaşa, and Mersin are like Abuzer's private estate. He pays the Customs Ministry from one to ten million Turkish lire [$50,000 to $500,000] for customs directors and chief guards . . . including the chiefs of police in Istanbul. . . .

"Bulgaria sends guns of every kind into Turkey, from Burgas and Varna by sea or overland by TIR truck. This traffic between Bulgaria and Turkey is run by Abuzer's right-hand man, Nadim Diskaya. On the other hand, I'm the one who used to organize the movement of weapons from Italy, France, Spain, and Czechoslovakia. *The Bul-*

garians, without checking the registration or arms licenses, would give guns of every sort to Abuzer [my italics]. In fact, two thousand high-powered rifles arrived by ship the other day, across the Black Sea. . . .

"Italy, Spain, France, and Czechoslovakia require licenses for arms sales. I used to get the licenses from the Arab Emirates or some African state, for twenty-five or thirty thousand dollars. And with the licenses, I would buy ten or twenty thousand guns, and four or five million cartridges, and load them on Abuzer's ships.

"Every month, at Hadarpaşa alone, fifteen to twenty thousand weapons would enter Turkey this way. . . . Now they are putting strong pressure on me. I had left a deposit for fifteen thousand guns and four million cartridges in Czechoslovakia, and they forced me to get them and load them on the ship. They threatened to kill me, and made me order another twenty thousand guns and five million cartridges. They have special riverboats without masts in Czechoslovakia, that carry the weapons down the Danube through Bulgaria to the Black Sea. There the guns are transferred to Abuzer's ships, and the riverboats turn right around. . . ."

Since false papers were essential to such operations, continued Telemen, "Abuzer has every kind of false passport, customs stamps, and so on. When Abuzer got me out of prison in Buca [Turkey], I immediately received three different passports. . . . All of Abuzer's men have more than one passport. They can go abroad whenever they please. Traveling on these false passports, the most dangerous assassins, smugglers, and terrorists can come and go at any time. They can unload TIR trucks full of arms, get their passports stamped with false stamps, and clear customs without moving from wherever they are. Abuzer has everything necessary to arrange all this. . . ."

Another prerequisite for this multilateral traffic was currency smuggling, Telemen went on. "Abuzer's men, carrying a suitcase with three or five million dollars, can come and go without trouble at the Yèsilkoy airport [in Istanbul]. These people are couriers. *They can have their passports stamped or not by border police, as they please* [my italics]. I myself have come and gone that way several times. . . .

"Generally, I made contact with Abuzer through [one of his men]. Abuzer prefers never to leave his house or studio. He doesn't telephone and doesn't answer the telephone. His phone number in Istanbul is 58-30-60, studio 38-17-50, Harbiye studio 46-25-95. . . .

"I've been thinking of making this break for two months. But I'm under tight surveillance. They never leave my side for a minute, they've become my shadows. . . . They could kill me at any time. . . ."

Ibrahim Telemen "fell" from his Istanbul hotel window before he could keep an appointment with Hasan Fehmi Gunes, then minister of interior.[2] Gunes, who had read his letter beforehand, ordered the arrest of everybody Telemen had named. All were released after a short trial.

To corroborate Telemen's story, *Cumhuriyet* carried two letters from another of Ugurlu's men: our friend imprisoned in West Germany, Suleyman Necati Topuz, who had provided the first damning information on Omer Mersan's Mafia ties.[3]

Topuz was frightened too, after denouncing the Mafia to the martial-law commander of Istanbul from his German prison cell, in October 1980. "My father was murdered in Turkey, and my brother-in-law in Germany, after that," he wrote. "The murders were organized by the Ugurlu brothers, and connected with the death of an old-timer in the Mafia who also tried to inform the Turkish authorities about them"—Ibrahim Telemen, in fact.

In one of his letters, sent after the Pope was shot, Topuz summed up Mersan's role in the Mafia: "This person—Omer Mersan—works for the whole Ugurlu family. Mersan, along with Celehattin Güvensoy and the family's plenipotentiary representative Fikri Koçakerim, directs the Ugurlu family's affairs in Bulgaria and other European countries. Omer Mersan is not a petty smuggler. He acts solely according to directives received from the Ugurlu family."

The nature of these directives might be presumed from his other letter. "I have worked with the biggest names in the Turkish Mafia since 1975, and directed their affairs in Europe and Sofia," Topuz wrote. "They do every kind of smuggling, from cigarettes to heavy arms, cosmetics, jewels, spare parts, drugs. They do everything: the financing and organization are shared, and so are the profits. That is why they are called a Mafia."

Then came a few lines that gave me an exhilarating sense of getting very close.

"The Turkish Mafia is under the control and direction of the Bulgarian secret service," Topuz declared. "The Bulgarian secret service has annexed the Turkish Mafia in the tightest way. Because in Bulgaria, everything—from cigarettes to heavy weapons—is sold to smugglers by the state company Kintex. Everything that passes in transit through Bulgaria is reexported through this firm. *The smugglers—the Mafia, I mean—are obliged to maintain all sorts of relations in Bulgaria through Kintex. This firm is essentially a branch of the Bulgarian secret service* [my italics]."

Why should anybody believe a jailbird doing time for pushing dope, and a dead crook? Because they ought to know, if anyone did, and risked their lives by telling, for one thing. And because of the man they'd chosen to send their letters to, for another.

Their choice, Ugur Mumcu, was a columnist for *Cumhuriyet* who had spent a lifetime on the pretty far left. He had gone to prison himself for his ardent political commitment in 1971, when martial law was imposed to cope with Turkey's first wave of terrorism. The thrust of his writing after that had been heavily anti-NATO and anti-American, filled with distrust for the capitalist West, with rarely a harsh word for the Soviet bloc. Nobody could accuse Mumcu of setting out to frame the Communist state of Bulgaria.

I had flinched away from meeting him, after reading an acid column of his on *The Terror Network*. (Later, we both got that behind us and became good friends.) But it was plain from his writings that he had long wrestled with his conscience before indicting Bulgaria as the Turkish Mafia's sponsor.

He could not forgive that country's betrayal. "I am in a position to state that arms in great abundance have reached Turkish terrorists through Bulgaria, coming from many places and especially Belgium, Italy, and France. These errors and crimes are a shame for a country calling itself Socialist, which permits freedom of action to traffickers in arms and drugs," he told the Italian Socialist paper *Avanti!*[4] "Drugs arriving from Turkey were exchanged for arms arriving from Europe. And Bulgaria had a part in this dirty traffic—so big a part that the notorious Bulgarian state firm Kintex was feeding arms to terrorists of the extreme right and left in my country. . . .

"We have struggled for years to demonstrate the external sources of internal terrorism . . . exposing the Bulgarian connection to this smuggling and the companies at the Turkish end," he wrote in *Arms Smuggling and Terrorism*, a best-seller in Turkey that winter. "We ran into incredible pressures because of this . . . tracing, with a sinking heart, who was being protected, and how, and why. . . ."

Mumcu's book was full of unpronounceable names and unfindable places on the map, from which emerged a commanding array of facts. He described the founding of the state export-import company

Kintex in Sofia in 1965, and Abuzer Ugurlu's debut as the Godfather in 1966. The first of Ugurlu's arms shipments to be discovered was seized in September 1967: 1,070 light automatics, 400 revolvers, and "a conspicuous quantity of ammunition," shipped "from Prague to Varna and from Varna to Trabzon" on Turkey's Black Sea coast.

Next came a warrant of arrest issued by a Turkish martial-law court in September 1973. The charges covered Ugurlu's known arms deliveries from Bulgaria to Turkey between 1966 and 1973: *70,731 guns of different makes, and 27,601,000 rounds of ammunition.* "Abuzer Ugurlu was a fugitive at the time," Mumcu wrote. "His address was Arh Milanov Sokak No. 18, Sofia, Bulgaria."

Mumcu went straight on from there to track the Godfather's heady ascent. But it is worth stopping at this point to look back. The years between 1966 and 1973 marked the passage of Turkish terrorism from infancy to full growth. The simultaneous rise of a Sofia-based gunrunning ring could hardly be accidental. There is clear evidence by now that Bulgaria had in fact set out deliberately to nurture Turkey's terrorist monster, by arming both sides; that this was part of an ongoing Soviet master plan to force the collapse of Turkey's democratic order; and that the Turkish Mafia was shaped by Bulgaria's secret services as an instrument toward this end.

When the day of reckoning came, with an international storm raging over Bulgaria's role in the papal plot, Western analysts would make singular efforts to skate around this awkward truth. If the Turkish Mafia was somehow involved with Mehmet Ali Agca, they suggested, that was strictly the Turkish Mafia's business. If Kintex was somehow involved with the Turkish Mafia, that was just business too; all Eastern-bloc countries are starved for hard currency. If Bulgarian customs police were closing an eye to the copious flow of weapons through their country, that didn't necessarily mean they were getting orders from above; even a Communist state can have bent cops.

But these efforts were either willfully or wishfully deceptive.

Some indication of the Turkish Mafia's broader political uses had come to light long before Mumcu began writing about it. A team of *Newsday* reporters had stumbled on Kintex a decade earlier, while tracing the heroin route from Turkey to the United States. The book incorporating their discoveries, *The Heroin Trail*, was now out of print and took some finding.[5] Its chapter on Bulgaria began like this:

"It was our last day in Bulgaria. Our car looped Liberation Square, past the outdoor cafés and statue of a Russian czar astride a bronze horse. It turned toward the onion-domed Alexander Nevsky Memorial Church, cut left at the TSOUM department store and eased into a narrow cobblestoned side street, busy with stores and people.

"We were riding with the two smugglers we had met in Istanbul. The car stopped near a squat, new, concrete-and-glass building without a name on it. Several men stood near the entrance, looking at us.

" 'That's it,' said one of the smugglers. 'That's the new head-quarters of Kintex.' "

The *Newsday* reporters were following drugs, not guns, which suggests the multiple functions of Kintex even then. Their description, going back a good ten years, starts with the kind of evergreen statements I'd been hearing myself.

"Galip Labernas, the former Istanbul narcotics chief, had heard of Kintex. During one conversation in his Istanbul apartment, he said: 'There is an important agency in the Bulgarian government that has given some of our biggest smugglers carte blanche to run morphine base through the country. We know it's happening, but we don't have many details. The agency is called Kintex.'

"A leading opium dealer in Istanbul who was perfectly willing to discuss his colleagues by name grew silent when asked about Kintex. 'I've heard of it; that's the Bulgarian arrangement,' he said. Then he pointedly changed the subject.

"A U.S. Embassy source in Ankara: 'We don't know much. We understand that Kintex is the official import-export agency of the Bulgarian People's Republic. The agency is supposed to promote exports and regulate imports. Sounds like a standard government bureau.' "

One of the smugglers traveling with the *Newsday* team offered a different version of this standard government bureau. " 'Kintex is immensely powerful in this country. . . . It's not just a governmental agency. If Kintex decides not to let you smuggle through Bulgaria, you can have a tough time here.' "

The second smuggler in their party added: " 'If you've got the right connection with that agency, you can pass morphine base through Bulgaria without the slightest ripple.' "

Speaking of the working arrangements up to 1972, the first smuggler went on: " 'Let's say you want to smuggle American cigarets into Turkey. You contact a middleman who has done business with

Kintex. *He puts your name through to Sofia for a check. Bulgarian agents in Istanbul run a background check on you. If you are reputable in the [smuggling] business and have no police connections, you start doing business with Kintex* [my italics].'

"Bulgaria is the only nation along the entire route from Istanbul to Marseilles to stop and check every car. But there is no problem for a man with Kintex connections," the *Newsday* team said. The first smuggler then added, " 'He sends a message to Sofia, giving a description and the license number of his truck or car. He also tells what time the truck is expected to cross the border. *Then Kintex sends a man to the crossing point to make sure that the truck goes through without any search'* [my italics]."

The operation would become considerably more elaborate over the years. But one particular aspect of the Turkish Mafia's relations with Kintex would endure unaltered. "The Bulgars had another interest in Turkey: the left-wing Dev Genc revolutionary movement," wrote the *Newsday* team, referring to the predecessor of Dev-Sol, the pioneer of Turkey's left-wing terrorist movement. "According to the smugglers, an Istanbul patron who was allowed to bring out his [morphine] base was required to occasionally reciprocate by providing smugglers to move guns and ammunition from Bulgaria for the Turkish revolutionaries. *The patrons were also expected, when asked, to supply intelligence information to the Bulgarian secret police* [my italics]."

Back in Washington, the *Newsday* reporters were told that "the State Department's files contained no data on Kintex." Nevertheless, "a U.S. source experienced in Bulgarian-American relations said it was possible that an agency such as Kintex could be operated as an arm of the Bulgarian secret police, reporting only to high Communist Party officials and unknown even to some high-ranking Bulgarian bureaucrats."

I don't know whether the State Department has opened a file on Kintex since 1972. The head of its Bulgarian desk looked blank when I asked him about it in Washington in 1982; and my telexed queries to the U.S. Embassy in Sofia remained unanswered. Whatever the reasons for such reserve, Washington was not unaware of the whole Kintex operation by then—or of Abuzer Ugurlu, either.

It was some months before I got to Washington and learned that, by which time I had a tidy file of my own.

The Istanbul "patrons," as the *Newsday* team had called them, were known now as the *buyuk baba*: the big grandpas. They dealt in everything movable that could be smuggled at a profit, from cocoa and coffee to cigarettes, liquor, electronic goods, diamonds, gold, currency, copper, weapons, drugs. Their particular value to Bulgaria lay in the last two items—guns in, heroin out—a two-way traffic that paid off in more ways than one.

Apart from the money to be made (a percentage for Kintex on every shipment), it provided the wherewithal for Turkey's systematic demolition—and, as time would tell, perfect cover for the papal plot.

The biggest of the grandpas in Istanbul were Abuzer Ugurlu and his brother Mustafa, handling the Turkish-Bulgarian end of the trade. Among the top two or three directing the Mafia's affairs abroad— in Italy, France, Switzerland, Germany, the United States—was a smooth-spoken and convivial man of the world named Bekir Celenk. He had a natural bond with the Ugurlu brothers, who came from the same part of Turkey: Celenk was from Gaziantep, the Ugurlus from nearby Malatya, Agca's hometown. While Celenk rarely returned to Istanbul, Abuzer Ugurlu practically commuted to and from Sofia. The two could talk over their business freely there at the Hotel Vitosha, where both made their headquarters. According to Interpol, they also shared an office. [6]

Celenk was certainly living it up in this Communist capital before fate overtook him. He had a villa of his own, rode around town in a big chauffeur-driven Mercedes, occupied a suite of rooms at the deluxe Vitosha, tipped royally at the hotel bar. His life-style was reported in the Istanbul daily *Hurriyet* late in November 1981, when its correspondent called on him at the Vitosha for an interview. [7]

Celenk's response was to summon three Turkish thugs, who stabbed the *Hurriyet* reporter and smashed his camera. Bulgarian security police, lounging about the Vitosha as always, watched but did not interfere.

A couple of months after *Hurriyet* carried this story, Ugur Mumcu wrote in *Cumhuriyet* that Bekir Celenk and Mehmet Ali Agca had met at the Hotel Vitosha in early July 1980. Agca was staying in Room 911, and Celenk in Room 1078, he said. [8]

Between them, Celenk and Ugurlu had performed signal political services for Bulgaria at this stage. Apart from everything else—a great deal about everything else would come out a year later—they had contributed decisively to the decline and fall of Turkish democracy by arming the nation's terrorists to the teeth.

Not only were both sides plied with more military hardware than they could ever use, but one side would occasionally pass some of it on to the other. Ugur Mumcu gave me an example. In 1979, a shipment of guns provided by Kintex was delivered by the Turkish Mafia to a local leader of the Gray Wolves' National Action Party in Samsun, on the Black Sea. This man in turn passed the guns on to Dev-Sol in nearby Fatsa. At the time, Fatsa had been seized and sealed off by Dev-Sol, which had set up a Leninist People's Commune. The atrocities it committed—extortion, torture, kangaroo trials, public executions—would lead to a mass trial of more than four hundred Dev-Sol activists in 1982. The guns passed on to them by the rightist National Action Party were still in their Kintex wrappings when the army moved in.

For all its habitual reticence, the Turkish General Staff finally did speak out on the whole arms issue, in an official volume called *Anarchy and Terror in Turkey*. Citing firsthand testimony from captured terrorists, the generals declared: "The arms found in Turkey came largely through central and Eastern Europe. . . . A certain nation on our western border fed—indeed, directed—the contraband weapons traffic in Turkey. Gunrunning on such a scale usually requires a lot of time, money, equipment, qualified personnel and juridical cover. [Yet] the arms furnished by a neighboring nation could reach buyers here within twenty-four hours. . . .

"The smugglers' organization sold arms to any terrorist formation, regardless of whether it was right or left. . . . Terrorist organizations themselves developed an important role in this traffic. . . . Those who were running such contraband collaborated with organizations controlled by a certain foreign state. . . ."[9]

A long list followed, of weapons consignments to left- and right-wing terrorists in every remote corner of Turkey—a country the size of Great Britain and France—or of Texas and Louisiana combined.

It was General M. who gave me this official army publication when I went back to see him, with the feeling that I was homing in at last. Though measured and meticulous as before, he was a little more forthcoming this time. He explained how the Mafia's two-way traffic had helped to build up such an enormous terrorist arsenal in Turkey. *By peddling the smuggled heroin in Western Europe, rightists in particular could use the proceeds to pay for their weapons.* Leftists, who were not used in the drug trade as a rule, had been enabled instead to acquire their guns at cheap "political" prices. Selected groups had been kept in particularly lavish supply. In southeast Turkey, for instance, the PKK (Kurdish Communist Party) and other Kurdish separatists had stashed away *844 Soviet-made RPG-7 rockets*, enough to equip a small army.

While a good part of the arms found in that region came through Syria from Palestinian sources, the general said, Kintex had seen to the rest. In fact, certain leaders of Turkey's terrorist left had specialized in procuring weapons from the Palestinians and Bulgarians both.

General M. paused at this point, gave me a long, considering look, then handed over a slim plastic folder. "These documents have not been published in Turkey," he told me. "They should help you grasp the situation in our country during the seventies. We are not making these facts public until they come out in the courtroom, where they can speak for themselves. Take them with you. But please don't show them to anybody here, or speak of them, or have them translated, until you leave the country."

The file was hardly out of my sight until I was back in Rome. Mostly, it had to do with one or another aspect of Russo-Bulgarian efforts to destabilize Turkey. Among the papers was a brief report on a left-wing terrorist leader assuredly specialized in the procurement of weapons, whose name had come up in the earliest days of Agca's interrogation in Rome: Teslim Tore.

Tore had been running guns for his Turkish People's Liberation Army since 1971. A fugitive in Syria after martial law was imposed in Turkey that year, he had started by procuring guns and explosives through the PLO's Fatah. Then, in 1974, he had "gotten in touch with the Bulgarian Embassy in Damascus." Over the next two or three years, Tore had "collected information for the Bulgarian Embassy," and maintained ever closer relations with the Bulgarians and Russians both. *By 1977, he was in a position to buy forty TIR trucks for his gunrunning operations.*

In 1979, under the civilian Socialist government of Premier Ecevit, Teslim Tore was indicted by the military prosecutor of Ankara for "giving secret information to the Bulgarians related to the security and political interests of the Turkish State." The specified charge was "political and military espionage." Sheltering in Damascus, he was not caught. In October 1981, Turkey's Second Military Court issued a renewed warrant for his arrest on the same charges.

In exchange for an unlimited weapons supply and a fail-proof delivery system, the leader of Turkey's largest left-wing terrorist formation had become a Bulgarian agent.

There was another short report of particular interest in the general's file, this one on Mehmet Ali Agca's movements in Turkey after his prison break. Two notorious Gray Wolf killers stood out for the help they had given him. One was Oral Celik, a constant companion who escorted him from one end of Turkey to the other: from Istanbul to Ankara to Malatya to Nevsehir (of fake passport fame) to Erzerum on the Iranian border and back to Istanbul. The other was Abdullah Catli, who reportedly had overseen arrangements for Agca's Faruk Ozgun passport, and had taken care of getting him out to Bulgaria.

Oral Celik, a fellow Malatyan, had been a rough right-wing hood from early youth and was rumored to be the real killer of Abdi Ipekci. I had seen his name right at the start, on the list sent out by Rome's DIGOS of seventeen Turks reportedly in touch with Agca during his travels. The list was "based on information received from the Turkish police," DIGOS had said.

The Turkish police in Ankara had given me some of this information too. Oral Celik was not only a right-wing terrorist, they told me. Apart from working for the Gray Wolves, *he also worked for the Turkish Mafia's co-Godfather, Bekir Celenk.*[10]

Abdullah Catli was on the same DIGOS list. Wanted in Turkey for a particularly gruesome massacre of seven left-wing unionists in Balgat, *Catli had been working for Abuzer Ugurlu in Varna, Bulgaria, since that massacre in December 1978.* The testimony came from two former Gray Wolf underlings. One had described Catli's Mafia dealings in detail, before being hanged in 1980 for his own role in the Balgat massacre. The other, hiding out in Scandinavia, had given press and television interviews to the same effect.[11]

Catli had "played a major role in shipping arms from Sofia to Turkey since January 1978," said this second penitent, Ali Yurtaslan. After the massacre the next December, Catli had "gone straight to Varna, Bulgaria, and started working with the Turkish underworld." With whom? "The names I know are Abuzer Ugurlu and Isamil Oflu," he had replied. These were the people supplying weapons to the Gray Wolves' National Action Party in Turkey, he added.

"When payment for the weapons was required in Europe, heroin was smuggled into Europe. . . . The Gray Wolves handled the heroin distribution and invested the cash in weapons purchases. . . ."

These were the two notorious Gray Wolves who, between them, had piloted Agca's movements from the day of his prison break, on November 25, 1979, until his arrival in Sofia the following July. Whether on the heroin or gunrunning end, or both, they were on the payroll of the Turkish Mafia in Bulgaria. "What could a gang of Turkish neo-Nazis have to do with the most orthodox Communist regime in Eastern Europe?" I had asked myself earlier that winter. This.

General M.'s report on Oral Celik and Abdullah Catli did not mention these Mafia ties. The first I'd heard of Catli's, especially, was rather late in the day, when a rough draft of my article for the *Reader's Digest* was already done. It matched so neatly with the picture I had pieced together that I could scarcely believe my luck. Then I went to Washington for a last try, and luck came with me.

During my few days there, I was given the gist of a confidential dossier on Kintex, put together by a major U.S. intelligence agency. It came from the sole member of the American intelligence community who was willing to discuss the papal shooting with me—then, before, and since. I had known him a long while, and trusted him.

We met in a pseudo-neocolonial eatery furnished in implacably cheery mock-maple, which served dreadful coffee. My friend had just reviewed the file that morning, at my request, without telling a soul in his agency. He read out his notes, which I scribbled down word for word. Obviously I cannot reveal his name; and I would hesitate to publish the material, if I hadn't found confirmation for so much of it on my return to Europe. What follows are my own notes of the conversation.

There was a preliminary reference to Agca himself, doubtless taken from a different file. It contained brief excerpts from a 900-page report prepared by the Italian Questura, the central police headquarters, in June 1981: a summary of what was known to the Italian authorities at the close of Agca's earliest interrogation. Agca, it said, had shown "excellent tradecraft," and had been "cleverly manipulated by others." It was an interesting citation to put side by side with statements emanating from Washington later. ("Mr. Agca was a 'known crazy,' 'too unstable to be included in an assassination plot,' " an unnamed but evidently authoritative U.S. official had assured the *Los Angeles Times* on January 31, 1982. Had he ever read this report in the U.S. government's possession since June 1981?)

After that came the notes on Bulgaria's versatile export-import agency.

"Kintex was founded in 1965. It is located on Anton Ivanov Boulevard in Sofia, has several safe houses in Sofia and offices in the ports of Varna and Burgas. It also keeps garages near Sofia for storing smuggled goods. It has close relations with other Bulgarian foreign trade organizations, such as Interpred and Intercommerz, to which it may be transferring some of its activities. Inside Turkey, it is connected with Balkan-Tourist, Balkan-Ship, and Tap-Ek.

"Kintex personnel appear to be trained in intelligence techniques and are clearly members of the secret service. They change cars and meeting places frequently, use passwords, and keep their meetings short. They will meet a customer at some designated place, pick him up in a Kintex car, and bring him to a safe house near the Pliska Hotel. They require references for reliable smugglers. Everything is negotiated in detail before a deal is made. Money must be paid on the line when the goods are loaded. If a smuggler is caught twice in his own country, Kintex severs relations.

"The smuggler must follow Kintex instructions to the letter. The smuggling is done by trucks overland, using international TIR trucks from Europe. If a shipment is to be loaded, the driver parks the TIR, leaving the keys in it, then comes back later and returns the truck to its original parking place. After that, the truck must move at once to the Turkish border, without inspection by Bulgarian customs.

"If the goods move by sea, the ship comes to Bulgarian territorial waters and is met by a Bulgarian patrol boat. The smuggler must have the password, after which he is directed to the transfer area. The crew is not allowed ashore. The ship loads and leaves by nightfall. The crew's leader meets a Kintex representative and is under Kintex control until the ship leaves Bulgarian waters. Or else, the smugglers' ship meets a Bulgarian freighter, ties up alongside, and transfers the cargo at sea."

A sample list followed, of operations involving Kintex in one way or another:

1978   Kintex smuggled Spanish small arms into Turkey.

1979   Bulgaria had purchased 5,000 Browning 9-mm
       automatics from Argentina in 1977, which surfaced in
       Turkey in 1979. The weapons were found in the
       possession of Turkish terrorists, and identified after
       Argentina gave Turkey their registration numbers.

1979   Turks seized a ship with 1,500,000 rounds of
       ammunition destined for Kurdish separatists in
       eastern Turkey. At this time, Varna and Burgas
       sea routes were heavily used for smuggling to
       Turkey. The shipment also included [Soviet-made]
       Makarovs and Czech Skorpions, in the new 9-mm
       version.

1979   Soviet arms entered Turkey from Syria through the
       southwest, and from Bulgarian ports of Varna and
       Burgas.

1979   Watertight containers filled with guns dropped by
       Bulgarian and Russian freighters, picked up by
       Turkish vessels.

1980   Soviet freighter picked up arms at Varna in January
       and carried them to Samsun and Trabzon [on
       Turkey's Black Sea coast]. From there they were
       moved to Erzerum [a largely Kurdish city in
       easternmost Turkey].

1980   Turkey's National Action Party is smuggling heroin to
       Germany, and using the profits to purchase weapons.

Along with these episodes were one or two illustrating the broader
nature of Bulgarian-Russian designs on Turkey:

1980   MLAPU [Marxist-Leninist Armed Propaganda Unit],
       trained by Bulgaria for years, is sending illegals to
       destabilize Turkey.

1981   Eight Turks accused of espionage for Bulgaria went
       on trial in January. The key defendant was Muzaffer
       Sengil, a ranking activist of Dev-Sol. Many quiet
       arrests were made, and persona non grata orders
       issued for Soviet military attachés caught *in flagrante*
       with material and information linked directly to Dev-
       Sol.

Then came a few short sentences to round out the story.

"*By mid-1982, numerous Soviet advisers held positions in Kintex at all levels, including senior posts.*

"Starting around 1969, Abuzer Ugurlu worked with Bulgaria. *In exchange for services rendered, he was allowed to run smuggling operations from Varna. In 1974, he was recruited as an agent of the Bulgarian secret service* [my italics]."

Practically every word of the report I was given was corroborated by firsthand testimony in Europe within the next few months.

What did it prove about the plot to kill the Pope? Everything necessary to show how the whole thing worked.

PART
TWO

·

PUBLISHING THE PLOT, DISTURBING THE PEACE

·

8

It was time to write the story.

From the early autumn of 1981 until late the next spring, I had been shuttling between Rome and Munich, Bonn, Hamburg, Ankara, and Istanbul, making side trips to Malatya, Vienna, Frankfurt, Zurich, Tel Aviv, Tunis, Washington, and Paris. The *Reader's Digest* had been tactfully forbearing as the choice date for publication— May 13, 1982, first anniversary of the attack in St. Peter's Square— came and went. I had talked the piece over a dozen times with the *Digest's* European director, John ("Dimi") Panitza, who kept shooting holes in my theory. A brilliant editor, he was a faultless marksman where that sort of shooting was concerned. Whatever I might come up with, Dimi would unfailingly advise me to go back and look for more. Now even he agreed that I had a solid circumstantial case.

It was going to be strong stuff for an anesthetized public. Misinformed in the first place, the outside world had then ceased to be informed at all. Judge Martella, appointed to head the investigation the previous November, had promptly submerged and had yet to be heard from. Agca, finishing his year in solitary confinement, might have dropped off the planet for all the attention he received. Nobody in high places had wondered aloud about the truth behind the crime of the century. The international press had dropped it long ago, seemingly for good.

Out of the blue, more than a year after the event, I would be saying in print that there really was an organized plot to murder the Pope. Worse, I would be tracing its source to the Bulgarian secret services, acting on behalf of the Soviet KGB. I thought I could imagine the uproar this would cause, but I underestimated by half.

Merely to assert that a plot existed—any plot—was to contradict practically everything the public had been given to believe. It did exist, though, however outrageous, improbable, uncomfortable, or awkward that might seem. Both the Turkish and Italian courts had ruled out widely held assumptions that Mehmet Ali Agca was pathologically deranged, or a religious crackpot, or an exalted political crank. Judge Santiapichi's court had in fact actually cited his "uncommon gifts of mental equilibrium" and "full psychic maturity." Once the evidence was assembled, furthermore, it demonstrated that he could not conceivably have acted on his own.

The proof of this last began at the scene of the crime, with those two accomplices in St. Peter's Square. Whether others were present besides, whether the two were there to help Agca get away or to kill him in turn, they were there. The one whose half-face appeared next to Agca's in the photograph had been identified tentatively by Turkish authorities as Omer Ay. The other, seen in profile from behind as he ran away, had not been identified so far. But he unquestionably had had a gun in his hand when Lowell Newton of ABC's Detroit Bureau took the picture. Having watched Newton reenact the scene at the Vatican for a television news team, I had no doubt of that. (Judge Martella, who invited him back to Rome for questioning, reportedly didn't doubt his story either.)

The first judge to interrogate Agca after the shooting, Luciano Infelisi, had spoken of other "documentary proof that Mehmet Ali Agca did not act alone." Not until the investigation was nearly over would its nature be revealed. But apart from that, there were the last-minute instructions jotted down in Turkish; the reservation for Agca's room at the Pensione Isa made by a man speaking correct Italian; the $50,000 or so spent on erratic wanderings around Europe by a Turkish fugitive supposedly without a penny to his name.

There was the matter of his Faruk Ozgun passport from Nevsehir, which somebody with plenty of clout must have arranged; its rigged exit and entry stamps at the Turco-Bulgarian border, indicating powerful protection on the Bulgarian side; his enigmatic terrorist career in Turkey, from the time he was put on a secret payroll to his peculiar arrest and confession for the Ipekci murder to his skillfully engineered jailbreak. And then there was the manner in which he was passed on to Bulgaria—by whom, and to whom—not to mention the tantalizing question of how he spent his fifty days there.

Plainly, the answer to the riddle in Rome lay somewhere in Agca's past. Stitching together what I had found, I was sure that the relevant part of his history began when he first acquired his faceless paymaster.

Whether or not that had come of his stay in a Palestinian training camp, I could not say. There was no proof that he had actually gone to such a camp in Lebanon. I had been to Israel twice to ask the Mossad just that, and come away empty-handed. ("They all used false names in the camps, and it happened five years ago, if it happened. We simply don't know either way," I was told in Tel Aviv.)

He might well have trained in a *Syrian* camp instead, which would have been harder to trace. Judge Santiapichi had told me that Agca had said so. Judge Ferdinando Imposimato, among Italy's topmost experts on terrorism, had referred to Syrian training too, in a report on Italian ties to international terrorism. I had been unable to get any further on that.

Palestinian sources were vehement in denying Agca's story. Abu Firas, heading the PLO mission in Ankara, had sent me a peremptory summons and delivered a stern lecture, warning me against bringing the Palestinians into this with Agca's tale of a training camp or anything else. (It was the Israelis who sent Agca to kill the Pope, Firas said, because His Holiness had been rude to the Israeli foreign minister a week or two before.)

Indeed, I did not believe that the Palestinians had anything to do with this plot. If Agca had in fact gone to a Habash camp, among hundreds of other Turks, he might merely have been spotted there by Teslim Tore as a promising young fellow. In and out of these camps since 1971, Tore had been a Bulgarian agent for three years by 1977, when Agca claimed to have met him in Damascus and gone on with him to Beirut.

With or without Tore's assistance, the then nineteen-year-old Agca had surely been picked up as a sleeper, and an expensive one at that. Eighteen thousand dollars, paid into his various bank accounts for more than thirteen months of idle anonymity, indicated that he was probably being held in reserve for very special assignments.

He might have been in the Turkish Mafia's pay all along, though not a shred of proof for that had turned up (then or since). It seemed more likely that the Mafia had taken him over after his arrest and imprisonment, when he was finished in Turkey, from whoever had been running him before. The state of affairs in his country between 1977 and 1979 suggested that he was on the payroll of some covert "operational" faction in MIT, Turkey's CIA, divided then into factions using tactics of infiltration and provocation on both extreme right and left. It might never be clear, and did not matter, whether the faction in his case was rightist or leftist. Either could plausibly have used him, and the Godfather was on the best of terms with both. What did matter was that by the time Agca left Turkey, he had acquired a perfect persona as an unregenerate Fascist killer.

The first hint that his all-purpose Gray Wolf tag concealed other connections had come from Agca himself. By naming Omer Mersan, he had in effect told whoever cared to listen of his contacts with the Turkish Mafia in Sofia. Mersan had confirmed their meeting at the Hotel Vitosha–New Otani (or the Park Hotel, or some coffeehouse, in various versions Mersan gave), in early July 1980. The columnist Ugur Mumcu had reported another meeting of Agca's at the Vitosha in those same days, with Abuzer Ugurlu's close associate Bekir Celenk. (Mumcu, in hot pursuit of the Turkish Mafia, had been keeping an eye on Celenk at the time.)

It seemed a safe assumption that Agca's stay in Sofia had been seen to by Abuzer Ugurlu. I knew from General M.'s confidential file that Agca's passage into Bulgaria, and the final pickup and delivery of his Faruk Ozgun passport, had been handled by Abdullah Catli. How Catli the Gray Wolf could have whisked a fugitive Fascist killer into Bulgaria for sanctuary might take some explaining. But it would have been a pushover for Catli the Turkish Mafia's gunrunner, acting on Ugurlu's orders and under Ugurlu's protection.

Who better than the Godfather had the pull needed to procure the Faruk Ozgun passport and the connections to get it stamped for Bulgarian entry at any time and place of his choosing?

Although hard proof was still lacking, I would have bet that Ugurlu had singled out Agca in prison as an ideal candidate for an exacting job: one of those "services rendered" for the Bulgarians in exchange for his own lucrative smuggling privileges.

The target need not necessarily have been Pope John Paul, as early as the time of Agca's prison break in November 1979. He might simply have been kept on tap for any similar exigencies that could arise.

Even if I were wrong, Agca's long Bulgarian summer would have to be accounted for. Bulgaria had (and has) inflexible rules for admitting Turkish citizens. They could get a thirty-hour tourist visa at the border, and no more.[1] To stay an hour longer would require formal application to police headquarters and standard security screening. Agca's presence in Sofia had been established from around July 10 to August 31. How did a Turkish murderer on the run get a visa for *fifty days*, with a false *Indian* passport in the name of Yoginder Singh? Who was paying the bills for "Yoginder Singh" at deluxe hotels like the Vitosha, which alone would have cost around $5,000 for that summer's stay, not counting food and drink?[2] And how did he pass his days there?

He must have had a grand time. The Hotel Vitosha–New Otani, built by the Japanese in 1979, was real-socialism's version of the decadent West's pleasure palaces. A modern white tower thirty stories high, it boasted a bowling alley, a sauna, a king-sized swimming pool, a reflecting lily pond in the landscaped garden, several bars and a panoramic restaurant, chic boutiques charging Paris prices, a naughty nightclub floor show, an abundance of prostitutes "licensed for foreigners," and a gambling casino featuring blackjack and roulette (for foreigners only).[3]

According to the French writer Gérard de Villiers, it also had a microphone in every room, concealed in the handles of electric bedside clocks. (The mike batteries were changed every Monday morning, says Villiers, to whom I am indebted for this firsthand account.)[4] The seventeenth floor, reserved for special guests, had hidden cameras in each room as well. Mingling night and day with the cosmopolitan clientele in the white-marble lobby were contingents of security policemen, doing what all security policemen do in police states. Guests of every nationality came under their scrutiny, but none so close as the many visitors doing business with Kintex: big-time smugglers of weapons, drugs, liquor, cigarettes, stolen cars, electronic goods, currency; their armies of couriers; their relays of hired TIR truck drivers.

The Vitosha was handily located, a stone's throw from Kintex headquarters, which in turn was within hearing distance of the muffled boom coming from an underground shooting range used to test its merchandise. The company had its own operatives keeping the Vitosha under surveillance as well. They were usually stationed across the street in their cars, black Ladas.

Dazzling as the life may have been for a country boy from Malatya, it could not have been different for him than for everybody else. Room 911 of the Vitosha, Agca's room, was bugged like all the rest. (Long afterward, when an Italian reporter asked a chambermaid if she could sneak him into Room 911, she pointed to the walls and signaled him silently to shut up.)[5] Not for a moment during those fifty days could the Bulgarians have been unaware of what Agca was up to.

And what was that? I was reasonably certain by now that Agca had been spirited to Sofia by the Godfather's men, that he'd met the Godfather's lieutenant, Omer Mersan, there, and the Godfather's business partner Bekir Celenk. I had found strong evidence of the Godfather's links to the Bulgarian secret service on the one hand, and, on the other, the neo-Nazi Gray Wolves—the Turkish Mafia's preferred gunrunners and drug pushers in Western Europe and Agca's principal contacts on his roundabout route from Sofia to Rome. I had heard of the money he threw around on that route, peeling bills from a thick wad in his pocket, never once cashing a personal check. For the time being, that was as far as I could get.

Agca had told the Italians that he'd received his Faruk Ozgun passport in Bulgaria (which was true), and his Browning 9-mm automatic as well (which proved untrue). He had also mentioned meeting a "Mustafaeff" there (which turned out to be true too, in the end). But all the wearying rounds I had made to follow these leads had brought me nowhere.

On the track of the shady gun dealer Horst Grillmayer, the last person known to have possessed the Browning, I had gone to Vienna. Austria's antiterrorist police refused to see me, its intelligence service turned me down cold, the U.S. Embassy had nobody following the case. I decided to call on Simon Wiesenthal, as much for the pleasure of meeting him as for any slender expectations I had.

Among the bravest and most incorruptible of men, the world's foremost authority on Nazi personalities living and dead, Wiesenthal was still running his planetwide manhunt from a modest apartment-house office with barely enough space to swing a cat. One room was filled with files and the other with Wiesenthal, relaxed in a comfortable sprawl as he waved me to the only remaining armchair. He listened with the concentrated attention of a true professional, as I told him what little I knew about Horst Grillmayer.

According to the Italian court, I said, the Browning had been in Grillmayer's possession until July 9, 1980, the very time of Agca's arrival in Sofia. SISMI, the Italian military intelligence service, had gotten to Grillmayer at once and asked about it, whereupon he had disappeared. Beyond that, I knew only that Grillmayer was reportedly an arms supplier for international terrorists of the right and left, and was said to come from "a family of fervent Nazis."[6]

Mr. Wiesenthal, no time waster, took me in for a look at his celebrated file on fervent Nazis. Alas, no Grillmayer. He turned up his hands ruefully, I shrugged, and we wished each other well.

From Vienna, I boarded an express for Munich, with Omer Mersan in mind. With a lively and charming young Turkish woman interpreter in tow, Özay Wallner, I headed for the Vardar Export-Import Company, in Bayerstrasse 43, just opposite the railroad station. Display cases for electronic wares were empty, and large packing crates were strewn around the shop, when we came in and asked for the owner, Selam Gultas. He was not there and not expected, said a harried-looking blonde woman who refused to give her name. Perhaps she herself might tell us about Omer Mersan then, I suggested. She looked as if I'd hit her. "We don't know this man, he has never worked here, he has gotten us into all this trouble . . . ," she replied, backing off toward a rear room. "But this is where the police found him, through Vardar's phone numbers," I protested, to her evidently growing alarm. Yes, she admitted at last, Omer Mersan had worked for Vardar "in a way," but not anymore. The fuss in the papers about him had ruined Mr. Gultas, all his creditors had immediately pressed for payment, Vardar was going out of business.

"Mr. Gultas is Turkish too," I pressed, my curiosity mounting. "Was he doing business with Turkey? Was Mersan taking care of that 'in a way' in Sofia? Did Vardar ship by TIR truck?" Yes, yes, she answered hastily. "But that's all finished now. . . ."

My last visit of the day in Munich was to the city's Polizei Praesidium. Though I had an appointment with the Police President, I could not get past a press secretary of his named Kissler. Our conversation was stilted, and visibly embarrassing for him. "At first, our police officer on the case said that press reports about Mersan's connections with Abuzer Ugurlu and contraband were not true. . . . We do not have a clear vision of the case. . . ."

Maybe the Vardar Export-Import Company could have helped to clarify the matter, I went on. The fact that Vardar was closing down just now had given me the impression that the police might indeed have looked into its possible smuggling activities. Was that so? "Many Turkish companies in Germany are involved in contraband," he answered. "Unless they break the German law, that is the last thing we think about here." The question was still whether Vardar itself had been investigated, I insisted. "We investigate many such companies. If there are no results, we stop. We're not the Gestapo, you know," replied Herr Kissler.

There was no point in asking if the absent Police President had gotten back from wherever he had gone. I knew an impassable roadblock when I saw one.

From Munich I flew to Zurich, in search of Abdullah Catli. The Godfather's emissary to Agca had been picked up in that elegant Swiss city on February 22, 1982, by pure chance. He happened to be cruising around with another famed Gray Wolf fugitive, his inseparable friend, Mehmet Sener, who had allegedly given Agca the gun to shoot Abdi Ipekci.

Sener himself was a prime example of the judicial incoherence—the kindest word—prevailing among presumably friendly states somehow entangled in this case. He had been on the run since Agca's arrest in Istanbul for the Ipekci killing in 1979. The West Germans had arrested him for a minor infraction in April 1980. Though Turkey had asked them to hold him pending extradition hearings on that murder charge, they let him go a month later.[7] He moved on to Switzerland.

Six months after that, on November 28, Interpol had issued an international search warrant for Sener on the same murder charge; it was bound to be in Swiss police files.[8] Two weeks after the Pope was shot the next May, Rome's DIGOS had sent out that list of seventeen "Suspect Turkish Citizens" reportedly in contact with Agca. It included Mehmet Sener too, along with Abdullah Catli and Oral Celik. The DIGOS circular, distributed through Interpol, had explicitly requested that persons listed be detained at any national frontier. This must have been in the Swiss files also.

Nevertheless, Mehmet Sener was not arrested in Zurich for murder, or for associating with the Pope's would-be murderer either. He was simply charged with carrying a false passport and questioned about nothing else.

Sure enough, Sener's beautifully counterfeited passport came from Nevsehir. So did Abdullah Catli's (he was born there). With Agca's and Omer Ay's, that made four. Were they all in this plot together? Was Nevsehir just a Gray Wolf town, or the Godfather's province? Was Abdullah Catli's inseparable friend Mehmet Sener another of those Gray Wolves in the pay of the Turkish Mafia—the Godfather's men?

The answers came along eventually, but not in Zurich.

Mehmet Sener was still in jail when I got there at the end of March 1982, but Abdullah Catli was not. For all his record of murder in Turkey, the Swiss authorities had released him in forty-eight hours. An urgent Turkish request for his extradition had arrived just forty-eight hours after that: too late. By then, Catli had melted into an indistinct mass of Turkish immigrant workers who all appeared to look alike in the Alpine light. No great manhunt was mounted for him. Murder or no murder, he was a political refugee for the Swiss.

IIe was a lost chance for the judiciaries of Turkey and Italy, and for reporters like me. No crumb of information came my way on Abdullah Catli's whereabouts. For the stolidly upright Swiss, apparently, he was just another among thousands of Turks fleeing harsh military rule at home. (Both Catli and Sener had in fact fled Turkey under the lax civilian rule of Bulent Ecevit's Socialist government.)

It was no good trying to explain that Abdullah Catli's name must be coupled with Abuzer Ugurlu's, and both with Mehmet Ali Agca's, in the papal plot. Even to myself, I began to sound as if I'd been reading too many mystery stories instead of authoritative documents provided by General M. Once again, I was struck by the sluggish flow of information from border to border in regard to this tremendous conspiracy. How many of the states directly concerned knew the first thing about the probable role of Abdullah Catli and Abuzer Ugurlu in the plot? Had Turkey tried to tell Switzerland about this, after Catli's arrest? Did their respective intelligence services communicate? How much was any country telling any other, anyway, on the Agca case?

The one country I'd found holding nothing back was Tunisia, which had little enough to tell. I had only a day to spare for a stopover in Tunis. The director of the Sûreté Nationale, Ahmed Bennaui, was an agreeable surprise: he seemed to *like* talking about the case. Warmly welcoming and crisply efficient, he took me step by step through Agca's visit to Tunisia from November 28 to December 12, 1980.

Traveling as "Faruk Ozgun," Agca had spent his first night at the Hôtel du Lac in Tunis, checking out the next afternoon at two. The hotel was big, impersonal, and full of transients whose bedside clocks were not bugged. If a "Mustafaeff" did come to Agca's room at noon, as Agca claimed, he could easily have passed unnoticed. Nevertheless, the police had no record of a "Mustafaeff" entering Tunisia.

Having no high hopes for this shadowy figure, I was not overly disappointed. The outlook improved when we came to Agca's mysterious Turkish companion in the tourist resort of Hammamet, Youssef Dag. His name had been nagging at me since I'd first read the batch of documents from Rome's central courthouse. A Youssef Dag had been seen frequently with Agca during the latter's two-week stay at the Hotel Continental, said an Italian police report. The report added only that he had boarded a Tunis Air flight for Rome the following April 24, landed at Fiumicino, and vanished.

Ahmed Bennaui could do better. Youssef Dag and Agca had been seen together three times outside the Tunisia Welcome Service travel agency in Hammamet. A girl at the desk there had picked out photographs of both men without hesitation, from a large assortment. *It was Dag who bought Agca's ticket for the overnight ferry to Palermo, presenting the "Faruk Ozgun" passport while Agca loitered across the road.* The girl was positive about it, M. Bennaui assured me. "She told us that she'd asked why Dag's friend didn't come in to buy his own ticket. Dag answered that Agca wasn't feeling well."

Apart from Omer Mersan, I had now come across a second living witness known from the outset to have crossed Agca's path during his travels: another enticing lead that was never pursued to the end.

Tunisia's Sûreté Nationale had lost no time in reporting the Youssef Dag episode, to Italy and Turkey both. What's more, Youssef Dag had been found—and, like Omer Mersan, turned loose.

I'd been back to Turkey twice before discovering that Dag had been there all along. In fact, he had boarded a connecting flight from Fiumicino and gone straight home. Detained and questioned by the Turkish police, he had denied everything and been released. "There was nothing to the Tunisia story," said a ranking official at the Interior Ministry in Ankara, with an impatient wave of his hand as if at a buzzing fly. Nothing to the positive identification, the dodge at the travel agency, the evident effort to deflect attention from Agca himself? It beat me.

There were no other finds for me to write about, no remaining avenues open to explore. Agca's established movements and contacts after leaving Bulgaria did not diverge from the predictable. His broad Gray Wolf tracks across half of Europe fit perfectly into the plot as I saw it now, and into no other. Any number of alternative theories had been plucked out of the air, theories involving Colonel Qaddafi, or Ayatollah Khomeini, the Israeli Mossad, the PLO, the fundamentalist Moslem Brotherhood, the Armenian terrorists' ASALA, the CIA. None was backed by supporting evidence, none could be made to fit the verifiable facts, and none could get around the most visible obstacle to all of them—the Bulgarian Factor—as the chapters to follow will make clear.

Before finishing the last draft of my article for the *Digest*, I'd had one more try at Judge Martella, to so little purpose that I wondered if he had given up. A DIGOS commissioner actually encouraged me to think so. "Do you have any idea when Martella might finish his investigation?" I'd asked, foreseeing calamity if the judge should produce something sensational that I knew nothing about, just when my article appeared. "Probably never," replied the commissioner, limpidly sincere. "If you ask me, he'll never get enough to arrest anybody, still less go to trial."

The man had only been doing his job, I realized with less than saintly resignation, when Judge Martella surfaced at last not two weeks later.

On June 2, 1982, on a warrant he issued, a Turk called Omer Bagci was arrested in Olten, Switzerland, for "direct complicity" with Agca in the papal plot. The DIGOS commissioner naturally had known this was coming—and a lot more—when we'd met last. Bagci, a local Gray Wolf leader in Olten, had no police record and had never cropped up in the case. He was charged with delivering the Browning to Agca in Milan four days before the shooting in Rome.

Only Agca himself could have told Judge Martella who this accomplice was and where to find him. The time bomb ticking away since May 13, 1981, must have gone off, or at least begun to rumble. A year after he had shot John Paul and lived to tell the tale, Agca was unmistakably talking.

Not that this did me much good. Bagci's arrest had demonstrated the existence of a plot, nothing more. After his swift extradition to Italy, the curtain of judicial silence came down again. There were no explanations, no leaks, no hints of future developments—save one: Judge Martella had slipped off to Istanbul to interrogate the Godfather, Abuzer Ugurlu, in prison.

The brief news item was doubtless incomprehensible to a Western public that had never heard of Abuzer Ugurlu. But it was a flaring beacon to anybody doubling back on Mehmet Ali Agca's trail. Not only was he talking, but he must be pointing in the very direction I had fixed on myself.

I couldn't use this tantalizing bit of news in my article because time had run out. The *Reader's Digest* release date was August 15, and could not be postponed. We had gone to press.

No sooner did that happen than my Turkish colleague Orsan Oymen got a magnificent scoop. His story in *Milliyet*, running to four installments starting that July 11, rated a couple of wire-service paragraphs in the Italian papers: enough to send me diving for the telephone. Where did Orsan get the information, and what exactly did he write?

He was in too much trouble to reveal his source publicly. Judge Martella was said to be in a white fury, and DIGOS in a black rage, over this arrant violation of the *segreto istruttorio*. But once Orsan had told me the source in confidence, I knew he was onto the real thing.

Agca had started talking in earnest to Judge Martella during a week of continuous interrogation, from May 1 to 7, 1982. The essentials of his confession ran to more than a hundred typewritten pages. The summary in *Milliyet* was a rare reward for the grueling months I'd spent on the chase.

This is the substance of what Orsan wrote:[9]

The hit man himself had described the organization that had hired him. It was the Turkish Mafia, Agca said. The "Fathers" smuggled arms and cigarettes to Turkey and the Middle East through Bulgaria, and had links with "an international Mafia extending from Turkey and Bulgaria to Switzerland and London." For the papal plot, they had made use of Turkish Idealists, the Gray Wolves.

The co-Godfathers who had sent him on his way were Abuzer Ugurlu and Bekir Celenk. He had met both in Sofia.

From what Orsan could learn, Agca had not linked the pair directly to the Bulgarian secret service. He had simply observed that "both Bekir Celenk and Abuzer were smuggling to Turkey with the knowledge of the Bulgarian authorities." For example, both were working in cooperation with Kintex in connection with the Bulgarian state tobacco monopoly, Bulgar-Tabac, manufacturing Marlboro cigarettes under license. The sales of the cigarettes had long been an immeasurably bountiful source of contraband, enriching Bulgaria and the Turkish Mafia alike. Its director, Agca now revealed to Judge Martella, was Mustafaeff.

There really was a Mustafaeff, after all, as neatly placed as if John Le Carré had invented him. He was director of the state monopoly producing those Marlboro cigarettes, which was a branch of Kintex, which was a branch of the Bulgarian secret service. Bekir Celenk and Abuzer Ugurlu were part of that circle—evidently the one Agca had moved in himself.

It was Ugurlu who helped Agca go first to Iran, and later to Bulgaria, after his prison break, and then put up the front money for Agca's onward journey. (Once out of Bulgaria, various Gray Wolf leaders passed more money on to him, Agca said.) Ugurlu in person had arranged for Agca's counterfeit Indian passport as Yoginder Singh, and the other as Faruk Ozgun, while "Ugurlu's men" did the legwork.

Omer Mersan, indeed among the Godfather's men, was "the middleman Agca met in Bulgaria"; Agca repeated this to the judge. Mehmet Sener was "Abdullah Catli's man," amounting to much the same thing—for the chief go-between in the first stage of Agca's flight from Turkey was Abdullah Catli himself.

As Catli's role in the whole passport affair unfolded, the puzzle of those exit and entry stamps at the Turco-Bulgarian border grew clear. Catli had picked up the Faruk Ozgun passport in Nevsehir (from Omer Ay, according to the Turkish authorities, though Agca did not tell Judge Martella so). Then Catli got it stamped for the purchase of 540 Deutschmarks in "tourist currency," at the Taksim branch of the Osmanli Bank in Istanbul, on August 27. From there, he took it to the Turkish border point at Kapikule—"Abuzer's private estate," as the late smuggler Ibrahim Telemen had put it. "In Kapikule, Catli obtained an exit stamp [marked "Edirne"] dated August 30, 1980, paying a bribe of 5,000 Turkish lire," Agca had declared.

The next day, said Agca, *"Catli and Ugurlu together acquired the August 31 entry and exit stamps from the Bulgarian border police* [my italics]."

Well, well.

Agca had seen a lot of Catli after that, in Sofia and later in Switzerland, often in the company of their mutual friend Mehmet Sener. At some undefined point, the role of chief go-between then shifted from Abdullah Catli to the other Gray Wolf leader I had read about in General M.'s file: Bekir Celenk's man, Oral Celik.

Oral Celik and Abdullah Catli had both had a hand in getting Agca out of the impregnable military prison of Kartal-Maltepe, Agca stated. Afterward, Agca had kept running into Celik in Sofia, and later in Austria, Switzerland, and Italy.

It was Celik who acquired the Browning from Horst Grillmayer in Vienna, where Agca and Omer Bagci joined him. The gun was then entrusted to Bagci for safekeeping in Switzerland.

After leaving Bulgaria, Agca had also kept in touch with Bekir Celenk. The two had met in Switzerland; and they had communicated by telephone during Agca's "holiday" in Palma de Majorca. He had spent a fortnight on the beach there at the Hotel Flamboyan, from April 25 to May 9, 1981. (The Browning was delivered to him on May 9, directly after his return flight to Milan.) At some time in those two weeks, he was finally told what "the ring behind him" had hired him for.

He was offered 3 million Deutschmarks—around $1,350,000—to kill the Pope, he declared. The proposition came "through Bekir Celenk," via a middleman whom Agca refused to name.

The first stage of Agca's confession stopped there. Though hardly more than a preview of the stunning revelations to follow in the autumn, there was no way of knowing that in the summer of 1982. Incomplete as it was, and still to be confirmed, the story he had reportedly told Judge Martella certainly bore out the one I had just written.

Much of it was confirmed already by evidence I had gathered myself. That did not make me so special. Any experienced professional reporter could have done as much, with the time, freedom, and resources I had behind me. The *Reader's Digest*, with its editions in sixteen languages and 100 million readers around the globe, was probably unique in its ability to back me all the way. No other publication comes to mind that would have been willing and able to keep a reporter on the move from country to country and continent to continent, for nine months, on a single story. Not many might have had the guts to print it, either.

The plot as I had reconstructed it was necessarily complex: there could be no such thing as a *simple* plot to assassinate the head of the Roman Catholic Church. I maintained that the Turkish Mafia, operating out of Sofia under tight Bulgarian control, had picked the suitable hit man and provided the suitable cover. The hit man had a ready-made image as a right-wing terrorist killer, an image polished till it shone as he was passed across Europe from one neo-Nazi Gray Wolf to another.

To all appearances, then, this would be an international right-wing conspiracy, as remote from the Soviet Union as half a century of political folklore could make it.

In reality, the Gray Wolves involved here were working for the Turkish Mafia, which was controlled by the Bulgarian secret service, DS (Darzhavna Sigurnost), which was working for the Soviet KGB. This last was my conclusion. Readers could draw their own.

The evidence spoke for itself up through the penultimate link in this chain of command. The final one, from the Bulgarians to the Russians, could only be a matter of deduction. Several degrees removed from the mechanics of the plot, the Russians had assured their safety from direct exposure. No piece of paper, coded message, tape-recorded message, firsthand witness, was ever likely to be found tying Soviet leaders to the crime of the century. Whatever might come to light, nobody was going to find a Russian with a smoking gun in his hand.

Furthermore, the very enormity of the crime should all but guarantee their immunity. It strained belief. This was 1981. Détente had been a way of life for a decade. Superpower diplomacy had become more or less civilized. The Russians wouldn't dare. Or else, they wouldn't be so primitive, incautious, foolhardy, maladroit. The Russians just don't do these things, people would say—not anymore.

The evidence was no more than circumstantial, and limited besides. All the bits and pieces I had put together in apparently logical sequence simply showed how the spurious terrorist hit had been mounted. There remained the matter of motive: a question conjuring up such unthinkable thoughts and improbable conjectures as to seem unanswerable.

9

"A cunning and dangerous ideological enemy," a "militant anti-Communist," a "malicious, lowly, perfidious, and backward toady of the American militarists," fighting socialism in the interests of his "overseas accomplices [and] his new boss in the White House": that was the Russians' stated opinion of Pope John Paul II in March 1981, published in the political journal *Polimya*, a few weeks before he was shot.[1]

The inelegant prose was customary, but not in this context. It was decades since the Soviet press had spoken of a Roman Catholic Pontiff in such paleo-Stalinist terms. But then, no Pope in decades had become such a threat to the Kremlin.

One look at the ocean of rapt faces on his first visit to Poland—at the adoring crowds running into the millions, spellbound by this commanding, radiant figure in white—was enough to take the measure of the man. His pilgrimage to Poland "would have the same effect on the masses as the Ayatollah Khomeini had in Iran," predicted Soviet Foreign Minister Gromyko at the time, voicing the apprehension of all official Russia.[2]

But it was not just Poland, let alone any single episode concerning the Poles. The case for or against Soviet guilt in the papal shooting most certainly does not depend, say, on whether or not John Paul sent an inflammatory letter to Brezhnev about Solidarity (a relevant episode nevertheless, which I will come to). It has to do with his challenge to Soviet hegemony over all of Eastern Europe, and to the Communist Party hierarchy in Soviet Russia itself.

From the day he was elected, on October 16, 1978, Pope John Paul II was viewed in Moscow with the blackest suspicion. His very election by the College of Cardinals was reportedly held to be a calculated anti-Soviet plot engineered by President Carter's national security adviser, Zbigniew Brzezinski, to destabilize Poland and dislodge it from the Soviet bloc. Obsessed for more than half a century by the conviction that the capitalist world dreamed only of encircling and annihilating their Communist state, Soviet leaders would see nothing implausible in this remarkable theory. In fact, it was said to be their underlying motive for deciding that this Polish Pope would have to go.

The man who said it was Bulgarian defector Iordan Mantarov, ranking officer of the Bulgarian secret service in Paris from 1979 to 1981, speaking to Nicholas Gage of *The New York Times*.[3] The French secret service believed him, whereas the CIA went out of its way to say it did not.[4] Whether or not we take his word for it, however, the motivation he suggested was by far the most convincing of the lot.

Like Mehmet Ali Agca in Turkey, Karol Wojtyla was a true child of his time. The first Slav to be chosen in the millennial annals of the Church, he was also the first Pope who had been formed in postwar Eastern Europe, under a Communist regime forcibly imposed on his country.

He was not only deeply religious, but a Pole to the marrow of his bones. There is no more devastating combination in history than religion identified with nationalism—as Great Britain has learned to its sorrow in Ireland, Israel with the Palestine resistance, Soviet Russia with its incorporated Baltic states and the Western Ukraine, Poland itself.

A Pole at the head of the Holy See! And this Pole! One can imagine the incredulous shock in the Kremlin when he was chosen: a man who had witnessed, and defied, the efforts of an alien government under foreign auspices to smother the Church in his own land; who had never accepted the Communists' right to play God as well as Caesar, there or anywhere else; who had been a worker himself and would not be resigned to the oppression and indignities workers suffered under Communist rule; and who now had the power to lead great legions into battle for religious and political liberty throughout the Soviet Empire.

Stalin had once asked mockingly how many divisions the Pope had. Brezhnev was about to find out.

Vatican policy changed overnight under John Paul. The two Popes preceding him, Paul VI and John XXIII, had bowed to what seemed the inevitable, abandoning a Church under siege and by now largely underground in the cause of peaceful coexistence with Moscow. The incoming Pontiff briskly turned that around, setting off a religious revival without precedent since the October Revolution in Russia.

Though much of what he did went unreported in the Western press, it is summarized in an excellent study for the Rand Corporation by Alex Alexiev, to whom I am indebted for much of the material in this chapter.[5] For a start, John Paul appreciably expanded Radio Vatican's broadcasting time in several East European and Soviet languages. He also elevated a number of prelates from these countries to important positions at home or in Rome. Within weeks of his election, furthermore, he had already begun negotiations for that stupendous visit to his native Poland. Once he had made it, in June 1979—just eight months after his election—the Russians' worst premonitions were borne out.

Some six million Poles, a sixth of the population, turned out for him. Delirious with joy at the very sight of a Polish Pope, they were intoxicated with the prospects he offered them.

He spoke not only of Poland, but of "brother peoples and neighboring peoples." He had come, he declared, "to speak before the whole Church, before Europe and the world, of those often forgotten nations and people, to cry out with a loud voice and to embrace all these peoples together with his own nation." He pronounced the Christian and Marxist world views to be diametrically opposed, accused the Communist system of allowing "evident privileges for some and discrimination for others," denounced the system's muzzling of the press by observing to half a million Poles at Gniezo: "It is sad to believe that each Pole and Slav in any part of the world is unable to hear the words of the Pope, this Slav."[6]

Not once did he oppose the Socialist system as such, then or since. What he evidently wanted was not to abolish it but to improve it— and more particularly, to nationalize it, freeing a sovereign state of a suffocating foreign hand. Peace and social harmony, he said, could be achieved only on the basis of "respect for the objective rights of the nation, such as the right to existence, the right to freedom." The task of the Church, he continued, with Polish Party Secretary Edward Gierek in the audience, is "to make people more confident, more courageous, conscious of their rights and duties. . . ."[7]

Then came a direct assault on Soviet domination of Eastern Europe, and on the Soviet-controlled Warsaw Pact. The validity of alliances depended on "whether they led to more well-being and prosperity for member states," he asserted. "No country should ever develop at the cost of enslavement, conquest, outrage, exploitation, and death."[8]

"Solidarity was not born of the disorders in the summer of 1980, but in the lap of the Church," the Soviet news agency Tass would say some years later.[9] Indeed, the Russians believed it was born of that first papal visit to Poland, and no wonder.

Surely the dream of a free trade union became a live hope for the Poles, on the strength of John Paul's words and presence in the summer of 1979. But the message went far beyond them, reverberating through what had been called the Church of Silence: from East Germany to Czechoslovakia to Lithuania, Latvia, and that most restless of USSR republics, the Ukraine. "The faithful will have only as much freedom as they manage to win for themselves," was his stout advice to the Lithuanian Catholics, quoted in their underground paper *Chronicle of the Lithuanian Catholic Church*.[10] The faithful got right down to it.

Lithuania, annexed by the Russians in 1940, is as Catholic as Poland and its close relative in culture, history, and incorrigible nationalism. Pope Wojtyla speaks Lithuanian and has said that half his heart resides there. His electric effect on its population was foreordained.

No sooner was he elected than Lithuanian priests set up a Catholic Committee for the Defense of the Rights of Believers. Its declared purpose was to publicize, and resist, perpetual violations of every Soviet citizen's constitutional right to worship as he pleased. One of its founders, Alfonsas Svarinskas, had spent sixteen years in a Soviet gulag (he was sent back in May 1983 to serve another seven years, for "anti-Soviet agitation").[11]

The committee's first official act was to declare the Lithuanian clergy's unconditional loyalty to Pope John Paul—a possibly constitutional but decidedly impolitic declaration in Soviet Russia.

By May 1981—that portentous month and year—all Lithuanian Church leaders save one had signed a statement announcing their determination to defy Soviet regulations harmful to the Church. They argued that the Church was responsible only to the Pope, and did not recognize the State's jurisdiction over its affairs. It was an unthinkable act of rebellion under a regime demanding undivided allegiance in all things.

The Pope's support never wavered. He refused to appoint Church officials named by Soviet authorities. He bestowed the cardinal's hat *in pectore* on the Lithuanian Catholics' acknowledged leader, Bishop Stepanovicius, consigned to internal exile for twenty years. He pressed for and finally won the release of another long-interned bishop.

Thus, after nearly half a century of implacable persecution, the Catholics of Lithuania—four-fifths of that Soviet republic's population—took to the streets, joined in religious processions and demonstrations, signed mass petitions. Underground, meanwhile, the Church blossomed with *samizdat* publications, a secret Catholic lay society, secret orders for nuns, a new secret seminary for priests.

"Fanatical agents of the Pope," under the influence of the Vatican's "vile fantasies," had become conductors of "the hostile strivings of the anti-Communists," said a top functionary of the KGB.[12] What he meant was that the Lithuanian Catholic Church had become the most militant religious movement in Soviet Russia.

Vying for that honor was the Ukrainian Catholic Church of the Eastern Rite: the Uniate Church, ever a thorn in the Russians' side.

The Uniate Church has five million followers in the Soviet bloc: one and a half million in Rumania, the rest in Czechoslovakia and the Ukraine. The latter in particular is the closest thing to an Irish problem that the Russians have.

The virulence of Ukrainian nationalism has survived every brutal effort to suppress it since the Western Ukraine was annexed by Russia after the Nazi-Soviet Pact of 1939. Hostile to Soviet occupation and Soviet socialism alike, the Ukrainians have been regarded and treated as intractable rebels, to be held down by all the formidable force of the State security police.

For centuries, millions of Ukrainians have looked to their Uniate Church for spiritual and political solace. Accordingly, it is the one church in Soviet Russia to be wholly outlawed. Its places of worship have been closed and burned, its priests imprisoned and exiled, its followers hounded, arrested, tortured, sent to Siberia, executed. Yet here too an invigorated Catholic population waded into battle with the advent of Pope Wojtyla.

Unlike his predecessors, John Paul II took up their cause energetically from the beginning. By the spring of 1980, he had convoked a first synod of Uniate bishops, which called openly for the reopening of their churches and restoration of their religious freedom. Not long afterward, the Ukrainians too organized an Initiative Group for the Defense of the Rights of the Church to back this alarming demand. Under the eyes of the world's most powerful security police force, an underground Uniate Church thereupon swelled to number five hundred priests.

In February 1983, Pope John Paul convoked another synod of Uniate bishops, which urged them on.

That year, he named three new cardinals from the Soviet bloc. They included Bishop Vaivods of Latvia, who had spent years in a Soviet labor camp. He was the first Roman Catholic Cardinal ever appointed inside Soviet Russia.

It was the same story in Latvia and Byelorussia as in Lithuania and the Ukraine, not to mention heavily Catholic states of Eastern Europe absorbed by the Russians directly after World War II. The religious renaissance was especially striking in Czechoslovakia, under Soviet military occupation since 1968. For all that daunting Russian presence, the Communist regime in Prague could not save its invaluable religious front group, Pacem in Terris, from the Pope's inexorable advance. A third of the country's Roman Catholic priests have been chivied into joining it. At a word from John Paul, all but a handful withdrew.[13]

Only his own sense of limits could contain the militant surge. The harder he hit, the greater was the popular response. In defiance of every Soviet tenet, an alternative pole of authority was emerging, essentially religious but with strong—and, for an inflexibly authoritarian Soviet system, extremely dangerous—political overtones.

No other leader in our time could have done as much. None has even tried.

What kind of menace that made Pope John Paul II may be gathered from the Russians' own ominous pronouncements. The Vatican was committing "innumerable acts" of "ideological sabotage," declared the Soviet review *Polititcheskoye Samoobrazovanie* ("Political Education"), as quoted by Tass.[14] It was "training and sending propaganda specialists . . . and smuggling subversive literature" into Socialist countries on a "vast scale." It had "inspired subversive activities in Poland" and furthered "the aggressive aims of imperialism and the enemies of détente."

Its "anti-Communist campaign for the defense of human rights" was an attempt to "activate destabilizing forces" in Socialist countries. "The subversive activities of the Vatican" did not stop in Poland, the author declared. They were directed "against all Socialist countries, and against the Soviet people first and foremost."

If Poland under the hypnotic sway of John Paul was bad enough, such a Poland against such a backdrop was insupportable.

Theoretically, there might have been a Solidarity movement without Karol Wojtyla. Polish longings for a free trade union went back to the imposition of Communist rule; Polish blood had been spilled for that on and off for more than three decades. But the difference this Pope made lay in the trust he inspired. With his blessing, backed by the colossal weight of the Catholic Church, the sobering lessons of experience gave way to an almost mystic confidence. This time was not going to be like other times. This time, a free labor movement could really come into being in Communist Poland, and survive.

Though the birth date for Solidarity is generally given as August 1980, it actually got started in December 1979—six months after John Paul's unforgettable visit. The occasion was an anniversary of the 1970 Polish strike wave, which had left some fifty workers dead. The strikes then had begun at the Gdansk shipyards, leading to formation of a Free Trade Union Committee of the coast. Having somehow survived continuing harassment ever since, the committee had organized commemoration ceremonies in 1979, provoking a rash of arrests. On January 25, 1980, the workers set up a five-man commission to fight for their comrades' release. An obscure electrician named Lech Walesa was on it.

The rest became history: the dizzying spiral of workers' demands and expectations; the growing disarray in Communist Party ranks; the strikes spreading uncontrollably until production slowed to a halt; the sinister warnings emanating from Moscow; the heartening signals from Rome.

By the summer of 1980, buoyant Polish workers were asserting their inalienable right to freedom of speech, press, and assembly, a free trade union, a free Church. The Pope was behind them all the way. Poland was paralyzed. The regime was on its knees. Soviet leaders seemed impotent, and stumped.

The Russians had responded to demands like these in the past by simply sending troops and tanks—to Budapest in 1956, to Prague in 1968. The West had looked the other way on both occasions and, for all its sonorous display of concern about Poland, would doubtless do so again. But the Church could not.

The Pope's divisions were massed across the country, in resolute workers' battalions from the Gdansk shipyards to strikebound Ursus, Lublin, Lodz, Wroclaw, Nova Huta, Warsaw. John Paul showed every sign of believing that God had chosen him for this unique and sacred mission: to reshape Communist Poland as a universal model for a free and sovereign Socialist state, respecting human rights and dignity, mindful of man's temporal and spiritual needs.

What would the Pope do with his divisions, when and if the Warsaw Pact armies moved in? A hot argument broke out over what he *would* have done in the autumn of 1982.

In an NBC White Paper, "The Man Who Shot the Pope," Washington's widely respected commentator Marvin Kalb had spoken of a handwritten letter in Russian from John Paul II, delivered by special courier to Brezhnev in Moscow. If the Russians moved against Poland, the letter reportedly warned, John Paul would "lay down the crown of St. Peter and return to his homeland to stand shoulder to shoulder with his people." The letter was sent in August 1980, Kalb said.[15]

Here was dramatic evidence that the Pope had intimidated the Russians into standing aside while Solidarity came into being—had indeed threatened to intercede physically between an invading army and his beloved Poles. It would have been a powerful motive for decreeing his death, if Kalb was right. But some of his colleagues could hardly wait to prove him wrong.

A skeptical column in *Time* pronounced the story most unlikely.[16] The rival television network ABC went to considerable trouble and expense to debunk it[17] (the program cost half a million dollars). A Vatican spokesman, choosing his words with care, denied that such a *letter* had been sent.[18] Those who had refused all along to believe in a Russian conspiracy now pounced on this point to argue that, without the letter, the whole case collapsed.

It would not have collapsed for the letter's sake in any case, but Kalb was essentially right. He may have been mistaken about the date of John Paul's warning, and the crown of St. Peter does not exist. Nevertheless, what mattered was whether or not the Pope did inform the Russians of his intention to defend Solidarity with all the strength at his command. There is little doubt that he did.

The veteran British correspondent Neal Ascherson, whose book *The Polish August* appeared several months before the NBC White Paper, placed the incident more precisely in December 1980. The message was conveyed to Soviet Party leader Vadim Zagladin during his confidential visit to the Vatican around December 15, Ascherson wrote. "The contents of the talks remain a secret," he noted. "But a few days later, two different sources reported that the Pope had told Zagladin that if Poland were invaded he would simply fly home to be with his own people."[19]

A more authoritative source was the Primate of Poland, Cardinal Stefan Wyszynski. Addressing the Academy of Catholic Theology in Warsaw on March 9, 1981, the cardinal said first: "Providence has placed in the Vatican a man who could be a Protector of Poland, and this he is. Providence knows what it is doing." The Primate then went on to speak explicitly of the "Holy Father's . . . letter to Brezhnev."[20]

The Pope's exact words would hardly have mattered anyway. Soviet leaders could have no illusions about John Paul's whole-hearted and militant commitment to the Polish workers' cause: in the summer of 1980, the next autumn, the following winter, the succeeding spring. Of all the obstacles to be reckoned with, he must surely have loomed largest in the Kremlin's calculations when the supreme moment of decision came, and went.

By the end of that Polish August, Soviet leaders were still holding back, and Poland's rulers caved in. On August 31, 1980, they stipulated a formal contract with Solidarity in Gdansk. It was the first agreement in the history of worldwide communism to legitimize a free trade union. Lech Walesa signed the agreement with a foot-high pen, a souvenir of Pope John Paul's visit just the summer before.

It was on August 31, 1980, that Mehmet Ali Agca left Bulgaria on his roundabout way to St. Peter's Square.

Was this by chance or design? We may never know. But what happened in Gdansk the day Agca left Sofia made a singularly compelling motive for his mission.

The Bulgarians, harboring the hit man all through that summer, had no motive of their own. Their orthodox Communist regime had no quarrel with the Pope, would be the last to feel the shock waves issuing from Poland, and had in any case never been known to make a move on the international scene except at the Russians' bidding. With the rise of Solidarity, on the other hand, the Russians themselves faced a shattering crisis on the vulnerable Western perimeter of their realm.

Solidarity was more than a mere trade union. It was a popular consensus, an expression of the people's will for better and more representative government, personal liberty, and, above all, national independence. Now it had become a recognized, organized force, playing a legitimate role in shaping the policies of a Communist state, altering and inevitably eroding the Party's entire power structure. Could the Russians tolerate this legalized freedom movement in Poland? Accept its intimate working relationship with the biggest organized church on earth? Risk the likely impact of both on the rest of Eastern Europe, not to mention the Russians' own heartland? Permit a massive and maverick body that they did not create and could not control to challenge the Party's absolute authority? Every rule in the Communist books since Lenin's day said they could not.

"When the Holy Father began defending Solidarity, Yuri Andropov ordered his assassination," declared Archbishop Myroslav Lubachivsky, a leader of the Ukrainian Church in exile, expressing in a simple declarative sentence a view held by practically the entire Catholic clergy in the Soviet bloc.[21]

That wasn't all. If Solidarity could hardly get along without the Church, neither could Poland's rulers. So remarkable was John Paul's hold on the Polish people during the troubles that the Church was coming to be the State's sole possible interlocutor. In the long run, as leaders of Warsaw's disintegrating Communist Party could see, only the Church would be in a position to assure popular restraint, national reconciliation, economic recovery. Coming to terms with that would necessarily amount to a kind of government partnership. In effect, a Communist regime would be taking on God's mightiest living spokesman as copilot.

And this copilot was, to the Russians' mind, "a cunning and dangerous ideological enemy," a "malicious, lowly, perfidious and backward toady of the American militarists," a conspirator elevated to the papacy for the primary purpose of destabilizing the entire

Soviet empire, by a Vatican cabal taking orders from the Soviet Union's archenemy, the United States.

Like Henry II, incapable of besting the indomitable Becket in an epic clash of wills, Party Secretary Brezhnev might well have said: "Will nobody rid me of this meddlesome priest?"

It was only natural, after the event, for Soviet leaders to point out that assassination has always been abhorrent to them. But there is half a century of indisputable evidence to prove that political murder, at home and abroad, directly or through proxies, has been an instrument of Russian state policy since the revolution.

Leon Trotsky was their most illustrious victim. One of the Soviet Union's Founding Fathers and a figure of worldwide fame, he was hacked to death in Mexico City in 1940, by a Soviet agent later decorated in Moscow as a "Hero of the Soviet Union."[22]

Times have changed since Stalin sent the Spanish-born Ramón Mercador, alias Jacques Mornard, alias Frank Jacson, into Trotsky's home with a hatchet.[23] In their quest for respectability, Soviet leaders shifted to less openly incriminating methods. According to the most expert of American writers on the KGB, John Barron: "The Soviet Union decided in late 1962 or early 1963 to entrust future assassinations not to Soviet personnel, but to hired foreign criminals and illegal agents of other nationalities, who could not easily be linked to the Soviet Union."[24]

The one known exception to that rule since then was the late president of Afghanistan, Hafizullah Amin, gunned down in his Presidential Palace in Kabul on December 27, 1979, by a KGB assassination team that also mowed down everybody else in sight. The decision to eliminate Amin had been made directly by the Politburo, evidently in great haste: the shocking carnage was a sure sign of how badly the hit team had botched the job. A full description of this plot was given to John Barron by a high-ranking KGB defector.[25]

At an extraordinary press conference in July 1983 at Washington's Smithsonian Institution, the Bulgarian ambassador to the United States indignantly denied that the Soviet Union or Bulgaria would ever resort to political assassination. Queried about these two extravagant examples of the Soviet Union's predilection for this practice—Leon Trotsky and Hafizullah Amin—the Bulgarian ambassador dismissed both as "irrelevant."[26]

An established practice when Barron's first book on the KGB

came out in 1978, the Russians' use of hired foreign criminals for such purposes would have presented no problems in 1981. In the Pope's case, indeed, it could be turned to notable advantage.

When everything else had faded from public memory, Westerners would still remember who shot Pope John Paul II: a convicted neo-Fascist Turkish killer, coming from a turbulent, remote and impenetrably mysterious Islamic land whose exotic religion was bound to breed fanatic haters of Christendom—and whose 600,000-man army positioned along Soviet Russia's southern border was unaccountably part of an otherwise all-Christian NATO, doubtless by mistake. A more perfect Pope-killer would be hard to find.

The real sticking point for Soviet leaders would have been whether this Pope might be less of a hazard alive or dead.

It was unimaginable that any Pope replacing him would take up exactly where he left off. The mix of forthright personality, Polish blood, working-class origins, and firsthand knowledge of life in a Soviet-occupied Communist state could not happen again. Karol Wojtyla was one of a kind. His own higher clergy in Poland was noticeably more conciliatory toward a regime that would have to be lived with after he was gone. Upper echelons of the Roman Curia showed much the same disposition, however discreetly masked. This could only be an extraordinary interlude for the Vatican, beginning and ending with John Paul's reign.

Yet all Poland might go up in flames if he died a martyr's death. Was that better or worse than a living Pope with the awesome powers of this one?

In the end it would probably be better, for the Russians if not the Poles. The country might get out of hand for a while, but not irrevocably so. Worldwide peace and stability continued to depend on the spheres of influence carved out at Yalta in the last World War. The West might sympathize with the reckless Poles, as it did with the reckless Hungarians and Czechs. But, judging by past performance, Western governments would not lift a finger to help them. Without the towering presence of this Polish Pope in Rome, rebellion was bound to peter out.

Or else, this too could be turned to Moscow's advantage. The Poles in full insurrectional spate, swirling wildly out of control, pulling out of the Warsaw Pact, breaking flamboyantly with the Soviet Union, would be the best possible excuse for military intervention. In this sense, Pope Wojtyla's most exasperating talent lay in checking the impetuous Poles at exactly the outermost limits of the possible.

Perhaps it was too soon, in August 1980, to judge just how far the Pope was prepared to carry the confrontation. Perhaps his repeated offers of mediation could be deftly turned toward what the Russians call a "normalization" of the situation. Perhaps he might even draw back voluntarily, once he perceived the enormous risks for the Poles themselves and for his own Church throughout the Soviet bloc. The next few months would tell.

During the next few months, Solidarity acquired ten million members, virtually the entire working class. Many were Communist Party members. Rural Solidarity brought organized farmers to the workers' side, over the regime's desperate opposition. The aged and ailing Cardinal Wyszynski, Primate of Poland, gave the farmers' union his blessing. Parish priests set up confessional boxes at the farmers' meetings, and helped openly to sign them up.[27]

"On December 14, a Sunday, the farmers came to town marching behind their banners through the empty streets of Warsaw," wrote Neil Ascherson, describing their founding Congress. "Their style was turbulent and uncompromising. . . . Father Sadlowski, a leading figure of [a local] Farmers' Defense Committee, spoke of the need for village schools to teach 'the spirit of the nation, of patriotism,' rather than 'traditions imported from the outside. . . .' "[28]

By the year's end, Poland was ringed by thirty Soviet divisions (not counting those stationed permanently within). Despite soothing Russian assurances to the contrary, Western chanceries were all but certain that an invasion must come sometime in 1981.[29]

On January 15 of the new year, the Pope received Lech Walesa in Rome. It was a solemn investiture for the first institutionalized free trade union in the worldwide Communist order, conducted with the ceremony usually reserved for a visiting head of state.

"In the Consistory Hall, with frescoes on the wall and a gilded ceiling, Lech Walesa arrived a few minutes before noon," reported the Roman daily *Il Messaggero*.[30] "A bit stiff in his gray suit, wearing a tie and vest, the Gdansk metalworker gazed above him where the gold on the ceiling reflected the photographers' flash bulbs. He raised himself almost imperceptibly on the tips of his toes and heaved a big sigh, as if to say, 'Well, we've made it—at last.'

"All that was lacking, for a visit by a chief of state, was the reception in the San Damaso court with the Swiss Guards standing at alert. . . . But there was something more. The Pope and Walesa, unionists and journalists in attendance, sang the old patriotic hymn together, 'God Save Poland.'

"Walesa dropped onto his knee at the threshold of the Pope's study, and for a few seconds ignored the Pope's delicate efforts to raise him. It was a scene of medieval flavor: the homage of a faithful vassal to his Lord. Then, for twenty-five minutes, the leader of Solidarity and the Pope were closed together in the study, with nobody else present.

"The union's canonization was completed in the public part of the audience: an exchange of gifts and speeches by the Pontiff and Walesa. . . . Walesa made obvious efforts to emphasize the non-political nature of the fledgling trade union. 'We are not interested in political problems,' he said. 'We are interested in the rights of man, of society, of the faith. . . . If these human rights will be respected, then man will feel himself a man and help others. These truths we have learned from you, Holy Father, and from the Church. They will be our orders.' "

In his reply, the Pope sealed this bond. "There does not exist, because there must not exist, a contradiction between the workers' independent social initiatives and the structure of a system that considers human labor the fundamental value of social and civic life," he said. "To undertake such an effort is a right confirmed by the entire code of international life. . . . We know that the Poles have been deprived of this right more than once in the course of their history, a fact that has not made us lose . . . our faith in Divine Providence, and in ever beginning again."

On Walesa's last morning in Rome, the Pope celebrated mass personally for the Solidarity delegation, in his private chapel. "I want to gather around this altar all working men, and all that their lives contain," he said. "If on this altar we can place all Polish labor, that strength which derives from on high will be restored to us, and man will become the son of God and give dignity to his labor. I beg you to carry my words to all working men in Poland. . . ."[31]

If the first supreme moment of decision had passed for the Russians, this extraordinary encounter in Rome marked the approach of another.

Walesa returned to wildcat strikes of indefinite duration in Poland. The Polish economy, mortally afflicted and staggeringly debt-ridden, was compared to a plague ship threatening to infect every

Communist state around it. The Polish Communist Party was nearing complete breakdown.

On February 23, 1981, Brezhnev solemnly warned a Soviet Party Congress that "the pillars of the Socialist state are crumbling in Poland." Strong action was required, he said, without specifying what kind.[32]

On March 19, two hundred policemen broke up a Rural Solidarity sit-in in Bydgoszcz, injuring twenty-seven farmers; several were hospitalized. The popular mood grew riotous.[33]

On March 26, the White House reported "indications that Polish authorities may be preparing to use force. . . . We are similarly concerned that the Soviet Union may intend to undertake repressive action in Poland," the spokesman said.

On March 27, Solidarity staged a nationwide four-hour strike, the biggest in the country since World War II, and called for an unlimited general strike beginning March 31. Maneuvers of the Warsaw Pact armies in Poland, "Soyuz '81," were prolonged beyond their time.*

On March 29, the Soviet news agency Tass ran a hair-raising story that Solidarity was launching a putsch, by blocking highways, occupying telephone exchanges, and seizing a television transmitter. Not a word of it was true.

On March 30, Walesa reached a zero-hour compromise with the government, and called off the impending general strike. His followers in Solidarity reacted so violently that he offered to resign. Even if he'd want to pull back, retreat was now cut off.[34]

On May 6, a Polish government with its back to the wall allotted regular radio and television time to Solidarity.

On May 7, a terse Brezhnev told a Czechoslovak Party Congress: "Polish Communists will, one must assume, be able to preserve the cause of socialism."

On May 12, Rural Solidarity too was granted full government recognition: the bitterest defeat of all for Communist hard-liners.

On May 13, a professional killer opened fire on Pope John Paul II in St. Peter's Square.

Had he not been shot and very nearly killed, the Pope might have been on his way to Poland again in another few days. He had reportedly just decided that he personally should administer the last rites of the Roman Catholic Church to Cardinal Wyszynski, now gravely ill, who would die in Warsaw two weeks later.[35]

10

"But what's it *about*? Can't you give me a *hint*? What do you *say* in the piece?" The disembodied voice filtering over the line from Washington to our farmhouse in the Tuscan hills sounded peevish.

"Well . . . I say the Bulgarians were behind it," I answered, realizing the hopeless inadequacy of saying that and no more, bound to silence until my article appeared.

"The Bulgarians? The Bulgarians! What on earth . . . ? We'll get back to you."

Nadine Mushin, the charming headhunter who kept Ted Koppel endlessly supplied with interviewees for his popular "Nightline" show on ABC, was amazingly good at getting back to me. From her New York office, on the day the Pope was shot, she had tracked me down to a pay phone in the pink powder room of the Brown Derby in Hollywood. The following winter, she had found me in a Stuttgart hotel at midnight, proposing to fly me to London for a 4:30 A.M. chat with Ted Koppel by satellite TV. She and her boss had followed the early twists and turns in the papal shooting with more interest than most, but on August 15, 1982, they fell away. Nadine never did get back to me.

I could understand that (I thought so, anyway). CBS "Morning News," the first to break my *Reader's Digest* story, had struggled bravely to comprehend and compress a plot built around layer upon layer of deception, full of strange foreign names, set in half a dozen countries. The piece had necessarily been cut to the bone to fit the space of a magazine article. Some of the bones would have to go too, in six or seven minutes of air time—time enough to make a few assertions, but hardly to explain them.

And this, of all stories, needed explaining. I was making grave charges against a superpower with which the United States and its Western allies had to maintain civilized relations. At the moment, these relations were hitting bottom. The Americans and the Russians were on a collision course over nuclear dis- and rearmament, with Soviet SS-20s on the ground, and U.S. Cruise and Pershing missiles due to be installed the following year. The controversy was making for serious cracks in the NATO alliance, and increasingly emotional demands on the United States to reach an agreement with Moscow at whatever cost. Was this a time to accuse Soviet leaders of attempted murder—*this* murder?

But then, would there ever be a suitable time?

My own feeling was that keeping the public in the dark was no way to go about maintaining civilized relations. Western governments have been trying it since détente began in 1972. The results have shown again and again that what we don't know can hurt us. By withholding information from the public on the true nature of official and unofficial Soviet policies, the Western establishment has inevitably encouraged Soviet leaders to reach further and dare more, in the conviction that Western silence meant tacit assent, or resignation. The worst strains on détente can be traced to that course.

To my mind, the best way to dissuade Soviet leaders from still more dangerous secret ventures was to see to it that they knew that we knew.

Not all of America's opinionmakers would be inclined to agree. Contrary to the conventional wisdom in Moscow, the American press and media do not generally leap at every chance to take a poke at the Soviet Union. The Russian view of the hawkish American view of the Russians has been out of date for many years. They might have perceived that, from the mixed reception I got when I flew to the United States for publication day.

Braced though I was for stiff questions, there weren't many. Indeed, the story got more extensive coverage abroad than at home. It did get a fairly big play on television, where time is generally too short to say much beyond gee whiz. But the big dailies and weeklies either skipped it or played it far back and low down.

The New York Times carried a short Reuters' dispatch on page 12. The *Washington Post* ran nothing on its news side (though the deputy director of its editorial pages, Steve Rosenfeld, came down on my side in an elegant Op-Ed column). The *Wall Street Journal* waited several weeks before noting it, although once the *Journal*'s editors did, they became my most outspoken, reasoned, and persevering defenders in the country. *Time* and *Newsweek* did not report it.

I have old friends on these publications who could have asked me about sources, documentation, unpublished details. Only one did, from the *Wall Street Journal*. To my knowledge, at that time, no major (or minor) publication assigned anybody to find out if my evidence held up. How ordinary Americans might have felt about the story, I could not say; it's a big country. Whether for or against my arguments, though, reactions in the press seemed curiously muted. The press did not seem excessively stirred—scandalized, outraged, even very curious—about the strong possibility that secret services of the Eastern bloc had conspired to assassinate Pope John Paul II.

If only I had claimed that the CIA was behind it instead, said a Congressman who called for more information: my fortune would have been made.

Colleagues I ran into, in Washington, New York, Los Angeles, San Francisco appeared to be oddly embarrassed by what I had written. Not that they challenged the facts, which they rarely mentioned. What they apparently minded was that I was somehow guilty of bad taste. Bad-mouthing the Russians went out with Senator McCarthy, they gave me to understand. It wasn't done nowadays.

For his inestimable services to Soviet Russia, the late Senator McCarthy should by rights have been decorated with the Order of Lenin. The coarse viciousness of the man, political evil incarnate, forged enduring bonds of solidarity among those who detested him. While that may have been good for our souls, it impaired our vision.

To be victimized by McCarthy was to win an automatic stamp of approval in democratic circles. The more he ranted against Reds and Russians, the more virtuous he made them look. His tireless efforts thus enabled the Soviet Union to pass itself off as every freedom lover's friend: the vanguard of antifascism, pioneer guide-state of socialism, foremost defender of peace and the world's oppressed peoples.

To suggest that the Soviet Union was in fact no better than it should be—that it was a totalitarian police state, expansionist, colonialist, militarist, and at least as sad a sinner in the dirty tricks department as the capitalist USA—was to play into McCarthy's hands.

Long after McCarthy was dead and gone, the axiom would still be with us, passed on from father to son as if nothing had happened to cast doubt on the Russians' democratic credentials (Hungary, Czechoslovakia, Afghanistan, Poland, Siberian gulags, dissidents' lunatic asylums, a decade and more of arming and training international terrorists).

Eventually, playing into McCarthy's hands became something in particular that cold warriors do, in their determined efforts to destroy détente. By this logic, as I would find in certain circles, my determined efforts to gather evidence on the papal shooting made me a cold warrior, therefore a rampant rightist and Red-baiting McCarthyite, because of where the evidence pointed.

"Even if it was true, you shouldn't have published it," said a righteous young Washington reporter, who did not seem to notice the doubt this proposition might cast on his own democratic credentials.

Two other descendants of the McCarthy age, both fresh out of Harvard, gave me a piece of their minds over The Palm's superb roast beef in Washington. Our host was Marty Peretz, editor of the *New Republic*, who had hired the pair as editorial apprentices after their completed internship in the State Department. Gathered at a big round table draped in red-and-white-checked cloth, we got down to my *Digest* article as soon as the drinks were served.

"What do you two think of the idea that the KGB plotted to kill the Pope?" Marty began.

"Ridiculous!" they replied.

"Tell me," pursued Marty. "What did you think of the story that the CIA plotted to kill Fidel Castro?"

"Oh, that! Of course!"

"Why are you so ready to believe that the CIA would kill Castro, but not that the KGB would kill the Pope?" Marty went on, intrigued.

"Because the CIA does things like that."

"And the KGB doesn't?"

"No, no. The Russians wouldn't do such things."

Indeed they wouldn't, agreed the Russians themselves in a Tass communiqué, dismissing my charges as "absurd."[1] Nor would the Bulgarians, said the Bulgarians, claiming that "in theory and practice," their People's Republic "excludes all thought and all idea whatsoever of contact with any extremist or terrorist movements."[2] Like my two young fellow diners at The Palm, they insisted that only the CIA would do such things.

Before very long, the Bulgarians would drop the conditional and simply say the CIA did it. They would keep saying so right to the end, describing the American government's intelligence arm as "the greatest center of terror and lies in the world."[3] The CIA did not reverse the charges. On the contrary, there would be times over the next winter and spring—I will come to them—when, in its efforts to get the Bulgarians off the hook, the CIA almost seemed to welcome their alternative version of the case.

Sooner or later, Bulgarians and Russians both were bound to get around to announcing that the CIA had ordered me to write my article. The Russians would state in Tass that "CIA operatives, specialists in fabricating foul anti-Soviet sensations," had planted the story.[4] The Bulgarians conceded that I had probably done some of the work myself, thus explaining "my agitated and frantic research, fantasies and inventions . . . as if taken from a penny novel."[5]

In practically no time, they would have me down as a lifelong CIA agent, recruited by James Jesus Angleton when I was barely out of my gym bloomers.[6]

I became a so-called "former American female journalist" who had "hustled out . . . the first false weapon with blank cartridges on an anti-Communist position"; the prime instigator of the Big Lie, comparable to the Nazis' frameup of Bulgarian (and Comintern) Communist leader Georgi Dimitrov for the Reichstag fire; the "fake journalist" who had "deliberately turned a reality into a ceaseless, multicolored, sparkling and hissing firework of lies and slander, aimed against Socialist Bulgaria, against the Bulgarian people and their historical traditions of a staunch follower of the brightest and most humane principles of freedom, democracy, and progress."[7]

One more jump and I became not just any old "CIA woman-agent and fake journalist," but the actual mastermind of the entire anti-Socialist plot, without whose resourcefulness neither Agca nor Judge Martella could ever have dreamed up a Bulgarian Connection.

Eventually, I would be denounced in Sofia as the "would-be twentieth-century annihilator of the Bulgarian people."[8] But that would take some months.

By that time, the Bulgarians had published a *Dossier on the Anatomy of a Calumny* running to 178 pages. The first communiqué in the pile, issued on September 8, 1982, would be too commonplace to mention if not for an oddly prophetic sentence tucked in near the end. Summing up "Sterling's untruths," it noted that "Ali Agca's 'testimony' eschews every logic." All the same, *"it changes so often and is so controversial that we would not be surprised if one fine day, on someone's suggestion and for some promise, he even 'confesses' that the Bulgarians ordered him to kill the Pope* [my italics]."[9]

That happened to be exactly what Agca was saying right around then, to Judge Ilario Martella. But nobody except the judge was in a position to know that. Certainly none of us journalists did. The only leak to the press since Agca had started talking, the previous May, had appeared in *Milliyet* in July. At that point, Agca had reportedly gone no further than naming the co-Godfathers of the Turkish Mafia in Sofia, Abuzer Ugurlu and Bekir Celenk.

Unless the Bulgarians were going in for premonitions, which was not their style, this looked very much like the opening move in a carefully planned campaign. The time bomb ticking away in an Italian maximum-security prison must be defused in advance. The hit man who could reveal the truth about his mission must be made to look like the puppet of "someone" telling him what to say. (In future Bulgarian communiqués, "someone" became Italy's secret services, the CIA and me.)

To believe that was to accept the proposition that the CIA must have suborned practically the entire Italian establishment. If Agca was making the whole thing up, then "someone" must assuredly have grilled him thoroughly to get his story straight; it proved to be a very involved story. Connivance on such a scale would have to mean that just about everybody remotely involved in the case was bent: Judge Martella, his associates and superiors, the attorney general and his aides, the courts, the police, the intelligence services, cabinet ministers, heads of parliamentary commissions, democratic party leaders.

A surprising number of people in the West were ready to believe it, all the same. Doubtless, the McCarthy syndrome was at work here. But so were the Western governments themselves.

It was a bizarre war of words that began with Bulgaria's first communiqué in September 1982, in that the presumably opposing forces would soon appear to be fighting side by side.

British, West German, and Israeli intelligence services would be quoted in the Western press as questioning the efficiency, integrity, and intelligence of the Italian police and judiciary.[10] (An unnamed source in West Germany's intelligence agency, the BND, was quoted in the British press as saying that Judge Martella had "taken Claire Sterling's article in the *Reader's Digest* too seriously."[11]) The CIA's deputy chief of station in Rome would tell the Italian minister of interior: "You have no proof."[12] The Italian defense minister, who had informed Parliament that SISMI had monitored abnormally intense coded radio traffic between Sofia and Rome on the day the Pope was shot, was said in Washington to be talking through his hat. (He was told this bluntly at a meeting with *New York Times* editors, who had been so informed by a CIA official.[13])

This convenient anomaly allowed Eastern-bloc spokesmen to have it both ways. While never letting up on their charges that the CIA was the guilty party, they would blandly invoke the CIA's statements to confirm their own innocence.

Such prospects would have seemed beyond imagining to me that September, when I had no idea that Agca would incriminate the Bulgarian secret service directly, naming names. Not until this happened did Western authorities show signs of genuine distress. As it was, Bulgaria's opening shot against my story, and me, seemed rather mild. Still, I felt pretty alone out there.

Late that September, Marvin Kalb presented his NBC White Paper, and I had company.

We had been comparing notes since midsummer, when I was asked by the show's producer, Tony Potter, to serve as a consultant. Rome was becalmed in the tropical heat and magically stilled by the holiday exodus when the three of us met in a white damask sea of empty restaurant tables to talk the case over. My own piece was finished and at the printers', while NBC still had a couple of teams in the field, where they had been for some months. Working independently of each other, we had naturally gone off on different tacks here and there. But it was exciting to see how often our findings matched.

Marvin was one of America's favorites in the media, and his White Paper could hardly be ignored. Even so, a number of his old cronies in the Washington press corps could not get over his assumption that the Russians would do such things. A small group of us had watched the program aired at the Kalbs' house when their phone calls began to come in. "It was a great show! Great!" they would say. "But come on, Marv. You don't really *believe* that stuff?"

It was then that Washington's intelligence community dropped a first hint that it did not choose to believe the stuff either.

The challenge was confined, for the moment, to Kalb's suggestions of a plausible Soviet motive: Pope John Paul's unyielding defense of Solidarity, the urgent letter to Brezhnev, a subsequent phase of "shuttle diplomacy" between Rome and Moscow, a Vatican undertaking to help finance the nascent free labor movement.

"U.S. intelligence officers told *Time* they had no evidence that the Pope was involved in either Solidarity's birth or funding," reported *Time* in its rundown on the NBC White Paper.[14] Was that how the U.S. government's eyes and ears abroad really saw Pope John Paul's role in the great Polish drama of 1980?

The grandfather of all "smoking gun" stories began on this unobtrusive note.

A smoking gun is what must be found when U.S. intelligence sources have their reasons for denying somebody's guilt—because there is so little likelihood of ever finding it. That is, the guilty party must be caught in the act, standing over the corpse with the gun in his hand. Short of that, in cases of political or diplomatic necessity, the fellow can be reasonably sure of getting away with murder.

I had become familiar with this line of attack since *The Terror Network* came out in 1981. For reasons I have yet to understand, the CIA had refused to concede what every intelligence service in Western Europe including NATO's had copious documentation to prove—about the Russians' heavy logistic support for international terrorism. I had failed to produce the smoking gun, CIA spokesmen told reporters in a succession of informal briefings. (In May 1983, the CIA's opposite number in Italy, SISMI, sent a twenty-five-page report to Parliament going much further than I did to incriminate the Russians. The KGB was actually "in a position to pilot the operations of major European and Palestinian terrorist organizations in an anti-Western direction," SISMI stated.[15])

Among a layman's many difficulties in ever getting to see a smoking gun is the reluctance of all intelligence services to part with the requisite evidence. Though understandable in principle, I had found it less so in practice. Under the U.S. Freedom of Information Act, an abundance of confidential information about internal American government activities has been made available on request, to American citizens and foreigners alike. But when I filed a request under the act for information on the far-reaching international operations of a known Soviet agent, I received one magazine article translated from French, and twenty-two typewritten pages of confidential material in which every relevant line—bar none—had been blacked out. (My legal expenses for procuring this material came to upward of $6,000.)

In the case of the papal shooting, the only smoking gun to be found would be Mehmet Ali Agca's. There was no *proving* a Soviet motive with courtroom evidence: nobody was going to see Pope John Paul peeling Polish zlotys off a big wad and telling Lech Walesa to get on with it. Nor was there much chance of spotting a live KGB agent giving Agca his orders and a packet of roubles, over Bitter Camparis at Doney's on Rome's Via Veneto.

What, then, would U.S. intelligence officers consider conclusive evidence of Russian guilt? Starting that September, their requirements would grow more exigent from month to month.

The more telling the evidence coming to light, the more resolutely they discounted it. Patronizing, discreetly amused, faintly bored, a little vexed, they would confide to correspondents that the whole story of a Soviet conspiracy was too preposterous to be taken seriously. Bulgaria's DS wouldn't be so clumsy. The Soviet KGB wouldn't be so reckless; its director of sixteen years' standing, Yuri Andropov, wouldn't be so stupid. Nor, suggested Vice-President George Bush, would Andropov be such a wicked scamp either. "My view of Andropov is that some people make this thing sound horrendous," he told a *Christian Science Monitor* reporter. "Maybe I speak defensively as a former head of the CIA, but leave out the operational side of the KGB, the naughty things they allegedly do . . ."[16]

Did the American Vice-President mean to imply that only the CIA would do such things?

Toward the end, this posture would so confound me that I felt obliged to discard any of a dozen trivial explanations that had been suggested. None had the necessary dimensions. Perhaps there was some deeply hidden factor, I thought, comprehensible only to the innermost circle of the U.S. intelligence community. Perhaps there were secret warriors here motivated by the highest patriotism, doing battle for a cause they could not reveal, marching like the British at Gallipoli straight into the enemy's line of fire without a thought for danger.

"C'est magnifique; mais ce n'est pas la guerre," a French general had remarked on that occasion.

Whatever the explanation, I never found it. From the time I returned to Europe that autumn, this would become a fascinating mystery of its own. The day was not far off when the truly unanswerable question was no longer whether the Russians were guilty, but why their arch-opponents in Washington were so anxious to absolve them.

11

"Was it the Bulgarians who sent you to Italy?"

"Yes, I said Bulgarians."

"Are you collaborating with the judicial authorities now?"

"Yes, I said that the attempt on the Pope was done by the Bulgarian secret service."

"And the KGB?"

"Yes, and the KGB. I said I have been trained specially by the KGB."

"Where? Who trained you?"

"I have been trained in Syria, in Bulgaria. I have said several times. I have been trained by special experts in international terrorism."

"Were you ever in the Soviet Union?"

"No. I have been in Soviet Union, but it doesn't matter. The Soviet Union doesn't have direct connection by the terrorists. It uses in the Middle East, Syria. In Europe, Bulgaria."

"Was Antonov involved?"

"Antonov, correct."

"And Aivazov?"

"Yes, yes, yes. Aivazov and Kolev. They are my accomplices in this action. . . ."[1]

Handcuffed, gaunt and unshaven, dressed in jeans and an Adidas sweat shirt, Mehmet Ali Agca shouted his answers to a jostling, yelling mob of reporters and TV cameramen. He was on his way to an armored police van waiting at Rome's Questura, where he had been brought for questioning about a kidnapped girl supposedly held to be traded for his freedom. He did not want to be freed. "I refuse all liberty. I condemn this criminal action. The Italian state should respond firmly," he cried out, plainly frightened stiff of his would-be liberators.

"I am with the innocent girl. I am with the family which feels pain. I am with Italy. I am with the Vatican," he went on. "I am doing very well in Italian jails. I thank Italian justice and the Italian state. I am a penitent for the attempt on the Pope. . . ."

The date was July 8, 1983. Judge Martella was on his way to Sofia, to see what he could see. His investigation was drawing to a close. Not a word had come from his office to confirm or deny millions of printed words speculating on the nature of the information he had gathered. Now, more than two years after the crime, the worldwide public was getting its first authentic account of Agca's secret testimony, from Agca in person.

Snatched up by television satellite, beamed into hundreds of millions of homes from San Francisco to Singapore, he had certainly made it to the planetary peaks of stardom. That was what he had been after all along—that and a pot of money. But was it enough, for a lifer? He'd had something of a manic look, with his burning eyes, chanting speech, manacled hands raised as if in benediction. Wasn't that what people had always said: that he was round the bend? And then, he'd seemed so sure of himself, rattling off his lines. Weren't people saying that too: that somebody had given him a script to learn by heart? Did he have somebody's promise: "Frame the Bulgarians, and we'll get you out"?

For all those who found his performance convincing, many more had black doubts.

Prodigious effort and some of the world's most expert craftsmanship had gone into generating such doubts. The operation had gotten under way the previous summer, and reached full force in the autumn, under the pressure of imperative need.

Between late November and mid-December 1982, three Italian judges held in high esteem, engaged in seemingly separate investigations going back months or years, revealed the existence of intersecting evidence that came to be known as the Bulgarian Connection.

On November 24, in the northern city of Trento, Judge Carlo Palermo announced orders of arrest for two hundred people of mixed nationality, working for the most colossal ring of arms and drug smugglers uncovered in our time.[2] The ring, running heroin westward and weapons eastward, dominated this two-way traffic from Turkey and the Middle East to all Western Europe and the United States.

The major components were the Sicilian Mafia, working in tandem with the American Cosa Nostra, and the Turkish Mafia, whose mightiest boss at the eastern end was the Godfather, Abuzer Ugurlu. The Turkish Mafia's liaison with other gangs in Europe was Ugurlu's co-Godfather, Bekir Celenk, whose arrest was ordered by Palermo some weeks later.[3]

The central meeting place to work out deals and carve up territories—a vital international summit for this purpose had been held there in January 1981—was the Hotel Vitosha in Sofia. Bulgaria, "demonstrably one of the main junctions between drug and arms suppliers," was the sole country that had failed to cooperate in Judge Palermo's three-year investigation.[4] "It did not even reply to our urgent requests for information," said Justice Minister Clelio Darida.[5]

Billions of dollars, powerful banks, men of unassailable repute, freemasons, ranking military officers, Vatican financiers, terrorists, murderers, Eastern and Western intelligence services—and remarkable eyewitness testimony—would make a heady brew for the press as Judge Palermo pushed on with his case. Part of this crossed my line of vision when I went back over my own ground, preparing to write this book.

Less than two weeks after the bombshell in Trento, another went off in Rome.

Judge Ferdinando Imposimato, a magistrate of exemplary independence and an outstanding expert on terrorism, had been interrogating a popular Socialist trade-union leader named Luigi Scricciolo since the latter's arrest in February 1982. Scricciolo, foreign-affairs director for his labor federation, UIL, had already confessed to having worked for a Bulgarian spy ring since 1976.[6] He had been accused of that during the Red Brigades' kidnapping of U.S. general James Lee Dozier. Among other things, he was charged with establishing contact at the time between the Red Brigades and the Bulgarians (who offered the Red Brigades money and arms to keep up the good work, in exchange for any information they could extract from their captive NATO general).[7]

Still uglier was the charge that Scricciolo, close to Solidarity since its birth, had passed delicate information to Bulgaria about the free Polish union. He had never admitted to this betrayal. Now, however, he did admit that the Bulgarians had approached him during Lech Walesa's visit to Rome in January 1981. They wanted him to help assassinate Walesa, he said, but he had refused.[8]

Not all news reports agreed on who spoke of this first: Luigi Scricciolo or Mehmet Ali Agca. Both did, though, within days of each other.

The two did not know each other, but their stories matched. Both were interrogated on this by the two judges concerned, Imposimato and Martella; and in the sensational ending to this story long afterward, both would turn out to have worked with the same Bulgarian agent in Rome—Ivan Tomov Dontchev, the chief of the Bulgarian spy ring there—whose arrest would be ordered by Judge Imposimato's collaborator, Judge Rosario Priore, the following July 28 (by which time, however, he was safely back home).

Killing Lech Walesa was one of the Bulgarians' "alternative plans," Agca had asserted.[9] He himself was supposed to be the hit man. He'd been in Rome all through Walesa's visit and for some weeks before, he claimed; police records confirmed this. (He had stayed at Rome's Pensione Hiberia from December 15 to 19, 1980; the Hotel Archimede from December 26 to January 17, 1981; the Pensione Isa on January 18–19, Walesa's last days in the city.)[10]

These details and many still more chilling would keep leaking to the press for months, until Judge Martella inherited the Walesa investigation and imposed his usual news blackout. While he would never confirm the Bulgarians' alleged "alternative plans" for Walesa, neither did he deny them outright. "What was your reaction to the news of a plot to kill Walesa?" a Roman reporter asked after the first leaked headlines that December. "I marveled," replied Judge Martella. "I marveled that certain details, such documents of proof, could be published. I also marveled that there could be somebody who was failing in his duty, somebody who was not a journalist. Somebody will pay. . . ."[11]

It was Judge Martella who touched off the other bombshell, in

Rome, just twenty-four hours after Judge Palermo's in Trento. This one went off with a truly awesome bang.

At 9:30 on the morning of November 25, 1982, Italian police showed up at an apartment house in Rome's comfortably middle-class Nomentana district. Sergei Ivanov Antonov, just leaving for his office, was apprehended, handcuffed, and carted off to jail. The warrant, signed by Judge Martella, accused him of having "taken part directly" in the attempted murder of Pope John Paul II.

Antonov had a civilian job, which did not entitle him to diplomatic immunity. An unobtrusive, rather meek-looking, bespectacled man of thirty-four, he had been stationed in Rome since 1977 as deputy director of Balkanair, the Bulgarian state airline. He was an "honest functionary," said the Bulgarian Embassy, very nearly struck dumb.

He had turned deathly pale when the police picked him up, and was said to have crumpled upon reading the four-page warrant at DIGOS headquarters. "Antonov read these pages with a bewildered look, at once incredulous and petrified," said the *Corriere della Sera*. "I couldn't be sure whether it was the face of somebody whose world has just collapsed and he doesn't know why, or who simply realizes that he is done for," observed a DIGOS detective at the scene.[12]

With the arrest of this obscure Bulgarian national, a political hurricane of extraordinary fury burst upon the West. It would rage throughout the many months of Judge Martella's investigation, during which time the public had no way of knowing what Antonov was actually supposed to have done.

Bound by the *segreto istruttorio,* Judge Martella was free to discuss the case only with the competent judicial authorities. Some of his knowledge, but not all, was shared with DIGOS and Interpol, handling his police work. Nobody else had the right to know—neither the prime minister, nor members of the cabinet, nor the secret services. The only man who had all the evidence against Antonov was forbidden by law to reveal it.

Antonov's lawyers, flinging their doors wide for journalists, said there was no evidence.

In between were the usual well-informed sources, unattributable, unverifiable, and frequently unreliable (often deliberately so). The best of them began to dry up soon after Antonov's arrest, under the stern strictures of the judge. Big leaks to the press from then on came largely from self-serving political tipsters, a kind of self-appointed intelligence bodyguard for the Western diplomatic corps, and professionals dispensing disinformation in an inexhaustible flow.

Upon ordering Antonov's arrest, the judge's office had issued a crisply uncommunicative communiqué. "Available information indicates that Mehmet Ali Agca carried out the assault against the Pontiff in criminal accord with other people, some of whom have been identified and others who have yet to be identified," it stated.[13]

Mindful of the vibrant reactions awaiting him in the world of international politics and diplomacy, the judge made it clear that he was not about to level charges against Bulgaria's entire secret service, still less the Soviet KGB, not to mention the Russian who had headed it for the past sixteen years—Yuri Andropov, elevated to the supreme leadership of his country in that very month of November.

"Any reference to complicity by other persons who are not the objects of the current investigation, and to the existence of alleged plots by international organisms, is without foundation at this point," the communiqué had carefully added.

A noninternational nonplot, involving several persons known and unknown of mixed nationality, meeting in two or more countries to plan a crime committed on Italian soil, was a tactful juridical nicety deceiving no one. "Antonov's arrest was sensational confirmation of an international plot to assassinate the Polish Pope, John Paul II," declared the normally far-from-downright *Corriere della Sera.* "Personages tied ideologically to the extreme right, Ali Agca and his Turkish Gray Wolves, were used to mislead investigators. . . . The plot was conceived and executed by the Bulgarian secret service."[14]

The plot was indeed shaping up to spectacular effect.

With the arrest of Sergei Antonov, Judge Martella had now identified five suspected accomplices of Agca's. In June, he had signed an arrest warrant for the Turkish Gray Wolf Omer Bagci, then a butcher in Olten, Switzerland. In October, he had issued warrants for three other Turks, whose names meant nothing to the West, but who made front-page news in Turkey. They were Musa Cerdar Celebi, head of the Gray Wolves' Federation in West Germany; Bekir Celenk, co-Godfather of the Turkish Mafia in Sofia; and Oral Celik, the Gray Wolf from Malatya, "Celenk's man."

The Bulgarian Antonov made five; and, in a matter of days, there were two more. On or around December 1, Judge Martella signed warrants for the arrest of Todor Stoyanov Aivazov, former cashier of the Bulgarian Embassy in Rome, and Major Želio Vasilev, former aide to the embassy's military attaché. Both had skipped to Sofia by then, Aivazov in the nick of time (he had lingered in Rome until November 12). They were accused of direct complicity as well.

Three Bulgarians working for a Communist state closer to the Kremlin than any in Eastern Europe; four Turks working for the neo-Nazi Gray Wolves and the Turkish Mafia, including a top Mafia boss; a convicted right-wing murderer as hit man; all eight of them acting "in criminal accord"—there was a plot to stagger the mind. We were no longer talking about a Bulgarian role behind the scenes and several degrees removed (about as far as I had been willing to go myself). The presumption now was that Bulgarian agents had been running Agca in the field and directing operations in Rome.

What folly! How could leaders of so potentially suspect a country take such wild chances? Wouldn't the KGB mind? What would Yuri Andropov say, when and if the agents were caught?

What he said to the Bulgarians is unrecorded. What the Russians and Bulgarians between them had to say to the West was designed to persuade their audience that the folly was not Bulgaria's, but Judge Martella's. A number of well-informed sources in the West concurred.

Off and running on a stupendous story, Italian reporters were heading straight for a brick wall. Only at the outset did they get anything like a real break, evidently from DIGOS (policemen are human too). Even that consisted of a surreptitious glance at some selected paragraphs or pages, or guarded conversations easily mis-interpreted and still more easily denied.

Practically all Italian papers carried the same background pieces when the judge made his first moves. This is what they said:[15]

Agca was thought to have been "loaned" to the Bulgarian secret service by Abuzer Ugurlu and the Turkish Mafia in Sofia.[16]

Omer Bagci, arrested in Switzerland and swiftly extradited to Italy, had held Agca's Browning in safekeeping, then delivered it to him in Milan four days before the shooting. He was said to have confessed.

Oral Celik, "Celenk's man," had acquired the gun from the shady Nazi gun dealer in Vienna, Horst Grillmayer. Agca was with Celik there when he passed it on to Bagci, on April 2 or 3, 1981. It was rumored that Celik was sheltering in Bulgaria.

Musa Cerdar Celebi, arrested in Frankfurt on November 3 and also extradited quickly, was part of the "Strategic Directorate" of the conspiracy. He had met Agca in Milan in December 1980, with several others present who confirmed the meeting. He had met him again in Zurich in February 1981, also with others present, including Omer Bagci and Oral Celik. At the end of April 1981, he had spoken to Agca by phone in Palma de Majorca. In between, he had met with Turkish Mafia boss Bekir Celenk in Frankfurt, where they were seen at lunch.

By all accounts, it was Musa Cerdar Celebi who passed part of the payoff money to Agca, on behalf of Bekir Celenk. The money bags were held by Bekir Celenk himself, on behalf of whoever was footing the bills (here the reports grew vague).

Celenk, too, had slipped out of Judge Martella's clutches at the last minute. He was in Munich until early October, when he must have gotten wind of what was coming. Whether on a tip or a hunch, he had packed his bags, driven off casually in his Volkswagen Golf (Swiss license plate number BE 352-9008), dropped by in Zurich and Vienna to wind up some business, and headed for his home away from home at the Hotel Vitosha. He was already installed in an opulent suite there when a second warrant for his arrest was issued in Trento by Judge Palermo.

Sergei Antonov was presented as the "anchorman" of the Rome operation, responsible for Agca's lodgings, day-to-day necessities, and eventual escape. He was supposed to be the mysterious caller who had reserved Agca's room at the Pensione Isa in "correct" Italian, shortly before the papal shooting.

Todor Aivazov and Major Želio Vasilev had reportedly attended a final planning session with Agca and Sergei Antonov, at the latter's home, a few days before the attack.[17] Vasilev had left Rome on August 24, 1982, Aivazov on November 12. Having thus dropped out of sight, these two Bulgarians seemed more or less to have dropped out of mind.

A few of the maddening gaps in these accounts were filled in on December 8, with a fresh round of background pieces in the press. The most detailed, in the *Corriere della Sera,* was accepted from then on as the seminal version of Agca's confession, Part Two. It went like this:

Agca, who had started talking to Judge Martella in May 1982, had begun to fill in the broader picture in September. His "stunning allegations," said the Italian daily, "ran to hundreds of pages, a detailed story full of information and so documented as to nail down inexorably the accomplices and sponsors behind him."

He told the judge that he had been selected as a hit man while he was still in Istanbul's Kartal-Maltepe prison. "A Turkish terrorist tied to the Bulgarian secret service"—Oral Celik—had helped him break out of jail, he said.

After his escape, he was helped to cross over into Bulgaria, where he remained for six weeks—his famous Bulgarian summer. There he was under the protection of Bekir Celenk, "a Turk who allegedly had enormous power in Sofia and resided in the luxurious Hotel Vitosha," as Agca did also. During Agca's stay, Celenk had introduced him to three agents of the Bulgarian secret service. They were Todor Aivazov, known to Agca as "Kolev"; Želio Vasilev, presented as "Petrov"; and Sergei Antonov, alias "Bayramic."

It was sometime then—between July 5 and August 31, 1980—that Celenk offered Agca 3 million Deutschmarks to kill the Pope. (*Milliyet*'s series on Part One of Agca's confession had said the offer was made nine months later, in Palma de Majorca.)

"The plan was for Agca to be completely isolated for some months, creating a desert around him, traveling constantly to cover his tracks," reported the *Corriere*.

At the time of his arrest, continued the Milanese daily, Agca was carrying a slip of paper with five telephone numbers. Two were for the Bulgarian Chancellery in Rome, one was for the Bulgarian Consulate, one for the Rome office of Balkanair, and a fifth, unlisted, for Todor Aivazov. (Other news reports around this time said that Agca had given the judge an unlisted home phone number for Sergei Antonov too.)[18] This was part of the "documentary proof" that Judge Infelisi spoke of after Agca's first interrogation, it turned out.

All three of the Bulgarian agents introduced to Agca in Sofia had worked with him in Rome, Agca claimed. He had picked their photographs unhesitatingly out of fifty-six mug shots of assorted diplomats, crooks, and foreign agents of varied national origin. He had visited both Antonov and Aivazov at home, and he provided their addresses to the judge, describing the rooms, contents, surroundings and even the view from the windows in precise detail. (The Tribunal of Liberty, ruling on December 5, 1982, stated that "Agca recalled details of Antonov's home, plants, flowers, garden, and even the position of the house telephone."[19])

On May 11 and 12, 1981, in Antonov's Soviet-made Lada 124, Agca had gone with Antonov and Aivazov to St. Peter's Square to run through dress rehearsals. They wanted mainly to settle two things: to pick the best place for him to stand in the crowd (close to the broad stone steps of the church, ten yards or so from where the Pope's limousine would pass), and to choose the best direction for a fast getaway to a waiting car (a few seconds' sprint past the colonnades).

On May 13, at 3:00 P.M., "Agca met Aivazov and Antonov in the Piazza della Repubblica" near Rome's railroad station. The two Bulgarians arrived in a rented blue Alfetta. Together, the trio drove to Aivazov's home at 36 Via Galiani, in the Tor di Quinto area. While the others waited in the car, "Aivazov went up to his apartment and came down with an overnight case." Back in the car, "he pulled out two guns and a panic bomb used for dispersing crowds. He put the bomb in his pocket and a gun in his belt, passing the other to Antonov." Agca had brought along his Browning.

With Antonov at the wheel, they drove to the Vatican. Antonov drew up before the Canadian Embassy to the Holy See, in Via della Conciliazione, the broad avenue leading to St. Peter's Square. "There the trio split up, agreeing to meet after the attack. For the last time, Agca looked back. He saw Antonov driving away in the Alfetta. . . ."

Agca seemed to recall that Antonov was wearing a beard at the time, though he, Agca, suspected it was false.

The Bulgarians had promised to smuggle him out of Italy in a TIR truck. If he was captured, they guaranteed his escape. "They did not keep their word, and Agca decided to reveal the plot," concluded the *Corriere della Sera*'s Marco Nese.

It was easy to pick holes in this sketchy story. Anybody might jib at that false beard. Foreign agents in paperbacks who engage in "wet work" do not customarily bring home the hired help. Paid professional killers, especially of Agca's notoriously boastful temperament, are not generally told of their assignments almost a year in advance. Nor are they sent in for the kill with five hopelessly incriminating telephone numbers in their pockets.

Taken separately, any of these points could be explained away. Several logical explanations came my way before the end, a couple of them very good. Taken all together, though, the plausible explanations narrowed down to two. Agca could be lying, which he was regrettably known to do, because "somebody" put him up to it in exchange, perhaps, for cosmetic surgery, a new identity, money, and freedom. If he was not lying, however, the Bulgarian secret service must be shot through with bungling incompetents.

Few could readily imagine this last. In books and movies, the subterranean world of covert action is peopled by fast-moving, fast-thinking, icily efficient secret agents who wouldn't touch a sloppy plot like this with a ten-foot pole. Nevertheless, the CIA did once plot to use the American Mafia to assassinate Fidel Castro with a poisoned cigar, an arrangement inevitably getting to Castro's ears long before the cigar could get to his lips.

The Russians ran a close second in 1979, in their efforts to assassinate Hafizullah Amin, president of Afghanistan. A highly trained agent of the Soviet Politburo's choice was sent to Kabul for this purpose. He was in the palace kitchen trying to slip poison into the presidential soup, while an alternative Soviet hit team was gunning down the president and everything else that moved—a fact of which the agent was blissfully unaware.[20]

These things can happen in the best-run security services and might very well have happened in Bulgaria's case. A tantalizing news item seeming to bear this out appeared in *Le Monde* of Paris and the Socialist *Avanti!* of Rome shortly after Antonov's arrest. A certain Jivkov Popov, coordinator of Bulgarian espionage in Western Europe at the time of the papal shooting, had been stripped of Party membership the previous March and sentenced to twenty years' imprisonment—"for large-scale theft of public weal," said *Le Monde*, "for criminal errors," said *Avanti!*[21]

If heads are frequently said to roll after some egregious blunder, it isn't often that we actually hear the thump.

Of course, there was always a chance that these early accounts of Agca's confessions were garbled. None of the background pieces carried in Italian papers before, on, or after December 8 was confirmed officially. In any event, December 8 was the last time an inside story of substance would come from authoritative quarters in Rome. With rare exceptions, the choicest headlines from then on were of the Bulgarians' making.

They needed time to pull themselves together. In its first statement from Sofia on the day of Antonov's arrest, the state news agency BTA scarcely mentioned Antonov himself or Agca either. It spoke generically of "unacceptable provocation," a "hostile, completely illegal, and absolutely unjustifiable act," a "ridiculous and absurd campaign of calumnies and sensational inventions," launched to ruin traditionally fine relations between Bulgaria and Italy, and to "put Bulgarian socialism in a bad light." This campaign, it said, was based on "a scenario elaborated beforehand" by Claire Sterling.[22]

"The Italian police, the Italian administrative authorities, the Italian courts, which had the greatest possibilities of getting to the bottom of every question regarding the terrorist act in St. Peter's Square, were unable, despite all their efforts, to find a single trace of accomplices coming from a Socialist country," continued the BTA. "Yet an ex-American female journalist in Italy is more competent and has more avenues open than the Italian state and other states where the terrorist stayed, than the Italian police and the Italian courts. In a fantasy-article published in an American magazine, it turns out that her personal investigation involves the Bulgarian, and in consequence the Russian, secret services. . . .

"And since nobody believes such accusations without proof, the campaign was dying down when somebody found the moment opportune to unleash a fresh campaign of falsification with the provocative arrest of a Bulgarian citizen. . . ."[23]

The Bulgarians had spotted this "somebody" as far back as September 12, evidently bracing for the day when Agca would make just such a confession. Now the same somebody was seen to be giving orders not only to Agca but to Judge Martella as well. The judge had visited the United States in October, observed the BTA. "It is useless to ask what he was doing there. . . . The signal has always come from across the ocean. . . ."[24]

Later, when the Bulgarian Connection in its entirety had been assessed fully in Sofia and Moscow, the Bulgarians would move heaven and earth to strip Mehmet Ali Agca of any shred of credibility. An elaborate machinery would be set in motion for this purpose, starting with an unprecedented four-hour press conference in Sofia, attended by 150 foreign journalists from all over the world. Day after day, month after month, Agca's "so-called" confession would be taken apart word by word and ground to dust.

But those directing the operation would always come back to my *Reader's Digest* article as the origin of it all: the artful fiction that Agca had read and memorized in his prison cell, or that Judge

Martella had handed to him with those orders, or that "somebody" had handed to Martella and Agca both; the mother cell of a cancerous growth, implanted on Italian soil to spread inexorably, directed "against peace, civilization, and humanity," destroying worldwide socialism and détente, opening the way to the Third World War.

I was in Tel Aviv on November 25, when Sergei Antonov was arrested in Rome and the Bulgarian press spokesman in Sofia tried to put the blame on me. The effort seemed laughably clumsy when I read the dispatch. A remarkable encounter when I got home made it less laughable, however.

The news from Rome, coming in on a weak BBC shortwave signal, had bowled me over. The Israeli press, which had its own troubles in November 1982, did not make much of it. Nor did my interlocutors in Mossad, who assured me that the Bulgarians "wouldn't be so dumb." As they had nothing to tell me about Agca's visit to a Palestinian camp—my reason for being there—I cut the visit short and caught the next plane for Rome.

I was hardly back home when a call came from the American Embassy. It was Frederick Vreeland, "Frecky" to his friends, among the multitude of whom I supposed I was one. I'd known him personally for twenty-odd years, running into him on several troubleshooting assignments in Paris, Rabat, Rome.

He wanted to see me urgently. I was just going out to dinner. Marvin Kalb, who had flown in from Washington to do an update on his NBC White Paper, would be at my gate in half an hour. He was bringing an old friend of mine along. Judy Harris, small, blonde, and smart as a whip, had been of invaluable help to Marvin and his producer Tony Potter for the documentary, and was still hooked on the subject. I was hoping to talk her into helping me also.

I really didn't have much time, I told Frecky. "It won't take long," he said. "I'm on my way."

He came in looking grave. We talked briefly of this and that, over a glass of fizzy white wine. Yes, my article had turned out to be quite a coup, I was doing a book on it now, wasn't the arrest of Antonov amazing, it was certainly getting to be a hot story. Then Frecky said: "Look, I don't want to frighten you, but we have reason to believe that you're on the Bulgarian hit list."

I asked how he knew. "We got it from the Italians," he answered. "Mind you, this isn't hard information. It's just a report they had, but we think you ought to know about it."

What precautions should I take?

"Well, Claire, you've been through this before with the Red Brigados, you know how these things go. . . . Maybe you ought to cool it for a while. . . . Get out of town. . . . Of course, that's up to you. . . ."

The house phone rang. Marvin and Judy were downstairs.

"Thanks, Frecky," I said, meaning it, and we left. I was shaken and told Marvin and Judy why as we walked toward the restaurant. They were shaken too.

We had little cause to doubt the warning, still less to take it lightly. Troublesome reporters have been removed before, and I was a peculiarly vulnerable target.

The Bulgarians had an unpleasant reputation for dealing with people on their hit list. They had used an umbrella tipped with a poison called recin to murder the exiled Bulgarian writer Georgi Markov in London, on September 7, 1978 (a quick jab injected the tiny platinum pellets into his right thigh as he walked down the street).[25] They were known to have used the same device at least twice again, in London and Paris.[26]

Exiled native writers, broadcasting on BBC or Radio Free Europe, were surely less threatening to Sofia than the prospect of having the crime of the century laid at its door. Bulgarians and Russians both were visibly rattled by one of the few international scandals that could really get under their skin.

Inner circles in Washington plainly did not care much for the prospect either, and in a sense this troubled me more. Grateful as I was to Frecky for the warning, I could not expect a warm show of solidarity from my government. Its reception had been cool enough the last summer, when I had published what was still just a reporter's theory, and Yuri Andropov was just one of several contenders for the dying Brezhnev's place. Now the Italian judiciary was going appreciably further than I had; and the man presiding over the KGB on May 13, 1981, had become the ruler of Soviet Russia.

More than ever, with Andropov in the Kremlin, Western leaders would not want this story told. Indeed, their ranks were closing— around Andropov—before our eyes.

"To many in the West, the consequences of concluding that the Soviets took part in the plot to kill the Pope are so appalling that the matter will simply not bear thinking about," wrote Harry Gelman, a recently retired ranking CIA official, in the *Washington Post* around this time.[27]

"The West's general reluctance to confront the possibility of Soviet and Bulgarian complicity . . . ," he went on, "is not surprising." For if the charges were known with confidence to be true, if it were once accepted that Soviet leaders had indeed adopted a policy of murdering Western leaders, what Western policy would be commensurate? What deals with the Soviet Union would then be appropriate? What place would the whole panoply of present Western interactions with the USSR—from arms control to commercial relations—have in a universe in which it was known that this was Soviet policy? And if the Soviets would do this, what else would they do?

"Since the implications here are intolerably dangerous, much better that the hypothesis not be true. It shouldn't be surprising, therefore, if many in the West have an unspoken conviction that the stability of the world-as-it-is demands that the Soviets be innocent."

If that was the prevailing view in Washington's upper echelons—and it was, as we will see—there would be no mighty American government standing foursquare behind me. It was a handy thing for the Bulgarians to know.

They had done well to single out an aggravating "ex-American female journalist" as their prime target. The very phrase had a ring of scatty-mindedness, food and fashion columns, menopausal hysteria—a cross to bear for my more sober, professional, and politically literate male colleagues. Tacking on a lifelong career in the CIA should take care of anyone who might still take me seriously. But all that was for public consumption. Privately, the Bulgarians could hardly be unaware of the genuine embarrassment I was causing my own government, CIA included, or of the ardent desire in high Washington quarters for me to shut up or go away.

It seemed to me, thinking things over after Frecky's visit, that I needed advice—more of it than he had offered, anyway. A discreet request through Italian government channels brought a courteous general from SISMI to my home, with his aide. I told him about the warning I'd had, asking not for protection but for information. If Bulgarian agents were in fact going after me, I wanted to know what to watch out for.

The general looked surprised. "You were told that this information came from us?" he asked. "But it couldn't have. Any report like that would have passed my desk, and I assure you that I saw none."

A moment of uneasy silence passed, while I tried to absorb this. If Frecky did not get the information from Italian counterintelligence, where did it come from? If the CIA had gotten it instead, why didn't he say so? If it did, and he had, I would not have written about this episode.

As it was, disquieting questions crossed my mind. Was it possible that there was no such information, that the report did not exist at all? Could this be a message originating right here in Rome, meant simply to frighten me off? Just who wanted me to cool it and get out of town—the Bulgarians, or fellow Americans?

The general was watching me with a faintly puzzled air. Doubtless he found the situation odd. "Naturally, we'll look into it. And, of course, we'll send somebody around to advise you about security," he said. "But I imagine that won't be necessary. I'm sure the American Embassy will be doing that anyway. Aren't your own people taking care of you?"

I did not tell him that I had asked the American Embassy to pass on my request to see the CIA's chief of station, who sent word back that the CIA did not talk to journalists. (Since I knew a number of journalists who had had the privilege, the rule was evidently flexible enough to be bent either way.)

"If you hear anything more about this, I'd appreciate your letting me know," I said, when the general and his aide got up to go.

The general from SISMI came to see me again a month later. This time he looked not only puzzled but a little frayed. A report to the effect that I was on the Bulgarians' hit list had finally reached his desk. It came from the Italian Interior Ministry, he told me. But the Interior Ministry has no agents abroad, and nothing to do with counterintelligence.

"Where did they get it?" I asked, and he hesitated.

"From the American Embassy," he replied at last.[28]

12

"What are the elements, according to your embassy, that prove Antonov's innocence?"

"We can list many: our foreign policy of peace and collaboration with all countries, including Italy and the Holy See. . . ."

"Yes, but what are the elements exonerating Antonov?"

"There are many. According to the press, he was in St. Peter's Square the day the Pope was shot. But we know he was in his office. That was confirmed by Antonov's office colleagues. They are Bulgarians. Some are Italo-Bulgarians. . . . Furthermore, Agca and Antonov speak different languages. One is a Turk, the other a Bulgarian. . . . Agca does not speak Italian, and even if he was in Bulgaria for fifty days, it is impossible to learn our language in such a short time. Antonov does not speak Turkish . . . though he does speak English pretty well. . . ."

"Where were Todor Aivazov and Želio Vasilev on the day of the shooting?"

"We don't keep records. . . . The embassy office hours are eight-thirty to one and three-thirty to seven. We are informed of everything done by our staff. Anybody who is absent, including drivers, must be reported to me personally. We can prove that Aivazov was in the embassy on May 13. . . ."

"Why did Todor Aivazov leave Rome?"
"He went to Sofia to work on our budget."
"Will he come back?"
"He must come back!"
"Aren't you sure?"
Silence.[1]

The Bulgarian consul-general in Rome, Stefan Ghenev, supplied these answers at a hastily summoned press conference on Sunday evening, December 5, 1982. It was the first official Bulgarian venture into the specifics of the case since Sergei Antonov's arrest a good ten days before. Even then, there was a shade of improvisation in the consul-general's replies. A couple of his errors might look distinctly criminal to his superiors.

For one thing, Todor Aivazov was not in his embassy in Rome on May 13, 1981—except, oddly enough, between three and five in the afternoon, just when he was supposed to be with Agca in St. Peter's Square. That is what he said himself when Judge Martella finally caught up with him in Sofia in the summer of 1983. By then he had a dazzling alibi, accounting for every minute of that evidently unforgettable day.[2] Checking it out would add weeks to the judge's labors, which he might have been spared if Aivazov had not slipped out of Italy when he did: just twenty-four hours after the judge had asked the Italian foreign minister whether Aivazov was protected by diplomatic immunity.

That was a minor slip of the consul-general's, compared to his boner about Sergei Antonov. Starting on February 22, it would be strictly forbidden to admit that Antonov spoke English, since Agca did as well. In Sofia on that date, Bulgaria's press spokesman Boyan Traikov settled the matter once and for all.

"Agca supposedly claimed that he spoke to Antonov in English. But Sergei Antonov does not know and does not speak English," Traikov stated firmly, reading off a ten-page, single-spaced catalogue of "Agca's lies."[3]

That was the first time Traikov presented what the Bulgarians claimed was irrefutable proof of Antonov's innocence—after his third month in jail. Until then, they had confined themselves largely to protesting that he *was* innocent. Asked how they could be so sure, Traikov had replied: "For the simple reason that no organization or person exists in Bulgaria who would have given orders to Antonov or any others to shoot the Pope."[4]

Nothing more could be said, insisted Traikov many times, because no official information had been given to the world press, let alone Bulgaria. This was only half true. The world press had no official information, but Bulgaria did.

Antonov could not be charged formally under Italian law unless and until Judge Martella recommended that he go to trial, at the investigation's end. Meanwhile, however, Antonov's lawyers would always be present while he was interrogated about the accusations that had landed him in jail. Two Italian lawyers hired personally by the Bulgarian ambassador in Rome and answering to him directly, Giuseppe Consolo and Adolfo Larussa, therefore had plenty of information. They heard the judge's questions and Antonov's answers, and received daily written summaries (*verbali*) of interrogations. They also had three amply substantiated court decisions—one ran to 120 pages—rejecting their appeals for Antonov's immediate release, the first as early as December 6.

An Italian investigating magistrate must have strong evidence to justify the arrest and continuing detention of a suspect until he has information enough to decide for or against a trial. The evidence must be sufficient to satisfy his immediate superiors, the Investigative Divisions (*Istruttoria*) of the Court of Assizes and Court of Appeals, the State Prosecutor's Office (comparable to a U.S. Attorney General's), and—on request—the Tribunal of Liberty, a special three-judge court meant to deal swiftly with possibly unwarranted detention.

All these bodies would consistently uphold Judge Martella's decisions to detain Antonov, confirming what the Tribunal of Liberty called "the absolute credibility of the elements gathered by the magistracy."[5] Copies of sentence and their motivation were consigned automatically to Antonov's lawyers (and to nobody else, unhappily for the rest of us).

As time went by, lawyers Consolo and Larussa would be a godsend to news-starved reporters by reading out selected bits from a court sentence here or a *verbale* there. "Out of respect for the *segreto istruttorio*,"[6] though, they would never show reporters a full text. "If there's anybody you can trust right now, it's me," Consolo said cheerily, lest some might wonder.[7]

In reality, the Bulgarians did not want to talk about the evidence at all. They made this clear in a peremptory summons to the Italian ambassador in Sofia within the first week. The Antonov case had caused "the gravest crisis between our two countries since the last World War," said Deputy Foreign Minister Liuben Gotsev. It was far too grave to be left to the Italian courts. The whole matter "must be shifted from a juridical to a political plane," Gotsev informed the ambassador, meaning that it must be settled through diplomatic channels.[8]

The ambassador explained that this was unthinkable in a country with an independent judiciary. Gotsev, uninterested, went on to indicate the sort of negotiations he had in mind.

Bulgaria was holding two Italian hostages for just this occasion. They were Paolo Farsetti and Gabriella Trevisin, arrested on their way to Turkey after a holiday on Bulgaria's Black Sea Coast, on what proved to be crudely rigged charges of espionage. A swap would appear to be indicated, Gotsev gave the ambassador to understand.

The two Italians had been arrested on August 25. The Italian ambassador was informed of the fact on September 12. The news of their arrest as "spies" was released to the public on November 27.[9] The time sequence suggested how, when, and why Bulgaria had taken out this kind of insurance policy.

By August 25, the Bulgarians knew Agca was talking (*Milliyet* had reported on his first confession, Omer Bagci had been arrested, my own article had appeared). September 12 was the day they announced that they "wouldn't be surprised if, one fine day," Agca should "confess" that Bulgarian agents had sent him to Rome. November 27 was the day the Italian ambassador got the blackmailing message for his foreign ministry—forty-eight hours after Antonov's arrest.

That more or less summed up Bulgarian efforts to get at the truth until the big press conference in Sofia on December 17. The sole newsworthy item up to then had been a razzle-dazzle fizzle giving them a score of one: a photographed face in the crowd at St. Peter's, flashed around the globe as Antonov's. It wasn't. (But whoever said it was—besides an editor trying to sell magazines?)

The press conference at Sofia's Moskva Park Hotel was a grand affair. Boyan Traikov chaired it, introducing himself as Bulgaria's press spokesman and a member of its Communist Party Central Committee. He was there in both capacities, he declared. Todor Aivazov, Major Želio Vasilev, and Antonov's wife, Rosica, were there too, and so was Bekir Celenk (produced from behind a curtain, with a theatrical flourish, halfway through the meeting). But four hours of multilingual give-and-take left correspondents little the wiser.

Bulgaria's score doubled to two, when somebody asked Aivazov if he was the chap in Lowell Newton's celebrated photograph, snapped from behind and seen in quarter-profile as he fled St. Peter's Square. Agca had reportedly said he was, and one look made it clear that he wasn't. Undoubtedly, Agca had lied. (Agca admitted as much to Judge Martella afterward. The fellow running away was a close Turkish friend he did not want to betray, he explained; and that was no lie, it turned out, when the runner was identified later as "Celenk's man," Oral Celik.)[10]

Boyan Traikov opened the meeting with a lengthy reference to this "anti-Bulgarian campaign, premeditated and planned, and now guided and directed . . . you may ask, by whom? It cannot have escaped you. The campaign began three months ago with an article in the *Reader's Digest.* . . ."[11]

With the floor open to questions, all four principals denied knowing Agca. The three Bulgarians denied knowing Bekir Celenk, who denied knowing them. Aivazov and Major Vasilev denied any part in the heinous crime. "Do I look like a spy to you?" asked the clear-blue-eyed Aivazov genially. Neither offered an alibi for May 13, 1981, perhaps because nobody thought to ask.

Major Vasilev was sure that "none of my compatriots could feel anything but absolute condemnation for such crimes." He had never visited Aivazov or Antonov at home. If Agca claimed to have Antonov's home phone number, it was probably in the Rome phone book, he added (it wasn't).

Rosica Antonova said she was longing to visit her husband in prison, if only Italy would give her a visa. Told that a visa awaited her at the Italian Consulate in Sofia, she was a little flustered (she never did use it to visit her imprisoned husband). Questioned about the beard, she said she had not seen Sergei wear a beard in the thirteen years she had known him. "I am stupefied by this question," she asserted.

Aivazov could not understand how Agca could have described his Rome apartment, unless somebody briefed him. "While I was in Italy, I noticed that strangers entered my apartment when I was not at home. . . . I informed my ambassador of this . . . ," he recalled.[12]

All three Bulgarians said they would gladly return to Italy for questioning, provided they had guarantees of a safe return. What kind of guarantees? That was up to the "competent Bulgarian authorities," replied Aivazov. Yes, but what kind did they *want*? "Let the Italian magistracy make the demand, and we will know how to respond," answered Boyan Traikov.[13]

Asked about the Bulgarians' proposal for a swap between Sergei Antonov and their two Italian prisoners, Traikov grew indignant. "The thought would not pass the antechamber of my mind that the Italian ambassador could have reported untruthfully on his talk with a representative of our foreign ministry," he answered. "I want you to be convinced that never, for any motive, under any circumstances, directly or indirectly, would Bulgaria propose an exchange between a person we know is innocent, and two Italians caught *in flagrante*, committing a grave crime against the security of the People's Republic of Bulgaria."[14]

(The "grave crime," for which Paolo Farsetti and Gabriella Trevisin were sentenced respectively to ten and three years' imprisonment that February, consisted of photographing a disused and obsolete Bulgarian tank.[15] Bulgaria's proposal for a swap had been confirmed in writing to Farsetti's brothers by two telegrams from the Italian foreign ministry, informing them that the Bulgarian government had "raised the possibility of the swap."[16] In Parliament on December 20, Foreign Minister Emilio Colombo rejected "any connection between the two cases" as "inadmissible."[17])

Questions about Bekir Celenk agitated Traikov to still loftier heights.

Celenk was already wanted by Interpol when he reached Sofia on October 24 (doing the last lap from Vienna by chartered plane, indicating a degree of haste).[18] Interpol's Paris headquarters had issued a first warrant for him in early September, based on Turkey's charges of smuggling and fraud.[19] (Although he was a Turkish national—whose passport had expired in 1980, at that—Turkey never got anywhere in demanding his extradition from Bulgaria.)[20]

Judge Martella's warrant of arrest for Celenk followed on October 26, for "complicity with other persons in the preparation of an attempt to murder Pope John Paul," and for "having provided the money to help Mehmet Ali Agca."[21]

A third warrant would be signed by Judge Carlo Palermo of Trento right after the press conference, on December 22, 1982. It accused Celenk of "organizing" an international traffic in arms and drugs, describing him as a "resident of Sofia, Bulgaria."[22]

For all that, Celenk was still living in style at the Vitosha. Far from arresting him, the Bulgarians had merely placed him "under control," whatever that meant, on December 9 (the sole restriction it seemed to involve was that they were never going to let him get out of the country again).

Queried about Celenk's life of ease, known criminal record, and suspected ties to the Bulgarian secret police, Traikov stated: "If we had any suspicion, any communication, any information about Celenk's illegal activity, we would not have put him under control; we would have arrested him and begun an investigation. The very fact that we have simply put him under control means that up to now no such information has reached us."[23]

"As for who Celenk may work for, we Bulgarians have an expression: God only knows!" concluded Traikov.

The remainder of the program was Bekir Celenk's. He presented himself as a world traveler, honest businessman, and dealer in fruits and vegetables, who was at present exporting mineral water from Bulgaria.[24] He had maintained offices in London and Munich, and tended to his affairs there and elsewhere—Frankfurt, Milan, Majorca—without the slightest police harassment. (That he had not been harassed by the police was perfectly true.) In fact, West Germany had only recently given him a residence permit.[25] He couldn't understand what the fuss was all about.

For all that, he did make a couple of worthwhile contributions to Judge Martella's investigation. He remembered, with some difficulty, that he had once lunched with somebody called Musa Cerdar Celebi in Frankfurt; and he was in the right place at the right time on a still more meaningful occasion. Obliged by popular demand to show his passport and read out its frontier-crossing dates, he was bound to admit that he had been in Sofia between July 5 and 11, 1980, staying at the Hotel Vitosha. That was when and where Agca claimed to have met him.

For reporters who had traveled hundreds or thousands of miles, there was not much more to write home about.

Some three weeks had now passed since Antonov's arrest, with nothing further added to the sum of public knowledge. Judge Martella's grounds for arresting and holding him had been examined and upheld by his immediate superior, Ernesto Cudillo, by the Istruttoria section of the Rome courts, by the State Prosecutor's Office, and by the Tribunal of Liberty. There could be no certainty of the legal evidence beyond that, now or for a full year to come.

Those who wanted to choose sides anyway, so early on, were essentially obliged to take one or the other on trust: the Italian judiciary or Bulgaria's Communist establishment. That was when Western leaders showed the first open signs of opting for the Bulgarian side.

On the day of the press conference in Sofia, *New York Times* correspondent Henry Kamm filed a story from Jerusalem.[26]

"Israeli and West German intelligence and security services with a special interest in international terrorism," the article began, "are skeptical of charges of a Bulgarian connection in last year's attempted assassination of Pope John Paul II by a Turk.

"The West German and Israeli agencies, which maintain close ties to their Italian counterparts . . . do not regard the Italian secret services as of the highest standard. They fear that rivalry within the Italian internal security agencies, suspect evidence, *or outright 'disinformation'* may have played a role in the disclosure of information that caused an investigating magistrate, Ilario Martella, to have a Bulgarian airline official in Rome arrested last month on suspicion of 'active complicity' in the attempted assassination.

"In the absence of evidence, *West European* and Israeli analysts and intelligence officials speculate over *the source and aim of the charges* of what is being called 'the Bulgarian Connection.' Much of the skeptical speculation centers on *'disinformation,'* the word in clandestine circles for the circulation of false information with the intent of embarrassing an opponent [my italics]."

Israel, for one, would formally deny thinking any such thing. Indeed, a top military official in Tel Aviv proclaimed just the opposite on January 2.[27] But the damage was done.

There was no room for misunderstanding the thrust of the article. If "disinformation" had been planted "to embarrass an opponent," only a Western intelligence agency could have planted it to embarrass the Soviet Union. And this allegation, said initially to come from West German and Israeli sources, had wound up in the article as "West European." If these were reputable sources speaking for their own national services—and they were dignified as such by a veteran correspondent of the West's most influential newspaper— then Italy's partners and allies appeared to be thinking along the same lines as the Bulgarians and Russians. The hoax of the century must have been perpetrated by the Italian secret service with the CIA's help, or vice versa.

Opinions leading inescapably to this conclusion would emanate from unnamed CIA officials themselves starting in another month or so, echoed by unidentified sources in the U.S. State Department and National Security Council, by the head of the CIA, by the presidential adviser on foreign affairs, by unidentified British spokesmen in Whitehall, and by still others in Bonn. There followed a display of East-West harmony on the subject such as the world had not seen in a decade of détente.

While Western sources continued to affirm that the East could not have done it, the East was cranking out its own *Dezinformatsiya* to prove they were absolutely right. Having said so all along, the Russians and Bulgarians now set out to demonstrate not only that the CIA did it, but exactly how it was done.

13

Boyan Traikov says that a fact exists that the [Italian] examining magistrate could investigate without visiting Sofia. It appears in the statement made by Todor Aivazov, ex-cashier of the Bulgarian Embassy in Rome, now in Sofia, regarding Agca's claim that he telephoned Aivazov's house several times. "There is no telephone in my apartment," Aivazov said.

With this article datelined Sofia, appearing on January 5, 1983, under the headline "No Bulgarians Under the Bed," an Australian named Wilfred Burchett obliged the British *Guardian* with a preview of things to come.[1]

Presented as a "world-famed writer" by Bulgaria's BTA, he was a hot source on the Bulgarian Connection.[2] It was Burchett, writing in the Bulgarian review *Otecestvo,* who described me that same month as "the would-be twentieth-century annihilator of the Bulgarian people," calling to mind the hated tenth-century Byzantine emperor Basil II, known as Basil the Bulgar-Slayer.[3] Reporters covering the Vietnam War might recall his excellent connections with Hanoi. Former American prisoners of war in North Korea would remember him well, for his frequent appearances in Chinese uniform to help in their interrogation.⁴

His article in the *Guardian* was a sign that Sofia and Moscow were finally swinging into action. Some three weeks had passed since the *New York Times* article of December 17, 1982, reporting the suspicions of anonymous Western intelligence analysts about the true source of disinformation on the papal plot. Now machinery to communicate concordant Eastern suspicions was set in motion.

The stories that follow began to show up in the Italian press and elsewhere in the West just after the new year.

•   •

In Italy, also on January 5, 1983, a rash of headlines spoke of "Strange Visits to Todor Aivazov's Home," said to have been reported punctually to the Italian authorities by the Bulgarian Embassy. "They Were Armed and Carried Cameras," ran a subtitle in the leftward-leaning *La Repubblica*.⁵

"Ali Agca's revelations are lies piloted by Western secret services, according to Bulgarian diplomats," ran the story below. "The Turk never went to Aivazov's apartment in Via Galiani, 36," these diplomats said. Tenants in his building, all employees of the Bulgarian Embassy, had "found doors open and locks forced at least fifteen times. . . . The intruders were not thieves, because nothing was ever stolen."

The intruders had been caught redhanded *on September 26, 1982,* two months before the first Bulgarian arrest, the story went on. "Diplomats coming home during working hours [that day] actually caught the mysterious visitors in the act. They hastily fled the building and drove off in a blue Alfa Romeo, license plate Rome W-L3933." The Bulgarian Embassy's many protests had "gone unanswered," reported *La Repubblica* along with most Italian papers.⁶

The following morning's papers—on January 6—carried a formal communiqué from the Italian foreign ministry.⁷ It said that the Bulgarian Embassy had lodged three complaints in all about intruders in Via Galiani, 36, each checked by the police. The complaint referring to armed men in a blue getaway car *had not been sent on September 26, 1982, but on December 9* (when a warrant was already out for Todor Aivazov, and Sergei Antonov was behind bars). The blue Alfa Romeo belonged to RAI-TV. The men in flight, armed or not, were a TV team from Channel One, filming the corridor and entrance to the fugitive's apartment.

Two earlier Bulgarian Embassy protests, on September 27 and December 7, were reports of thieves who had stolen money and passports. They had broken into an empty ground-floor apartment and two others in Aivazov's building, inhabited by an embassy functionary named Batcharov and an interpreter named Marcevski. None of these burglars entered Aivazov's apartment.

Memories of mysterious armed intruders would linger long after the story's swift and ignoble death. But few would remember that it was not Agca who lied in this case. It was Todor Aivazov who had spoken of "strangers entering his apartment," to 150 foreign correspondents at the December 17 press conference in Sofia.[8]

(Nobody I knew seemed to remember another whopper, offered by Bulgarian press spokesman Boyan Traikov at a later date. His assertion that Antonov spoke no English—and so could not speak to Agca—was accepted almost universally as gospel truth right to the end, though Bulgaria's consul-general in Rome had said at the start that Antonov "speaks English pretty well.")

•   •

No sooner did the Italian press drop the story of fifteen break-ins at Aivazov's building than another was discovered at Sergei Antonov's.

On January 14, 1983, a fresh round of headlines appeared. They were generated by a scoop in *Paese-Sera,* a Communist daily recently saved from bankruptcy by benefactors close to a hardline pro-Moscow faction in the Italian Communist Party.

"Somebody Entered Antonov's House. They Said: 'We Are Policemen,' " announced *Paese-Sera* on its front page. One of its reporters had visited "the elegant building in Via Pola," and "talked with the *portiera.*" She was quoted as saying that the so-called policemen had come about ten days before Antonov's arrest—"on the very day that Agca described the apartment" to the judge, the reporter observed. "Antonov wasn't home, but they went up and got into his apartment anyway," the *portiera* allegedly declared.

To journalists flocking to see her the next day, the woman denied the whole thing.[9] Evidently, *Paese-Sera*'s correspondent had gotten it mixed up. The policemen who did enter Antonov's apartment had done so on the morning they came to take him away: a legitimate visit and search, duly reported at the time in the Italian press.[10]

•　　　　　•

A week earlier—on January 6—*Paese-Sera* had featured another big scoop. This one was delivered to its editorial offices by anonymous messenger. It purported to be the photocopy of a letter from the Ministry of Justice to the director of Agca's maximum-security prison in Ascoli-Piceno, authorizing "three 'persons' known to you to have 'special' talks with the prisoner Agca, without time limits and also outside his prison cell."

The letter, dated March 14, 1982—two months before Agca got started on Part One of his confession to Judge Martella—was stamped *Riservatissima* ("Top Secret"). Whoever sent the anonymous messenger had tacked on a message of his own. The letter, he said, had been "used by three men disguised as monks" (wearing cassocks, that is), who met with Agca "several times, in secret places."

Even *Paese-Sera* admitted that the missive was "probably" false. In fact, the Ministry of Justice pronounced it a "gross forgery," as anyone could see at a glance (I have a copy).

To strengthen the impact of the fake letter it was printing, *Paese-Sera* ran an item from *Pravda,* the Soviet Party daily, on the same day, on the same page. "Only a blind man could fail to see that the Bulgarian Connection was a creation of the CIA," *Pravda* said.

•　　　　　•

That forgery was modest compared to another appearing some months later (July 21, 1983) in an equivocally financed weekly called *Pace e Guerra,* put out by ex-dissident Communists. This was delivered by anonymous messenger too. It purported to be a true copy of two secret cables sent by American ambassador Maxwell Rabb, suitably dated August 28 and December 6, 1982.

The first (following on the heels of my *Reader's Digest* piece) spoke of a "possible and promising campaign in Italy to draw public attention to Bulgarian involvement in the attack on Pope John Paul II." The "key issue" was "to provide the evidence of Ali Agca's links to the Bulgarians," for which "friends from SISMI . . . are ready to cooperate."

The second (twelve days after Antonov's arrest) rejoiced in the campaign's "resounding success." The "European media have enthusiastically developed themes on the lines anticipated: that the gunman was directed by the Bulgarian secret police," ran the text. Success had been assured by "prearrangement" with Socialist labor leaders and others in "the Craxi Party" (the Italian Socialist Party led by pro-Western Bettino Craxi), as well as newspapers happily exposing "the spy-nest, Sofia."

Whoever wrote the stuff certainly knew something about American Embassy communications. The typewriter was right, as were several code signals and some addresses. But he must have been thinking of some other ambassador when he dreamed up "the spy-nest, Sofia"—a grating phrase for Ivy League ears at State—and "the Craxi Party," an epithet coming more naturally to diplomats from Eastern Europe.

Among thirty-odd more technical errors, several stood out. The cables were not numbered, an impossible oversight in any diplomatic correspondence. The addressees included "USIS Washington," an acronym changed in Washington years ago to USIA (United States Information Agency). The code letters "SU," used by American diplomats to mean the Sudan, were taken to stand for the Soviet Union.

Pace e Guerra wouldn't vouch for the material either, but ran it anyway under a blaring headline: "How Many Strange Facts Around the Bulgarian Connection!"

As a matter of routine practice, Italy's state news agency Ansa carried a summary of *Pace e Guerra*'s story, whereupon it followed the classic *Dezinformatsiya* route. The Soviet *Pravda* and Bulgarian news agency, BTA, picked up the plant *as an Ansa story*.[11] ("The Italian news agency Ansa, which has raised the curtain slightly on highly significant facts . . . ," ran an earlier BTA dispatch, citing the "fifteen break-ins into Bulgarian flats," the "three secret agents in monk's cassocks," etc.[12]) From then on, *people would quote Ansa* as the source of these strange facts regarding the American ambassador's deplorable behavior.

•   •

It did not matter that all this was crude and easily exposed. What mattered was that some always stuck. Little by little, accumulating mounds of artifice hardened into conventional wisdom on the subject. Diligently applied, the tactics did wonders to build up public faith in the innocence of Sergei Antonov.

Much depended on perpetuating the image of Agca as an incorrigible liar, and of Judge Martella as a decent but beaten man, discouraged, deluded, and at the end of his rope.

Time after time all during that year, he was reported in the Western media to be on the verge of quitting in disgust. The first story to that effect appeared less than five weeks after he had ordered Antonov's arrest. On December 26, the universally respected Paris daily *Le Monde* reported that Judge Martella "had asked to be relieved of his job." Its cited source was the *Daily American,* an ad-filled, essentially small-town paper for Rome's English-speaking expatriate community. The *Daily American*'s source was an unidentified "Christian Democratic Deputy."

Combined with this was the persistent rumor of Antonov's eternally imminent release, for utter lack of evidence. ("The impending release of a Bulgarian official . . . may herald further important developments in the investigation . . . ," said *The Times* of London on January 5—just six weeks after Antonov had been jailed, and only a month after the Tribunal of Liberty had upheld his detention. "The Italian legal authorities now admit there is no decisive proof involving Sergei Antonov . . . and his release is believed imminent," reported the London *Sunday Times* the following April 24.)[13]

Despite Antonov's continuing detention, and three unconditional court decisions upholding it, the rumors never died. On the contrary, people began to say: "What? They're *still* not letting him out? Something fishy there."

Plea bargaining became another indestructible fiction. Agca was supposed to be "singing" (a Whitehall spokesman's word) to get his prison sentence halved, as scores of Italian terrorists were doing under Italy's new Penitents' Law. ("In Italy, a convicted terrorist's sentence can be cut in half if he confesses fully," said *The New York Times* in this regard, on December 28, 1982. But the new law applies only to those who confess *before* they are convicted and sentenced. Agca, a condemned lifer, was not eligible, as Italian judicial authorities had stated categorically and repeatedly.[14])

Other fictional accretions revolved around three pillars of the Bulgarian defense: Antonov's Alibi, Antonov's Wife's Alibi, and what became known as the Mystery of the Folding Door. How this defense stood up in its entirety under Judge Martella's inexorable interrogation, we were not given to know. But the larger holes were clearly discernible.

Antonov's alibi for the day of the shooting depended on what his lawyers considered "the time that counted": shortly after 5:00 P.M. on May 13. They claimed that he had heard the first news of the attack at his office, and rushed down for the portable radio in his car so that everybody in the office could hear the next bulletins.[15]

Of ten witnesses swearing to this alibi, nine were Bulgarian employees of Balkanair. The tenth corrected her testimony after a four-hour session with the judge: she had spoken to Antonov by phone at the Balkanair office not after the radio news around 5:00, but after the first news announcement on television at 7:00.[16]

This wasn't necessarily the time that counted, anyway. Judge Martella had never revealed exactly when Antonov was supposed to have been in St. Peter's Square that day. But in the seminal version of Agca's confession published by the *Corriere della Sera* on December 8, he had described the trio breaking up in Via della Conciliazione well before the shooting. "For the last time, Agca looked back. He saw Antonov driving away in the Alfetta," the paper had said. That would have been around 4:00 P.M.

This quasi-official account published in December was forgotten by January, and deliberately falsified by February.

On February 22, Bulgaria's spokesman Boyan Traikov accused Agca of "changing his story" *in January*: of moving up the hour he had last seen Antonov from 5.00 to 4:00, "*after he was told of Antonov's alibi* [my italics]," so as to get around it. That was one of "Agca's lies," he said.[17]

Agca did tell lies to the judge, some of which doubtless slipped through even after seven months of checking and cross-questioning. "Nobody is transformed from devil to angel overnight. It's always a gradual process: two steps forward, one step back," Judge Martella once told a visiting American senator. "Agca has the typical attitude of a penitent, who stakes his future on his confession and feels obliged to make it believable," said another judge close to the case. "Thus, Agca does not remember, or guesses perhaps, or even invents. But if it is right to discount some of his declarations, it would be too much to throw out everything he says because of some imprecise statement, or even a lie."[18]

Nevertheless, most of the lies on Traikov's list looked more like Traikov's.

It was a wrathful Boyan Traikov who produced his ten pages of accusations, in an interview by his own state news agency on Bulgarian television.[19] By the time he did, on February 22, lawyers Consolo and Larussa had already lost in the Italian courts on Antonov's alibi not only for May 13, but for May 11 and 12, the "dress rehearsal" days. "How can we explain that ruling against an innocent Bulgarian citizen?" demanded Traikov. "Judicial incompetence? That would be too ingenuous!"

"We want Bulgarian and world opinion to know," Traikov went on, "that the charges against Antonov were based on absolutely false testimony by Agca, *which he could not have prepared and invented alone*, that somebody is passing on the lies . . . and piloting him constantly, that he is lying continually *with the help of the secret services and the collaboration of Italian magistrates*. This is not a normal judicial investigation. . . . *The Italian Ministry of Justice* is carrying out a plot to defame Bulgaria and socialism, to justify the aspirations of American and NATO militarism for world domination [my italics]."

He was explicitly accusing the entire Italian establishment of participating actively in a monstrous conspiracy; and if everything else he said were accepted as fact, it would have to be true. Agca could not indeed have prepared and invented such an elaborately circumstantial story alone.

It was quite an accusation. Yet Western analysts—or those who spoke in their name—were already accepting the idea with equanimity, on the apparent assumption that sunny Italy was more operatic than real (whereas, presumably, Bulgaria was the other way round).

Then came Traikov's list of "Agca's lies," the biggest of which he claimed were these:

1. Agca said he spoke English with Antonov. But "Sergei Antonov does not know and does not speak English."
2. Agca "rectified" his story of being with Antonov at 5:00 P.M. on the day of the shooting, to "annul" Antonov's alibi.
3. Agca had probably never been in Bulgaria, except in transit. A check of frontier records showed that nobody of that name had entered the country. Did the Turk claim to be using a false Indian passport as Yoginder Singh? Well, *eighteen* Yoginder Singhs were in Bulgaria in 1980. "Which one was Agca, if one *was* Agca?"
4. Agca was supposed to have provided home phone numbers for Todor Aivazov and Antonov. But neither had a home phone in Rome.

5. "Despite what he was told and shown in photographs," Agca still didn't get the descriptions quite straight about Aivazov's and Antonov's apartments. "He speaks of a folding wooden door in Antonov's house. There is such a door in the empty apartment above, but not in Antonov's." (A curtain hung over the opening there instead.)

6. Agca "suddenly" remembered—six weeks after Antonov's arrest—that he had attended a final meeting in Antonov's house on May 10, 1981. Among those present, Agca now said, were Agca, Antonov, Todor Aivazov, Major Vasilev, four unnamed Turks, Antonov's wife, Rosica, and a child of ten, helping to serve tea. Although "several witnesses exist who say that Rosica was in Rome at the time of the papal shooting, they have poor memories," asserted Traikov. "Rosica left Rome on May 8 by car," driving through Yugoslavia with friends, arriving in Sofia by May 10. Her ten-year-old daughter, Ani, was at school there.

The first charge was taken care of already. Antonov did speak English, according to Bulgarian consul-general Stefan Ghenev, who must have dealt closely with the deputy director of his own country's airline in Rome.

The second was disposed of too. The story that Agca was supposed to have "rectified" in January had been published in early December by several Italian papers. Antonov's alibi for May 13 was not "annulled" by Agca's trickery. It simply did not convince the Italian court.

The third charge might have held up, if Agca hadn't provided the essential clue to his presence in Sofia from the outset. Western police were meant to believe that he had only passed through Bulgaria in transit, on August 31, 1980 (the dates of entry and exit stamped in his fake Faruk Ozgun passport). But the Turk he named, Omer Mersan, had spent time with him at the Hotel Vitosha in early July. Just one Yoginder Singh registered at the Vitosha would have straightened that out.

Judge Martella had formally asked the Bulgarian authorities—on January 28, a month before Traikov's harangue—if they had checked the hotel register "for the period from early July to the end of August 1980."[20] After "a thorough check," the Bulgarians replied, they had found "no proof" of Agca's presence.[21] In an unguarded moment, however, the Vitosha's manager, Aleksandur Andreev, admitted to

The New York Times that "he never checked on this after the assassination attempt and the Bulgarian authorities did not ask him to. He had never inquired whether any of the staff recognized Mr. Agca from photographs."[22]

The fourth charge could almost certainly be written off. One of the few points that sources were willing to confirm at DIGOS, SISDE, SISMI, and three or four judges' offices was that Aivazov and Antonov both had unlisted phone numbers in Rome. As far back as December 3, 1982, *La Repubblica* reported that "it took investigators considerable time to learn that this number *was* used by Antonov for special conversations."

The fifth charge, known as the Mystery of the Folding Door, was a washout as mysteries go. Boyan Traikov was talking about Antonov's apartment *in February 1983,* whereas Agca claimed to have seen it *in May 1981.* Rome is full of flimsy, accordion-pleated jobs like that, unusually accident-prone. Judging from folding doors I have known there, this one might just have fallen down.

More to the point was the allegation that Agca could have made such a howler with all the lowdown he was supposed to be getting from the police, the secret services, the examining magistrates, the Ministry of Justice. The police didn't need to break into an empty apartment above so as to know what Antonov's looked like. They had searched his own apartment, legitimately, when they arrested him.[23] Why would they tell Agca to describe a folding door that wasn't there? A four-hour judicial inspection of the premises had been made the following January. If Agca had somehow gotten it wrong before, why didn't the judge—his "pilot"—set him straight?

The last charge could at least be discounted halfway. There was nothing "sudden" in Agca's recollection of a meeting at Antonov's house on May 10, 1981. Such a meeting had been reported in the *Messaggero* of Rome five days after Antonov's arrest. The article, dated November 30, 1982, said that Agca, Antonov, Aivazov, and Major Vasilev were present for this "final planning session."[24]

What was new, at least for the public, was Agca's claim that Rosica and a girl sounding like her daughter were there too, serving tea.

Antonov's Wife's Alibi became Bulgaria's biggest card. Lawyers Consolo and Larussa assured reporters that Antonov's always imminent release was now only days if not hours away. Names were named: a Bulgarian couple, Kosta and Donka Krastev, allegedly took Rosica from Rome to Sofia in their car on the specified dates (May 8–10, 1981). Documents were waved at reporters (but not handed over), purporting to prove her overnight stay in a Yugoslav motel (the Staro Petrovo Selo) on May 10.[25]

A nameless Italian frontier guard posted at the Trieste border was said—by the lawyers, to *La Repubblica*'s correspondent—to have identified the Krastevs in one car among several thousands crossing the border daily—this nearly two years before.[26]

Lawyers Consolo and Larussa announced that Rosica had been obliged to leave Italy *before May 9*, because that was when her visa expired.[27]

It is a very long time since Italy has expelled a law-abiding foreigner because of a visa about to expire. In this instance, the Questura in Rome told reporters that Rosica's visa *had been renewed before it expired on May 9*.[28]

The Bulgarian couple came to Rome to tell Judge Martella about their three-day drive with Rosica. Questioned in separate rooms for many hours, the Krastevs emerged looking harried. Why didn't they bring along Rosica's passport, the judge wanted to know; that could have settled everything. The Krastevs replied that Bulgaria automatically took back a citizen's passport after a trip abroad, held it a year, and then destroyed it. The Bulgarians then announced that *Rosica's passport had been trashed on September 15, 1982*.[29]

Once again, the court turned down an appeal for Antonov's release. The Bulgarian couple "did not convince the judges," wrote the *Corriere della Sera*. "There were no new elements seriously undermining the case."[30]

Lawyers Consolo and Larussa were apparently dumbfounded. They had always maintained up to now that Judge Martella was "correct, scrupulous, and loyal."[31] They had read out some lines to reporters from Martella's previous explanation for turning them down. "How could the Turk indicate the dates?" the judge had written, to justify Agca's credibility, "if in January Rosica Antonova were not in Italy and not in Rome? And what if on Sunday, May 10, Antonov were not at home and his house were shut? If on May 13 Antonov was in Bulgaria, or in another Italian city, not in Rome but at Fiumicino Airport, in a place with documentary proof that he was there? What could the Turk, with his accusations, have done? He would have been clamorously given the lie!"[32]

How to explain Antonov's continuing detention after a statement like that? Perhaps Judge Martella had mentioned a lot of other "ifs" that the lawyers skipped, diminishing Rosica's overall importance. What if nobody else in Agca's scenario was in the right place at the right time, either? Supposing his two other leading Bulgarian characters—Todor Aivazov and Major Vasilev—had been out of town on those three consecutive days in May 1981? What would become of Agca's credibility then? Lawyers Consolo and Larussa could have clamorously wiped the floor with him.

Or else, Rosica's alibi may simply not have been good enough. Antonov himself had provided the most compelling reason to disbelieve it. Starting with his first interrogation after arrest, up to and through the Bulgarian couple's interrogation in Rome *half a year later,* Antonov had consistently maintained to Judge Martella that *his wife, Rosica, was with him in Rome on May 13, 1981. She had met him at the Balkanair office around seven that evening and they had gone home together,* he said. His own lawyers could not deny that, strain as they might to get around it.[33]

•   •

Throughout these stormy months, Italy came under all but unbearable pressure from the East and West both: get the Bulgarian out of jail, make a deal, call off the judge. Many an Italian politician would have dearly loved to do so. But the cost to the nation's independent judiciary and free institutions would have been prohibitive.

Italian leaders knew, if their allies abroad might not, that Judge Martella and the entire judicial structure upholding him could not be called off just like that.

If they did not know everything Martella knew, furthermore— he was not required to tell all even to the secret services, and didn't— they knew that the prisoner under his scrutiny could not conceivably have been "piloted" from beginning to end.

They made that plain, or thought they did, soon after the balloon went up: during the last weeks of that December, and especially in a solemn parliamentary debate just before Christmas.

Only a day before "West European intelligence analysts" expressed their suspicions in the *New York Times* article filed December 17, Italy's incoming Christian Democratic premier Amintor Fanfani had told Parliament that the Bulgarian Connection was "not a hypothesis but a fact." The papal shooting was "the gravest act of destabilization the world has seen in sixty years," he said.[34] The preceding day, a Parliamentary Oversight Committee for Italy's intelligence services had come to much the same conclusion. It was "convinced that the plot was almost certainly conceived and organized by the Bulgarian secret services—a true act of war, if undeclared," *Corriere della Sera* reported.[35] On December 20, the ministers of interior, defense, justice, and foreign affairs rose to discuss it in Parliament.

They were not just talking about Agca and John Paul. To Italians, the Bulgarian Connection meant what three separate judicial investigations were bringing to light: that to all appearances, their country had been used with insolent contempt as a kind of colonial outpost, to promote a multibillion-dollar traffic in contraband arms and drugs, to assist and manipulate the nation's murderous Red Brigades, to spy on Poland's Solidarity for the benefit of the Warsaw Pact, to conspire to take Lech Walesa's life during his stay in the Italian capital, and to eliminate an inconvenient Polish Pope besides.

For all their resignation to a reasonable amount of espionage and foreign meddling, the revelations of the past few weeks had been too much. "We wanted the Russians to know we knew," the Socialist defense minister Lelio Lagorio told me after the parliamentary debate.

It was "an act of war in times of peace," Lagorio had said in Parliament of the papal conspiracy, echoing its oversight committee but still earning a stiff jab from several quarters in and out of Italy for "playing politics." Certainly, he was more outspoken than many of his Christian Democratic colleagues. For a number of reasons, not least the need to cohabit in Italy with the West's largest Communist Party, leaders of the ruling Christian Democratic Party had long been obliged to play a different kind of politics. It was a good quarter of a century since they had shown the smallest inclination to stir up trouble with the Russians.

Not once since the storm blew up had a plausible theory been offered to explain *why* these Christian Democrats should set the secret services, the police, and the courts on course to "pilot" Agca so as to frame the Bulgarians. Far from being overjoyed by the situation, many of these Catholic leaders were miserable and some were acutely unhappy: notably the incumbent ministers of interior and foreign affairs. Nevertheless, they were unanimous in defending the integrity and independence of the Italian judiciary.

Interior Minister Virgilio Rognoni, unhappiest of them all, had been directly responsible for Italy's police and domestic intelligence service, SISDE, during the whole affair. The very thought of his sanctioning a sinister anti-Bulgarian plot was ludicrous. "The data emerging from the three judicial investigations" involving Bulgaria "did not flow down from heaven," he told Parliament. There were "facts, circumstances, and hence, in the judiciary perspective, evidence of guilt, thanks to a long, complex, determined, and continuing action by the State's institutions. . . .

"It is a fact," Rognoni went on, "that in the three investigations there surely exists . . . a common reference point in Bulgaria, whether in regard to its citizens and diplomats or its secret service." In a broader sense, "the exploitation of terrorism by foreign secret services, or indeed the direct actions taken by them, constitute a constant danger, a threat, a sort of surrogate war. . . . These are the facts, and they give the lie to unfair criticism."

Foreign Minister Emilio Colombo, who had scarcely uttered a mean word about the Russians or their allies in his long and distinguished career, spoke of "the most serious questions emerging, in regard to the possible use made by the Sofia government of diplomatic privileges and prerogatives."

One of the uses Sofia's government had made of the Italian foreign minister himself was to cover Todor Aivazov's urgent flight from Italy, as Colombo described it to Parliament. Judge Martella had asked him about the three Bulgarians' diplomatic immunity on the preceding November 11. Colombo had informed him of Aivazov's diplomatic immunity on November 12. The Bulgarian ambassador, summoned to the Foreign Ministry on November 26, "was asked formally" if his government would renounce immunity for Aivazov. Evidently, the ambassador needed time to think that over. *Only on November 30* did he inform the foreign minister that Aivazov "had left Italy about a month before." In fact, Aivazov had boarded a Balkanair flight for Sofia on November 12.

For all the criticism against him for "playing politics," the Socialist defense minister, Lagorio, was not much bolder than the normally circumspect Interior Minister Rognoni. He too spoke of a "surrogate war" waged on the West by "foreign government bodies, in the framework of East-West friction." Responsible for Italy's military intelligence agency, SISMI, he was also in a position to provide some background information on the Bulgarian Connection.

Public attention had been deviated by "the most subtle and devious attempts at 'disinformation,' " he declared. Italian counterespionage had singled out a Bulgarian state society for import-export—he was referring to Kintex, of course—as the bearing structure of the illicit international arms-drugs traffic, he said. The Italian labor leader jailed for suspected espionage, Luigi Scricciolo, "had identified three Bulgarian officials known to him only by code names," from an album of mug shots prepared by SISMI. "From the same album, Agca recognized his three Bulgarian accomplices in the papal shooting."

In the Red Brigades' 1982 kidnapping of General James Lee Dozier, "our counterespionage had reported two noteworthy anomalies in respect to the Bulgarian security services' normal broadcasts. An increased rate in the radio traffic was noticed during the days of the kidnapping, detention, and liberation of General Dozier," especially on the day he was freed. That also happened on the day of the papal shooting, Lagorio said.

As for the shooting itself, "our counterespionage was convinced . . . of a plot from the beginning. It carried out intensive activities abroad, to verify the identity of people with whom Agca might have been in contact." At home, it had also "established direct contact with Agca" on December 29, 1981, in a visit made together by SISMI and SISDE, "authorized by the judiciary." On that occasion, "it first appeared possible that Agca might abandon his silence."

It was a question whether this last could be taken to mean that Agca was talked into talking that day. Judge Martella denied flatly that the visit "produced anything relating to Agca's subsequent confession, which did not begin until four months later" (around May 1).

There remained the fact that Italy's secret services did meet Agca in prison on December 29, with the knowledge and consent of the Ministry of Justice and the magistrates concerned.

It was the only known and authorized visit of this kind from the beginning to the end of the investigation, and there was nothing incorrect or irregular about it. What country in the world would not have called on its own intelligence services for assistance in a case like this?

Naturally SISMI would have been doing its own investigating abroad, in so entangled an affair of international contraband

and espionage. Weren't West Germany's BND, and Britain's MI-6, and Turkey's MIT, and the French SDECE looking into it as well? They were quoted as saying they were, though the CIA said *it* wasn't.[36]

Indeed, Judge Martella could see for himself that SISMI's help was indispensable in certain designated areas, and he availed himself of it. He had met with its director, General Nino Lugaresi, on September 20 to discuss that.[37] On November 1, he had then asked the incumbent Republican premier, Giovanni Spadolini, to authorize investigation by SISMI "in areas the judicial police could not reach.[38]

Under all but intolerable strain, the Italian establishment had held up with authority and dignity. In an editorial headlined "Heroism Italian Style," the *Washington Post* praised Italy warmly as a "model among Western nations of legal correctness and political courage. What they are doing—arresting suspects, and subjecting them to rigorous but fair trials, naming foreign names and accepting the international complications—is uncommon and difficult and brave."[39]

But few such words of praise from the West would be coming Italy's way again; for, seeing the way the world was already turning, the *Wall Street Journal* warned against being "mainly concerned with explaining away the abominable deed. We suspect that what is going on here is the same temptation to deny reality that we have seen on other occasions. . . . Rather than face up to these grim realities, ways are found to avoid confronting them. Excuses are made for our adversaries. We look for scapegoats among ourselves. We whistle past the graveyard."

Sure enough, the scapegoats would be found, the excuses made. Before the year was out, Western intelligence analysts would be standing the evidence on its head. Over dinner, or drinks, or somewhere safe from observation, through links, hints, raised eyebrows, avuncular pats on the back, solemn warnings or jocular laughter, they would be passing on their curious version of the case to dozens of reporters who had every reason to take their word for it. Their considered opinions follow.

14

On November 9, the day before Leonid Brezhnev died, Italian Interior Minister Virgilio Rognoni received a visit from the CIA's vice-chief of station in Rome and a staffer from the U.S. Senate Intelligence Committee. The Americans wanted to know about the Bulgarian connection to the shooting of the Pope.

Mr. Rognoni explained that the Turkish gunman had been informed a few months before that Italy could not afford the cost of keeping him in solitary confinement much longer. To Mr. Agca, that meant he would be transferred to an ordinary prison and would promptly be murdered. That induced him to talk about the Bulgarian Government officials who hired him to kill the Pope.

"What proof do you have?" asked the CIA man.

The man in charge of Italy's internal security laid out the facts . . . [as he knew them at the time].

The CIA man waved all that aside. "You have no proof," he said.

When columnist William Safire reported this episode in *The New York Times* on December 27, 1982, the Bulgarian Connection was already a highly visible and inflammable issue. But the meeting he described took place on November 9, when it was not. The phrase had not yet been coined, the Bulgarian Sergei Antonov had not yet been arrested, and such evidence as there was had not yet been revealed to anybody outside a restricted judicial circle—not even to Interior Minister Rognoni.

Yuri Andropov had not yet been chosen as the new leader of Soviet Russia either. If some future need might be felt by the West to spare him a possibly deadly blow, that could not yet be used as an excuse.

The man from the CIA could not reasonably expect Rognoni to produce definitive proof of Bulgaria's guilt: that was the judiciary's job, not the interior minister's. Nevertheless, Rognoni did tell his visitors something the public still did not know: that the gunman who shot the Pope was actually saying the Bulgarians had hired him to do it.

Far from taking a deep interest in this remarkable news, the CIA's deputy chief of station in Rome "did his best to convey to the Italian Government a high degree of skepticism from the American Government," Safire wrote. "According to one report of the meeting, the CIA representative continued to view with distaste the conclusions being reached by Italian investigators."

The same local CIA deputy chief would tell an NBC reporter shortly afterward: "You people [referring to Marvin Kalb and myself] are making things up." But even he could not say the same of this story. I have talked with the staffer from the Senate Intelligence Committee who was with him at this meeting with Rognoni. Safire's account of it was true, he said, adding that the interior minister seemed taken aback.[1]

Whether the senior CIA officer was speaking for himself or his government, there was no mistaking his intent. He was leaning on a highly influential member of the Italian cabinet (who was apprehensive enough already), with all the weight of an American in his daunting position. Prejudging the case on its political merits, without waiting for all the evidence to be in, he was implying that the Italians might do well to drop it before it came into the open—judge or no judge, confession or no confession. Otherwise they might incur not only the wrath of the Russians but the grave displeasure of the United States.

And they did.

The official American posture was irreproachable. The State Department and White House merely expressed a wish to keep out of it while the Italian magistrates got on with it. Supposedly, that meant the United States would await with serenity the outcome of an Italian court investigation in which three Bulgarian nationals—two on the Bulgarian Embassy's staff in Rome—had been formally accused of "direct complicity" in the attempted assassination of the Pope.

In time, however, this apparent policy of benevolent neutrality proved to be not so benevolent, and not very neutral. The Kremlin somehow came out looking like the injured party, whereas the Italian judiciary, and by inference Italy's entire governing class, stood accused of ineptitude, perjury, subornation, and criminal collusion.

The Americans were not alone in manipulating public opinion to this effect. That the Russians and Bulgarians should do so was understandable and inevitable. But several Western governments did much the same. Most of the talking was done through their unnamed spokesmen—a time-honored practice adopted on many a trying occasion by governments of every political persuasion.

Ordinarily, though, such leaks to the media would be used to send reassuring little signals to the other side in a crisis, or weaken the other side in an argument, or push a point of strong interest to the spokesman's side. I don't know of another occasion when spokesmen for the West were used to push a point of vital interest to the East, at the expense of a close Western partner and ally.

The first sign of what was coming had appeared in the *New York Times* article of December 17, 1982—the one in which unnamed West German, West European, and Israeli intelligence analysts "feared that . . . suspect evidence, or outright 'disinformation' " might have been planted on Judge Martella, by what could only have been some Western agency bent on embarrassing the Russians.

A bemusing headline in the *Corriere della Sera* on December 30 underlined this curious meeting of minds between East and West. "Russians Accuse the CIA of Terrorism; American Government Cautious On Bulgarian Connection," the headline ran.

The story beneath dealt with several ferocious comments from Tass, *Izvestia*, and *Literaturnaya Gazieta*, accusing the CIA of plotting to murder not just the Pope, but also Italian statesman Aldo Moro (killed by the Red Brigades in 1978), Sicilian Communist leader Pio La Torre (gunned down by the Mafia in 1982), and the founder of Italy's state petroleum board, ENI, Enrico Mattei (who died in a mysterious plane crash in 1962).

Side by side with these charges in *Corriere della Sera* was a report from *The New York Times* of December 29 that said:

"United States intelligence officials remain intrigued but unconvinced by allegations in Italy that Bulgaria instigated the attempted assassination of Pope John Paul II. . . . Officials familiar with the Central Intelligence Agency's work in the case said there was considerable evidence linking Bulgaria to espionage and terrorist activity in Italy. . . . But the information available to the United States, much of it provided by the Italians, has failed to convince American officials that Bulgarian agents hired Mehmet Ali Agca . . . to shoot the Pope."

To say that U.S. intelligence officers "remain unconvinced"— after the CIA had worked on the case, and Italians had provided much of the information available to the United States—was not quite so innocent as saying that these same U.S. officers would "wait and see," as they said they would in the same article.

The next day, *The New York Times* carried another story headlined: "Plot on Pope: On Basis of Evidence, A Bulgarian-Soviet Link Can't Be Proved." This one, quoting "many professional political and intelligence analysts," was filed by Henry Kamm from Rome.

He reported that what had emerged from Italy's daylong parliamentary debate on December 20 "was a clear Government belief that Judge Martella's actions were based on substantive information." Nevertheless, Kamm's unidentified sources could think of no plausible Soviet motive for the papal shooting.

While Italian defense minister Lagorio had accused the Soviet Union "of committing 'an act of war' by choosing to assassinate the Pope rather than invading Poland," wrote Kamm, "Mr. Lagorio did not elaborate on the sources that provided him with the information on such a Soviet dilemma."

According to Kamm's own intelligence sources, he said, "subsequent events proved that the Soviet Union had entirely Polish means at its disposal to solve the Polish issue. . . . They doubt that the Soviet Union, which they consider cautious in international affairs, would have taken so great a risk as plotting a political assassination of Shakespearian magnitude, entrusting its execution to a 23-year-old Turk of doubtful emotional stability. . . .''

A week later, Italian papers reported a close identity of views on the affair in Washington, London, and Bonn.

"The British and American governments fear that a campaign to involve the KGB in the assassination plot could compromise crucial East-West negotiations," reported *Il Giornale Nuovo*'s London correspondent on January 6. "The news reaching London is that the

Reagan Administration's Sovietologists continue to be skeptical about the whole thing, maintaining that it is virtually unthinkable that the Soviet Union could have acted with such reckless imprudence."

A "Whitehall spokesman," quoted in the same dispatch, warned of "the need to separate certified proof from the suppositions and confessions 'sung' by somebody who wants to get out of jail or cut his sentence." (Considering the harsh provisions of Italy's Penitents' Law, that would have to be a pretty mixed-up songbird.)

The article also cited British press reports about the West German secret services' "skepticism regarding alleged Bulgarian and Soviet complicity," as well as their "concern over the enlargement of Judge Martella's investigation to Germany." (The judge was trying, around that time, to track down Bekir Celenk's financial hanky-panky in Germany.)

Unnamed German authorities were also said to feel that Judge Martella had "attached too much importance to Claire Sterling's article in the *Reader's Digest*," implying that he must have snatched at my piece as an excuse to nab Sergei Antonov. (Bulgarians aside, no unnamed spokesman yet had made the judge out to be quite so brainless.)

Another anonymous German source came up with the notion that "the Bulgarians might merely have given a 'scholarship' to Agca and other terrorists," to keep them on tap. "Agca and the others might then have advanced the assassination plot on their own and surprised the Bulgarians," he suggested to *Newsweek* on January 3, 1983. He did not say what for.

By January 27—three days after a second Italian court ruling upheld Antonov's detention—more substantial leaks to *The New York Times* made the front pages in Italy. "CIA Does Not Believe the Bulgarians Wanted to Kill Pope Wojtyla," was the headline in the left-leaning *La Repubblica*. Its subtitle said: "Italian Foreign Ministry Invites Washington to Be Cautious on the Eastern Connection."

The subtitle was quickly disposed of. It referred to a Washington source telling *The New York Times* that "the Italian government has urged the United States to use caution in speaking publicly about this matter." A prompt and categorical denial from Rome made it likelier that the urging toward caution had come from the other direction.[2]

The rest of the *Times*'s own front-page story by Bernard Gwertzman on January 27 was not so easily disposed of. It was the fourth major story provided to *The New York Times* by unnamed Western spokesmen since the issuance of Italian arrest warrants for the three Bulgarian nationals in November. This time the sources were all American—intelligence analysts, administration officials, State Department spokesmen—whose transparent purpose was to display open-minded detachment while getting Bulgaria off the hook.

Officially, the American government still came through in the story as wanting to keep out of it while Italian magistrates got on with it. The State Department's spokesman was "very concerned" about reports to the contrary. "It is certainly not United States policy to discourage journalists or the Italian authorities from investigating this case," he declared firmly.

The same went for the various intelligence agencies, said a spokesman of theirs. Despite a reference in the same paper a month before to "the Central Intelligence Agency's work on the case," a senior intelligence officer now announced that "no U.S. agency was conducting a separate American investigation into the case. It is an Italian matter, and it would be inappropriate for the United States to interfere."

Since intelligence gathered in Bulgaria, Turkey, West Germany, Austria, and Switzerland would in no way interfere with Italian justice—would indeed be most welcome to Judge Martella—this was rightly dismissed by an American senator as "the most illogical explanation I ever heard."[3]

Even so, what followed scarcely reflected a seemingly commendable posture of restraint.

"American officials familiar with the evidence of links between Mr. Agca and Bulgaria say he spent some time in Sofia in 1980. . . . But the nature of his connections with the Bulgarians remained unclear," ran Gwertzman's piece in the *Times*. "He told Italian investigators that the three Bulgarians helped him plot the assassination attempt, but as far as American sources know, the Italian Government has been unable to confirm this."

In point of fact, the Italian government was unable to confirm or deny this or any detail of Agca's confession, until Judge Martella's work was done. It was expressly forbidden to do so by law.

Other intelligence analysts then revealed that they not only knew more than they had owned up to so far, but were racked with indecision about how to explain it.

By now, they were willing to "rule out the possibility that Mr. Agca's connections with Bulgaria were completely innocent," Gwertzman wrote. "They said that because of tight security in Bulgaria, it was highly improbable that Bulgarian authorities were unaware of Mr. Agca's presence in Sofia in 1980, or his background as a convicted murderer."

Thus, Gwertzman continued, "intelligence analysts are working on two theories to explain the Agca-Bulgarian connection. One is that the Bulgarian secret service had hired him as an assassin or drug-trade enforcer, in an arrangement that had nothing to do with the Pope or the Soviet Union. According to this theory, the Bulgarians were not aware that in 1979 Mr. Agca, after escaping from a Turkish prison, . . . had threatened to kill the Pope."

If the Bulgarians knew all about Agca's background, that certainly looked like a singular oversight. But it was minor compared to the next. "Later, this theory goes, *when Mr. Agca found himself in Rome on a mission for the Bulgarian secret service*, he independently plotted to kill the Pope, without the support or knowledge of the Bulgarian authorities [my italics]."

Those who had trouble accepting that as a sound working hypothesis were offered a more straightforward, alternative theory: "Moscow, concerned about support Pope John Paul II, a Pole, might give to the Solidarity union in Poland, [might have] asked the Bulgarian secret service in 1979 to find someone who could someday assassinate the Pope."

Although some senior intelligence analysts plainly must have preferred the second theory, Gwertzman's sources here didn't give them much of a break. "In 1980 and 1981, when Solidarity's influence in Poland was increasing, the Vatican communicated frequently with Solidarity's leaders and gave it advice and other assistance"—this was the lackluster reason advanced for a drastic Russian decision that this Pope would have to go.

Evidently these intelligence analysts talking to *The New York Times* thought poorly of the alternative theory, as did the CIA. Despite the Agency's "confidence in the judgment and abilities of Judge Ilario Martella . . . [and] his reputation as an independent nonpolitical jurist . . . the CIA remains skeptical about Bulgarian involvement," Gwertzman's sources concluded.

In just another four days, on January 31, 1983, a fresh CIA assessment that might reasonably evoke a certain hilarity was leaked with an apparently straight face. This one—the fifth important leak since November—was given to Robert Toth of the *Los Angeles Times*, reproduced in the Paris *Herald-Tribune*, and relayed to the press of all Western Europe.

"The Central Intelligence Agency," Toth reported, "has concluded—with what is said to be 99% certainty—that officials of the Bulgarian government *had advance knowledge* of the assassination attempt," but "the CIA is also convinced that neither the Bulgarians nor the Soviet Union *instigated the attack* [my italics]." According to Toth's source, "No 'smoking gun' or absolute proof of Bulgarian complicity had been found by U.S. intelligence officials."

Evidence is unlikely to be found by those who are not supposed to be looking for any. U.S. intelligence agencies had gone on record just four days earlier as "conducting no separate American investigation into the case." Now, however, it appeared that the CIA had been conducting its own investigation after all.

"There is no doubt," continued Toth, "that the CIA has been following the issue intensively, through its agents in Europe, its contacts with Italians and other friendly intelligence agencies, and its analytic experts here. Its conclusions, which have been discussed with key members of the Administration as well as a handful of Congressmen, are said to include:

"—There is a 99% certainty that Bulgarians—and by inference the Soviet KGB, which has controlling ties to the Bulgarian intelligence agency—knew that Agca intended to shoot the Pope but apparently chose not to stop him. Agca's public threat to kill the Pope during John Paul's visit to Turkey a year earlier had been front-page news. . . .

"—The three Bulgarians who have been implicated . . . *were intelligence agents* with whom Agca was working on some unknown matter [my italics]. Presumably it involved drugs and arms smuggling. Bulgarian intelligence is said to be heavily involved in such smuggling. . . .

"—Agca was a 'known crazy' . . . too unstable to be included in the assassination plot, let alone be trusted to do the shooting, and almost certain to be caught."

In a word, said a "source familiar with the CIA's views": "Agca was operating in cooperation with the Bulgarians, but they were not his employers."

The leak ended with an emphatic reminder to the *Los Angeles Times* that "these conclusions [!] rest solely on circumstantial evidence. . . . The odds are overwhelming that the truth will never be known with 100% certainty."

How could the CIA be 99 percent certain, solely on the strength of circumstantial evidence? Did the overwhelming odds against absolute certainty depend on the missing 1 percent? What was the public to make of this extravagant mathematical exercise, tacked onto a story that made no sense?

It was helpful to learn that the three Bulgarians named by Agca really were intelligence agents; the CIA ought to know a spook when it saw one. The same applied to its assertion that the Bulgarians knew all about Agca while he was in Sofia; any Bulgaria-watcher in the business would say the same. But the rest simply did not add up.

First of all, no Bulgarian agent would be caught dead running a drug-trade enforcer in Rome or anywhere else outside his country's borders. Bulgaria judiciously leaves that kind of job to foreigners. Judge Carlo Palermo's investigation in Trento was making that clear, and I had a mass of evidence to the same effect.[4] Skeptics in Robert Toth's article had indeed observed that "very little evidence has been unearthed connecting Agca to the arms-drugs traffic, [whereas] there is overwhelming evidence that Agca could be hired to kill."

If the Bulgarians did hire Agca as a killer, who did they have in mind as a target? Bulgarian dissident writers abroad? Enemies of the Bulgarian People's Republic? Why did the CIA source omit any mention of Lech Walesa as at least a potential target, when Bulgarian plans to have him killed in Rome had been described to two different Italian judges by two firsthand witnesses—the imprisoned ex–labor leader Luigi Scricciolo and Agca himself—both employed by the Bulgarian secret service?

It also "strained credulity," observed *The Times* of London, that the Bulgarians and Russians would have known a crazed killer was on the loose with plans to shoot the Pope—a killer in Bulgaria's pay, what's more—without saying or doing a thing about it.[5] What if this "known crazy" were caught, as they supposedly thought he was bound to be? Wouldn't he also be bound to reveal that he was working, in whatever capacity, for the Bulgarian secret service?

In any event, Agca was no crazed killer. As we have seen, the Italian court's Statement of Motivation in October 1981 had referred to his "full psychic maturity" and "uncommon gifts of mental equilibrium." Turkish and Italian medical examiners had both pronounced him sane, and every other competent authority dealing with him in both countries had found him so.

The London *Times* could "not help suspecting that whoever had leaked this version of the CIA's conclusions—presumably someone close to the Reagan Administration—has a political motive. The effect is to blacken the Bulgarian communist regime and by extension its Soviet masters, but not to the point where the conduct of normal international diplomacy, including proposals for a summit meeting, would become impossible."[6]

A nameless American source in Toth's story confirmed that. "If Bulgarian-Russian guilt were proved unequivocally, Reagan could never sit down with Andropov," he said.

While there was no denying the gravity of that dilemma, there was every reason to question the wisdom—let alone the propriety, ethics, and sheer believability—of trying to save the day with such charades.

These were still the months when the Bulgarian Connection was something new and a shaken Western public was struggling to come to terms with it. The implications were so calamitous that even people well aware of the Soviet Union's faults longed to be told that the Russians could not have done this.

The temptation to tell them so must have been strong in Western governing circles, but giving in to it could be almighty dangerous. The Italian investigation was long under way, and the very anxiety of certain Western leaders to head it off betrayed their qualms about the outcome. Unless Italy's government agreed to an intolerable degradation of the country's legal institutions—assuming it could get away with that—the truth was going to come out sooner or later.

To insist on Russian innocence as evidence mounted to the contrary was to invite just the kind of popular overreaction confirming the West's first fears. Deprived of the available information—indeed deliberately deceived and reassured—ordinary people everywhere in the West would be perilously unprepared for the truth when it hit them. The predictable result in such situations is what is called a self-fulfilling prophecy.

In a reasoned column for *The New York Times*, Flora Lewis warned of just this possibility. "The clues are adding up," she wrote. "The sinister aura of this spy story too fantastic for fiction is enhanced, not diminished, by the remarkable caution of Western governments. Even President Reagan, who did not hesitate to accuse the Russians soon after taking office of reserving 'the right to commit any crime, to lie, to cheat,' is ducking the question of possible Kremlin complicity now.

"That is obviously because it is so dreadful to contemplate the consequences if more damaging facts do emerge. They should not and probably cannot be stifled. History and Western dignity demand the truth. So the warning must be to prepare against impetuous action and an emotional response that could make St. Peter's Square comparable to . . . the bullet at Sarajevo that set off World War I."[7]

Yet the cult of disbelief died hard, sustained by the one source that should by rights have been above suspicion. If anybody ought to be seizing triumphantly on the Russo-Bulgarian conspiracy theory, it was the redoubtable CIA. Precisely because it had come to be seen so widely as the world's primeval anti-Communist force (and prime evildoer besides), its exceptional efforts now to exonerate the KGB and the Kremlin were irresistibly seductive. Those who had never believed a thing the CIA said about anything else were happy to take its word on this.

Thus the pacesetters of Western public opinion continued to transmit the steady leaks flowing from Washington and tributary flows from like-minded capitals in Western Europe. The honorable exception was France, whose ambassador to Rome had declared bluntly from the start: "The French government has the same opinion of the Bulgarian Connection as the Italian government's."[8]

By that spring, France alone seemed to be upholding this view. The United States in particular appeared to be turning dead against it.

On May 3, 1983, Marvin Kalb stated on NBC's "Nightly News" that CIA Director William Casey had "changed his mind and now believes there may not have been a Bulgarian connection in the papal plot." What, then, became of the CIA's assertion a good three months earlier (on January 31) that Agca's alleged accomplice, Sergei Antonov, was a known Bulgarian agent?

Twelve days later, Judge Martella ruled—for the third time—that "sufficient evidence exists" to warrant Antonov's continuing detention.[9]

By the end of May, nonetheless, yet another unnamed spokesman told Robert Toth of the *Los Angeles Times* that both the director of the CIA, William Casey, and the President's national security adviser, William Clark, now felt that "efforts to find a Bulgarian Connection . . . have 'run dry.' "

"Casey's view now, which the CIA has presented convincingly, is that Agca probably was not hired by the Bulgarians," a knowledgeable source told Toth on May 28. "Clark's position," he added, "is somewhat short of that": somewhere between a possible but unprovable connection, and none whatever.

The conversion of CIA Director Casey, spectacular if true, appeared to be recent. He had reportedly believed in the Bulgarian Connection since the previous November,[10] and he had been reinforced in this belief as late as February, upon the return from Rome of Republican senator Alfonse D'Amato of New York.[11]

Senator D'Amato, an Italo-American with a large Catholic constituency, had the President's ear. He was also well connected at the Vatican, and well informed from other sources after five busy days in Rome. No sooner did he get back home than he made a beeline for the White House.

The senator had already tangled with the CIA about what *The New York Times* called his "one-man fact-finding mission." A senior staffer for the Senate Intelligence Committee who was to have gone along was advised at the last minute to "cancel the trip," said the *Times*.[12] (As the staffer told it to me, Senator Barry Goldwater had passed on the message from the CIA, which had considered this particular staffer a "troublemaker" since his visit to Rome in November—the visit William Safire had written about.)[13]

Once in Rome, Senator D'Amato was a fox among the chickens at the American Embassy. Ambassador Maxwell Rabb, an old friend, had cabled asking him to put off the visit, and nobody there seemed glad to see him.[14] Only by dint of "working the phones furiously, pleading, cajoling and pressing officials to meet him," did his aides get the right appointments, wrote *The New York Times*'s Philip Taubman, traveling with the senatorial party.[15]

Nevertheless, he did get the right appointments. (I was in Tuscany at the time, but Judy Harris, still following the story for NBC, made the rounds with him and kept me up to date.) Among those who briefed him on the papal shooting were judges Martella and Imposimato, Interior Minister Rognoni and Foreign Minister Colombo, several key lawyers, and Erminio Pennachini, the Christian Democrat heading Parliament's liaison committee with the secret services.

Pennachini especially was frank in telling him: "My impression is that the CIA has attempted to becloud the results of our investigation, and diminish their significance. We got no help from them."[16]

How much else the senator picked up along those lines in five days, I couldn't say. But he had evidently learned enough to perceive an unaccountable gap between the information available in Rome and indications coming from authoritative American quarters there. "The CIA has conducted a war of silence, obstruction, and disinformation in this investigation," he declared at a farewell press conference; and its own investigative efforts, he said, had been "shockingly inept."[17]

He was incensed to hear from the U.S. Embassy, furthermore, reported Taubman in the *Times*, that "not one person has been assigned to follow developments in the case." (Taubman recalled top U.S. officials in Washington as having "said privately that the Papal shooting is not a subject of intense scrutiny.")[18]

At lunch with Taubman and other American reporters, the senator described comments he'd gotten from "a senior U.S. intelligence official in Rome." This is how he said they went:[19]

"Antonov? We don't know if he was an agent. He didn't know much about running an airline." (But hadn't a CIA source said that Antonov *was* an agent, in the *Los Angeles Times* of January 31?)

"We don't have a copy of Agca's confession. Apparently it contains some mistakes . . . about rooms and so on . . . a wrong house . . ." (Antonov's, that is).

"Lagorio knows he's wrong about the jump in the Bulgarian Embassy's radio traffic when the Pope was shot." (The CIA, asserting that modern espionage techniques can cover such telltale signs, had in fact advised *New York Times* editors to challenge Italian Defense Minister Lagorio on this when he visited their paper in January.[20] Both Lagorio and SISMI, controlled by his Defense Ministry, were baffled by this outright charge that they must be lying.)

"Maybe it's all the arms and drugs racket." (Asked if Agca was ever identified with this racket, he replied: "Well, no.")

"We're not whitewashing. . . . We just want to keep our options open."

Here the conversation lagged, said the senator, as the senior intelligence official got out an aerosol can, sprayed his leather briefcase, and began polishing. ("What color?" asked Taubman. Light brown.)

For Taubman, Senator D'Amato's Rome visit was " 'a working

trip' that plays well back home,"[21] as doubtless it was. Let the senator who doesn't care how it plays back home cast the first stone. For all that, D'Amato had hit on something that few of his countrymen could know and many might be shocked to discover.

No U.S. Embassy anywhere—not in Rome, or Ankara, or Sofia, Vienna, Bonn—had assigned anyone to follow developments in the investigation of a crime that might well affect the future course of international politics and diplomacy.[22]

No U.S. intelligence officer in Rome was setting forth the *ascertainable evidence*, in frequent if unauthorized talks with resident and visiting foreign correspondents, American and otherwise. In fact, they were doing just the opposite.[23]

No U.S. intelligence team was gathering information in Turkey or Bulgaria, regarding Agca's crucial links to the Sofia-based Turkish Mafia—or so the Senate Intelligence Committee was told by a CIA spokesman.[24]

No U.S. intelligence agency had passed on to the Italians a cardinal fact I knew to be in American files, connecting Agca to the Bulgarians: the fact that Abuzer Ugurlu, the Godfather of the Turkish Mafia who arranged to get Agca out of an Istanbul jail and see him safely installed in Sofia, had been an agent of the Bulgarian secret service since 1974.[25]

The Christian Democratic Deputy who told Senator D'Amato "we got no help from them" was surely right about that.

To my knowledge, indeed, the Italians got very little help from anybody. Not only the United States, but West Germany, Great Britain, and practically every other Western state that Italy turned to had been dragging its feet since the investigation began.

A top general in Italy's military intelligence, SISMI, told me that not a single Western intelligence service was collaborating actively and wholeheartedly on the case. On the contrary, he said, nearly all were withholding information. "We got no help at all from the CIA," he added. Judge Severino Santiapichi and the judge at his side in Agca's trial, Antonio Abate, spoke to me about running into impenetrable barriers of silence abroad, in their earliest efforts to find a trace of Agca's possible accomplices. ("It is established that the investigation did not succeed in piercing the thick curtain of silence covering this affair," they wrote in their Statement of Motivation.) Judge Martella mentioned to me a delay of eight months—from February to October 1982—before U.S. authorities cleared the way for his requested visit to consult with the FBI and question witnesses.[26]

While Senator D'Amato could hardly have learned all this in five days, he had picked up enough in Rome to make an interesting tale for a supposedly hard-line Republican President in Washington.

Directly after D'Amato's call on presidential adviser William Clark, President Reagan spoke out against "an international crime deserving the deepest possible investigation." He commended "the courage of the Italian government in bringing the problem to world attention."[27]

Not long afterward, the word went out that three top CIA officials in Rome had fallen from grace. "The station chief and his two deputies are the subject of a secret investigation in Washington and may soon be fired," reported Marvin Kalb on NBC. On the State Department's insistence, an in-house CIA mission went to Rome to review their performance. The three were thereupon cleared, and back in business.[28]

By then, the CIA had evidently recovered from a head-on collision with *The New York Times*, brought on by an article asserting that there really was a Bulgarian Connection.

Sent by the *Times* to make an independent study of the case in Italy, Turkey, and West Germany, Nicholas Gage had written on March 23, 1983: "Authorities in Western Europe have information that supports testimony given to them by a Turkish assassin, Mehmet Ali Agca, that when he tried to kill the Pope . . . he was acting at the behest of Bulgarian intelligence agents."

Gage's report was packed with substantial information: evidence confirming Agca's confession, indirect corroboration from Luigi Scricciolo, indications by a key witness that Antonov "has lied repeatedly, even in small matters, and the Italians can prove it." But his big coup was the discovery of Iordan Mantarov, the defector who had been second in command of the Bulgarian secret service in Paris and who claimed firsthand knowledge of the conspiracy.

Mantarov, whose cover job at the Bulgarian Embassy was that of deputy commercial attaché, had told French intelligence that he had learned of the plot from a higher-ranking Bulgarian agent, Dimiter Savov, his close friend. He said it was conceived because the Soviet KGB became convinced, soon after Cardinal Wojtyla became Pope, that "his election . . . had been engineered by [President Carter's national security adviser] Zbigniew Brzezinski to inspire the Poles to strike out against the Communist system." When unrest mounted in Poland and the Pope supported Solidarity's aspirations, these suspicions hardened into conviction; and "the KGB began discussions with the Bulgarian intelligence service on a way to eliminate John Paul II."

Agca was picked as hit man "because he was known throughout the world as a rightist . . . killer and had no links to any Communist country," Mantarov maintained. "He was supposed to be killed in St. Peter's Square after assassinating the Pope," he added.

Of all the suggested Soviet motives for murder, this was the one with the clear ring of truth. The French believed Mantarov's story, said Gage. But the Bulgarian Telegraph Agency and the CIA both hotly attacked *The New York Times* for printing it.

The Bulgarians said this was yet another plant by "Western intelligence services panting for breath in their helplessness" to prove Bulgaria's guilt.[29] A CIA source denounced it as third-rate "hearsay," refusing to believe for a moment that the French could have believed it.[30] If they did, they would have shared it with the Americans, said another CIA source.[31]

This wasn't necessarily so. The French are notoriously close with their information. They have also been markedly reluctant to share it with the CIA since Watergate—lest it "show up in the next day's *New York Times*," I was told in Paris on the highest authority, as far back as 1979.

Mantarov's story had no part in the Italian judicial investigation; Judge Martella had never heard of him. But it was a big factor in changing William Casey's mind about the whole Bulgarian Connection, as reported in the *Los Angeles Times*.

The California daily's story of May 28, 1983, said that the director of the CIA had finally decided the Bulgarians were out of it mostly for three reasons: "lack of progress in the Italian investigation . . . ; reports from Rome about a possible trade of Mr. Antonov for two Italians jailed in Bulgaria on espionage charges"; and "persuasive denials . . . by CIA professionals" of Mantarov's story in *The New York Times*.

A decision made on such grounds seemed all but incredible. The Italian investigation had not slowed down at all, still less run dry: "Where do they get their information? It does not come from me," was Judge Martella's reply when I asked. The swap proposition for Antonov had been turned down indignantly and repeatedly by Foreign Minister Colombo, dove though he was, and did not materialize then or since. The Mantarov story, true or false, was juridically irrelevant.

Yet those were the reasons given to the *Los Angeles Times* for Casey's conversion to "the earlier view of CIA professionals"—the self-serving, contorted, improbable, if not preposterous view that "the Bulgarians very probably did not direct Agca to shoot the Pope, *although they probably knew his intentions and chose not to stop him* [my italics]."

With this sixth big leak in six months, the old-boy network in the CIA appeared to have won. Step by step, between December 17, 1982, and May 28, 1983, the idea was instilled in the public mind that Western "disinformation" had been planted on Judge Martella to embarrass Russia; that the Italians had no case anyway; that the Russians had no plausible motive to want the Pope dead; that the Bulgarian-Russian connection could not be proved, in the foreseeable future or ever; that the Italian investigation had reached a dead end and was folding up; and that Agca was an unemployable nut case, who would never have been hired as a hit man by the Bulgarians or anyone else.

Any information to the contrary in Judge Martella's hands was thus discounted in advance as unreliable in substance and sinister in intent.

By May 28, these were no longer mere hints from unnamed spokesmen. Two of the men closest to the topmost peak of power in Washington—William Casey and William Clark—were now identified publicly with this position, which hardly differed from Bulgarian press spokesman Boyan Traikov's. For if there was no such thing as a Bulgarian Connection in the papal plot, then the known Bulgarian agent Sergei Antonov could not have been Agca's accomplice. That left only one explanation for his continuing detention: the Italians were framing him.

Did the government of the United States really believe that? How could it accept the sleazy artifice and deliberate distortion pointing public opinion in that direction? Why was the U.S. intelligence community resorting to such scandalous practices? Whose interest could be served by denying the increasing likelihood that the Russians had resorted to spectacular political assassination as an instrument of national policy? If the Russians had done it once, were they not capable of doing it again, whenever and wherever a Western head of state might get in their way? Didn't the public have the right to know and consider the tremendous implications of such a Soviet policy?

No answers have come from the incumbent administration in Washington.

Others, unburdened by the weight of office, have not hesitated to speak their minds.

Former CIA director Richard Helms came right out and said that the papal shooting "had all the earmarks of a KGB operation."

Former secretary of state Henry Kissinger fully agreed.

A former President's national security adviser, Zbigniew Brzezinski, was still more forthright. "It takes an act of faith *not* to believe the Bulgarians did it," he declared.[32]

From the White House, silence.

PART THREE

·

ANSWERS
AND
ENIGMAS

·

15

At a White House briefing on December 9, 1982, presidential press spokesman Larry Speakes was asked if he had any comment on reports from Italy linking the Bulgarian secret service to the attempted assassination of the Pope. No, he did not. Could he confirm the integration of the Bulgarian secret service with the Soviet KGB? No, he had no information on that. Would he look into it and reply at a later date? No, he had no interest in doing so.[1]

Where the White House led, makers of public opinion—for once—followed. Memories failed, and time receded to the days when the West knew little and understood less about life in the Soviet bloc.

"The would-be killer might have found help in Bulgaria solely from a flourishing underworld of arms and drugs smugglers," wrote *The New York Times,* expressing widespread hopes. "Or zealous Bulgarian security agents might have acted on their own, without clearance from their Soviet allies. Or a government's ambiguous signal might have been construed as a wink of approval. . . . That Yuri Andropov willed an attack on John Paul II is possible but hardly proven. That his people became mired in a sleazy conspiracy on imagined authority is a likelihood Americans should be the first to understand."[2]

None of these propositions could be made to fit the known and demonstrable facts.

Bulgaria, a small Balkan nation of nine million souls with an endlessly tormented past, has long been the most placid, pliant, and constant of Soviet Russia's vassal states: the USSR's sixteenth republic, people call it. Its Communist regime has scarcely caused the Kremlin a moment's worry since taking power in 1947. Its enduring leader, Todor Zhivkov, has vowed allegiance to the Soviet Union "in life and in death."[3]

Unlike other East Europeans, Bulgarians seem more relieved than restless under their powerful neighbor's protection. Many *like* the Russians, drawn to them by millennial ethnic and religious bonds; and everybody loves "The Liberator," Tsar Alexander II, who delivered Bulgaria from five centuries of brutal Turkish rule under the Ottoman Empire. (His statue on horseback faces the Communist Party headquarters in Sofia.)

Only here, in all Eastern Europe, does a delegate from the Soviet Politburo sit in regular attendance at local Politburo meetings.[4] Here, too, is a prime minister born on Soviet soil, a man who has spent more years in Moscow than in Sofia.[5] And here as well, under close Russian tutelage, is the single security apparatus in the Soviet bloc ideally equipped to arrange for the Pope's assassination.

Among the more popular of Western self-deceptions is the one about the devil-may-care Bulgarian security agent who took it into his head to rub out the Pope, without telling the Russians a thing about it. That one "is for the birds," observed the London *Economist.*[6]

There are no devil-may-care Bulgarian secret agents, as anybody who has been one will tell you. Some may act independently, and even brashly, on matters affecting their own nationals. But none would have the temerity to make a move of international importance without consulting the Russians first.

A number of Bulgarians fleeing to the West have described the inner workings of their country's security service, the Darzhavna Sigurnost, or DS. Several are men of many decades' experience and elevated rank. Colonel X., now living discreetly in Switzerland, had been trained in espionage by the Russians and served in the DS for thirty years. Colonel Stefan Sverdlev, the highest in rank ever to defect, organized DS operations abroad and attended meetings of the Warsaw Pact security services. The archives he brought out with him in 1972 have furnished priceless information to the West. He spent the next eight years working for Greek intelligence, which had kept him smartly up to date.

These men and others are unanimous in saying that the DS is wholly answerable to the Soviet Union. KGB officers, reporting straight to Moscow, are stationed in the DS top command and in all seven of its departments: Intelligence, Counterintelligence, Military Counterintelligence, Technical Support, Security and Vigilance, Propaganda, and Information and Analysis.[7] An estimated 400 KGB officers fill these jobs, of whom some 300 are concentrated in the First and Third Departments: Foreign Intelligence and Military Counterintelligence.[8]

Every DS section abroad is also monitored on the spot, by an officer in each Bulgarian embassy reporting directly to the KGB. "You can recognize the DS man in any embassy because he is abusive to everyone except the ambassador, and the KGB man because he is abusive to everyone including the ambassador," says the dissident writer Vladimir Kotov, who very nearly died of a jab from one of those Bulgarian umbrellas in Paris.[9]

"Never—never!—could the Bulgarians make such a decision on the Pope independently," said Colonel X. in a lengthy, three-part interview with the French *Le Quotidien de Paris*.[10]

"There are KGB agents in every department of Bulgarian security. If anybody had acted on his own, there would have been a wave of purges. . . . There were none. . . . Sofia has absolutely no strategic international autonomy," said two senior French intelligence agents to the left-wing Paris weekly *Le Nouvel Observateur*.[11]

"It is absolutely impossible for the Bulgarians to act on their own initiative abroad. . . . Every important decision must pass through Russian hands. Nothing can be decided without consulting the KGB officer in charge, who must refer it to Moscow," said Colonel Sverdlev in an exceptional interview filling two pages of the ultra-left Paris daily *Libération*.[12] In the Pope's case, he added, "a decision that big would have to be made in the Soviet Politburo, by Brezhnev himself. Only then would the head of the KGB be entrusted with its execution."

The head of the KGB when such a decision would have been made—between late 1979 and May 1981—was Yuri Andropov. Any ambiguous signal at the time would have had to come from Brezhnev. The one Russian in a position to construe that as a wink of approval would have been Andropov himself.

However the order came, Andropov's decision to pass it on to

Bulgaria would have followed naturally, Colonel Sverdlev told *Libération*.

The Bulgarians are notorious among their Warsaw Pact allies for their willingness to take on the dirtiest jobs farmed out by the KGB: kidnapping, terrorism, and murder—"wet work," in Soviet parlance. And they are good at it. ("Our killers never miss," boasted Party leader Zhivkov to columnist Cyrus Sulzberger.)[13] But Bulgaria's importance was far greater than that in the Kremlin's larger scheme of things.

For a decade and more, under the supervision of a special KGB section in Sofia,[14] Bulgaria's security services have played a major role in the resurgence of international terrorism, in the destabilization of Turkey, Italy, Yugoslavia, and Greece (in order of priority), the arming of the Middle East, and in the moral, physical, and financial degradation of the West (by pumping massive supplies of heroin into Western Europe). This last was a matter of deliberate policy established by the Warsaw Pact countries, the colonel said.

With the expertise the Bulgarians thus gained, the infrastructure they built, the network of couriers and informers at their disposal, their contacts with and hold over major terrorist bands of the right and left in Turkey and Europe, all the ingredients were in their hands for what should have been a perfect crime.

It certainly *looked* perfect for a good year and a half, at least to Western eyes. A more knowing Eastern eye could spot the telltale signs, however.

First of all, said Colonel X. in his lengthy Paris interview, "nothing—absolutely nothing—on Bulgarian territory can escape the vigilance of the state security forces. Sofia isn't Paris, or Rome. . . . An enormous machine of surveillance keeps strict watch even on tourists passing through for a few hours. . . . It is unthinkable that two foreigners could meet in a hotel in the capital, or even on the street . . . without the special services being informed."

Then, the choice of a hit man was a dead giveaway, noted Colonel X. "A Turk, a Moslem, an extreme rightist, and a notorious fugitive to boot: it's like a signature." And again: "Agca stayed at the Hotel Vitosha, which could not conceivably have escaped the services' notice. . . . The Vitosha is State Security's hotel. That's where they put people they are particularly anxious to protect or keep under close watch." (This doubtless explains those tapped bedside clocks, whose mini-tape-recorder batteries are changed regularly by the chambermaids every Monday morning.)

Furthermore, said Colonel X., "Agca met there with Bekir Celenk, a Turkish Mafia boss who could only have done this by arrangement with the security police. Not a word, not an intonation of their conversation could have been lost on the services, since Celenk is their accredited agent. . . ."

The final, unmistakable sign was the use of Balkanair and its deputy director, Sergei Antonov, directly on the scene in Rome. All East-bloc security services use their national airlines for undercover work abroad, said Colonel X. Unfailingly, in any foreign capital, the airline's number-two man—the one who handles passports—is necessarily a trained and trusted security agent. (A Balkanair stewardess fleeing to the West, who knew Antonov well, assured Judge Martella that there could be no doubt of this.)[15]

If nothing else, Antonov's involvement with Agca should have given the whole game away.

I did not have a chance to meet Colonel X. But in January 1983 I talked for hours with Colonel Sverdlev, in the safe anonymity of a large and busy Munich hotel lobby. Square-set, heavily built, his broad Slavic features stolidly expressionless, a practiced eye roving constantly around the crowded hall, he looked every inch the kind of professional he had been all his adult life.

Over coffee in a dimly lit corner, he gave me a rundown on just how he thought the papal plot must have worked.

Ordinarily, a Bulgarian agent would be used for "wet work" assignments, he said. But that was out of the question in this case. "For one thing, the agent himself would have to be killed afterward, by another Bulgarian agent. This would be bad for morale in the service," he explained.

For another, this particular murder must never be traced to the East. It must be done, *and seen to be done*, by right-wing extremists.[16]

In such cases, continued the colonel, "any hint of collaboration between Eastern security and Western right-wingers is altogether impermissible. Therefore, the Gray Wolves used for backup here would obviously be dealt with through the Turkish Mafia, which was ours, of course. The only exception might be Turks actually recruited by the DS, and sent back to infiltrate the Gray Wolf movement. One or two like that were bound to be mixed up in the Agca affair," he said.

Agca himself was neither from the right nor left, although he had a useful right-wing front, Colonel Sverdlev went on. "He was simply a professional killer for hire. The DS had dozens of foreigners like him. I worked with some myself."

Before a mercenary like Agca was sent into the field, continued Sverdlev, he had to undergo intensive training inside Bulgaria. "The big thing was mental conditioning. The hit man would have it drilled into his head that nothing could possibly go wrong, that we would never let him down. Our heroic Bulgarian agents always took care of their own, we'd say.

"We would tell endless tales of our thrilling exploits in getting our people out of tight corners or arranging their escape from prison. Our agents would always be there to cover for him or get him out of jail if he was caught—so he would be told over and over again.

"In the last week or two before sending him into the field, we would drop the formal training and concentrate on making the man feel strong and confident. We'd take him to fine restaurants, we'd all get drunk together, we'd bring him home to show how much we liked and trusted him—that he was one of us. He must never be allowed to suspect that he would be killed as soon as he'd done the job—which he had to be, of course."

Had things gone smoothly, said Colonel Sverdlev, not only would Agca be dead "but not a single man close to the truth would be left alive. Agca would have been shot in St. Peter's Square, or right after he got away. The others would have disappeared in a matter of days."

Things did not go smoothly, though, because of the stubborn little nun hanging onto Agca's arm in the square. Immobilized, with the carabinieri bearing down on him, Agca could not be shot. Neither could his foreign accomplices, wherever they were. Should word of their deaths somehow get back to Agca in jail, he would be sure to tell the Italians every last thing he knew.

Alive and a captive, Agca was a ball and chain for the Bulgarians running him in Rome, explained Colonel Sverdlev. They wouldn't dare leave the country, for fear of losing any trust he might still have that they would get him out. They couldn't afford to leave anyway, until some way might be found to have him murdered in prison while there was still time (he did wait a year before starting to confess, after all).

Coming from the highest-ranking officer ever to defect from the

Bulgarian services, such thoughts might give Western skeptics pause. Agca's story about Todor Aivazov, Sergei Antonov, and Želio Vasilev—his three Bulgarian accomplices—no longer sounded so implausible. Aivazov and Antonov might well have given him their private phone numbers and invited him home, to make him feel he was one of them. And all three would have had compelling reasons to stay on in Rome as long as they did.

Not until August 27, 1982—after excerpts from Agca's first confession were published in *Milliyet*—did Major Vasilev leave Italy. Aivazov hung on until the following November 12, when his ambassador almost certainly got wind of Judge Martella's interest in him. Antonov held out until his arrest on November 25, though Italian police had been trailing him for months.

We know now that, during all those months, Agca lived in perpetual fear of being killed.

So did Judge Martella, who received repeated threats against himself, his wife, and his children.

More important to an understanding of the plot were the special facilities Bulgaria could draw on: a deeply entrenched espionage ring in Rome, and the unique institution called Kintex in Sofia, both objects of three independent but intersecting judicial investigations by judges Carlo Palermo, Ferdinando Imposimato, and Ilario Martella.

Colonel Sverdlev could tell me something about the one, and a good deal more about the other.

Bulgaria's DS had been slipping agents in and out of Italy with no trouble at all since at least 1968, he said. This was not because Bulgaria had a particular interest in Italy—it didn't—but because the Russians did. All the ring's work was reported back to the First and Third Departments of the DS in Sofia, and relayed to Moscow.

From 1968 on, Colonel Sverdlev said, the Bulgarian spy ring in Italy had gone after anything and everything of possible use to the Russians: information on NATO; recruitment of Italian agents in labor unions, student circles, and government ministries; penetration of the Red Brigades complete with offers of arms and money.

Within a few months of our talk, developments in Judge Imposimato's investigation bore this out fully.

Italy had also been turned into a huge staging area for West European distribution of heroin flowing through from Bulgaria, the colonel went on. That was part of the policy agreed on by the Warsaw Pact states, and one of the places where Kintex came in.

This was borne out too, by Judge Carlo Palermo's investigation in Trento.

Kintex was a branch of the DS First Department, said Colonel Sverdlev. Founded under a different name in 1955, it grew into a multipurpose, multibillion-dollar state conglomerate starting around 1965. Its main dealings were in every kind of international contraband: cigarettes, liquor, electronic goods, jewels, currency, and especially arms and drugs. It also went in for straight legal trade. Both, stated Sverdlev, were used to maximum effect for espionage purposes.

The entire top floor of the modern Kintex headquarters on Boulevard Anton Ivanov in Sofia was given over to an ultrasophisticated global communications network, for coded and open traffic. Both kinds of traffic were used to serve "purely political goals."

"Kintex," the colonel declared, "is an instrument of the Bulgarian security service—which is to say, the Soviet security service—whose purpose is to help subversive movements in such a way that Moscow will not be discredited.

"Earning hard currency is a secondary purpose. But this too is used for subversion, and not to improve the Bulgarians' lot. In the Bulgarian services, we use the term 'self-maintenance,' meaning that security activities should pay for themselves, without taking too much from the State bank. That's where the Kintex money goes."

Operating through "dozens of front companies, dummy corporations, and related foreign subsidiaries, Kintex stretched its tentacles around the world." The Turkish Mafia was its good right arm in Sofia. The Russians, whether inside the company or as "advisers" on "planning commissions," were its real directors behind the scenes.

The spy ring Colonel Sverdlev spoke of was already partly exposed by January 1983. Over the next few months, Luigi Scricciolo exposed it further in a confession described by Italy's Tribunal of Liberty as "ample and extremely detailed."[17]

Luigi and his wife, Paola, had been in Bulgaria's employ for some years—he since 1976, she since 1979—receiving "conspicuous funds" for their services.[18] They had spent some time in Sofia in August 1980—Agca's summer there, though he didn't meet them then. Their Bulgarian control in Rome was the chief of the DS spy ring, Ivan Tomov Dontchev, who fled Italy in October 1982. (Luigi's big confession had gotten started four months earlier.)

A warrant for Dontchev's arrest was issued by Judge Rosario Priore the following July 27. It charged him with "serious acts of espionage"; creating "an information network to gather confidential information on the Italian labor movement"; recruiting Italian students studying in American universities, so as to gather U.S. scientific and technological knowledge; gathering sensitive information on the activities of Solidarity in Poland; and establishing "a structure of collaboration with the Red Brigades."[19]

There was no mention of the Lech Walesa plot in these charges, because that whole matter had been turned over to Judge Martella. Before this was done, however, Luigi Scricciolo had admitted to Judge Imposimato that he knew of Dontchev's plans for assassinating Walesa, during the latter's visit to Rome on January 15–19, 1981.[20]

So did Agca, who picked out Dontchev's picture from the same mug shots months before he identified his three alleged Bulgarian accomplices (Antonov, Aivazov, and Vasilev). "That one? Oh, that's Dontchev," he had told Judge Imposimato, who showed him the mug shots on a hunch, following up on Scricciolo's story.[21] Later, Agca confessed to having attended meetings at Dontchev's home, where the Walesa plans were discussed.[22]

Agca did not know Scricciolo or name him, merely asserting that Dontchev was getting information on Walesa from "some Italian labor leader." Scricciolo, denying the information came from him, nevertheless admitted that Dontchev had pressed him for the smallest details of Lech Walesa's hotel reservations, appointments, and itinerary. Eventually, and reluctantly, Scricciolo also admitted that the plan did exist, but fell through for reasons unknown to him.[23]

Agca, in Rome from the preceding December 26, had actually checked in at the Pensione Isa—his takeoff point for the papal shooting four months later—on the night of January 18: Walesa was to meet privately with the Pope at the Vatican the next morning. Not only did Agca say he was supposed to be the hit man on this occasion too, but he revealed a precise and comprehensive knowledge of Walesa's visit that astounded judges Imposimato and Martella.

Agca's report was "rich in particulars," said *La Repubblica* on March 25, 1983, although few of these particulars were known to the public as yet.

He said some rooms were being painted at the Hotel Victoria just before Walesa checked in there, something nobody else had noticed. Judy Harris, dropping by the hotel to check, found that the painters had indeed been at work there at precisely the time Agca mentioned.

His description of Walesa's crowded five-day itinerary was not only faultless, but more accurate than SISMI's own report on Walesa's visit: a fact revealed to a few of us in confidence by an unimpeachable source.

The plot to kill Lech Walesa never caused more than a flurry of interest in the press, perhaps because so much of it remained under wraps. But all of us close to the case knew how strong the evidence looked to Italian authorities involved. Among others, Giuliano Torrebruno, Luigi Scricciolo's lawyer, freely assured any reporter who asked that the Walesa plot most assuredly existed. (After he said as much for publication to NBC and Nicholas Gage of *The New York Times*, he received a bullet in the mail.)

That certainly put the attack on Pope John Paul in a different light. Evidently, Agca was not merely hired for a special occasion: he was an all-purpose hit man at the disposal of a Bulgarian spy ring operating in Italy and reporting to the Russians. In that event, no overeager subaltern in the Bulgarian services could possibly have hatched a plot against the Pope on his own. The ring's designs on Lech Walesa indicated a calculated policy, with fallback positions. Agca himself told the judges that this was one of "several alternative plans" that Dontchev's ring had in mind.

Knowing this much about Agca's mission in Rome did not require high-powered intelligence gathering. Half a dozen Italian court reporters could have passed it on as background information. They could also have set anybody straight on the "drug enforcer" rumor showing up in the foreign press. There was no shred of evidence linking Agca to the drug trade in Rome. It was in a different context altogether that Judge Martella went to Trento that winter, to confer with Judge Palermo and question some of his star witnesses.

After three years of formidable labor, Judge Palermo's nets had been flung wide. Tens of thousands of pages of testimony now documented the largest organized band of international arms and drugs smugglers ever uncovered. Practically every country in Eastern and Western Europe, and the United States as well, turned out to have had dealings with this ring that their governments would rather not talk about. But only one country was involved *as a state*, providing the infrastructure and wherewithal accounting for three-quarters of the heroin reaching Western Europe, and four-fifths of the arms reaching the Middle East.[24]

That was Bulgaria.

Variously described as the "hinge" or "junction" or "linchpin" of this immense two-way traffic, Sofia was said by Judge Palermo himself to be "a central meeting place for the big dealers in the arms-drugs trade. The top people stay at the Hotel Vitosha, or meet in the Café Berlin. . . . They had a most important meeting there in January 1981 to regulate the whole traffic among themselves. We've learned this from dozens of witnesses."[25]

Most of these witnesses spilling the beans to Judge Palermo had been arrested on returning flights from Sofia. One was Wakkas Salah Al-Din, the prisoner Judge Martella went to Trento to see because of his prolonged stay and high-level contacts with Turkish Mafia bosses at the Vitosha while Agca was there.[26]

Henri Arsan, kingpin of the ring's operations in Italy, was reported by Judge Palermo to have "had decisive aid from Bulgaria." Abuzer Ugurlu, "a prime organizer of this traffic," according to Italy's Criminalpol,[27] had run his end of the traffic from Istanbul, Sofia, and the Bulgarian port of Varna before the Turks arrested him.

Bekir Celenk, right-hand man to Henri Arsan and principal liaison for the drug traffic moving westward, made his main headquarters in Sofia (where, as Interpol in Ankara had told me, he and Abuzer Ugurlu used to share an office).

Celenk's business partner in Germany, Atalay Saral, assured me that "everybody" smuggling into Turkey went to Sofia once a month. He also told *The New York Times*'s Nicholas Gage that "the Bulgarians helped us in return for 10% of the cargo's value in hard currency. . . . It was worth it, because they not only provided storage facilities but many services, even sending gunboats to escort our ships out of Bulgarian waters and rescue vessels . . . if they ran into rough weather."[28]

Much of this was confirmed in the *Wall Street Journal* on May 13, 1983: "Western drug experts . . . believe that Bulgaria has been a vital link in one of the most massive arms-for-drugs smuggling schemes Europe has known in recent years. Heroin was shipped across Bulgarian borders to northern Italy, the experts say, where it was received by Mafia groups who then marketed it in Europe and America. . . . The proceeds were used to buy arms . . . for sale in the Middle East. One of the fronts for the arms sales was Kintex, a Bulgarian foreign trade organization officially described as an exporter of small arms and sporting goods. . . .

"Kintex . . . is a highly secretive operation, handling most Bulgarian arms exports, according to Western diplomats. 'We are never allowed near the building. . . . But we can watch the big black Volga sedans bring the arms buyers to its doors,' " said one.

According to *The New York Times*'s Henry Kamm, "Many diplomats attribute Bulgaria's suspected tolerance of the narcotics traffic to political motivation. They believe that Bulgaria, as the Soviet Union's most faithful follower, considers that anything bad for the West, such as addiction among its youth, is good for the Soviet bloc. . . ."[29]

Kamm went on to say that "American Ambassador Robert L. Barry had complained to Bulgarian [officials] last July that the Hotel Vitosha–New Otani was a meeting place for smugglers, and urged the authorities to take action." The Bulgarian officials replied, however, that they could not help the American ambassador there because "he had no facts." No smoking gun, that is.

For all this sudden exposure, relatively little had been published exploring the role of Bulgaria and Kintex in depth. Early in 1983, however, an illuminating two-part series on the subject appeared in Belgium's biggest paper, *Le Soir*.[30] It spoke of "an enormous fleet of Bulgarian trucks on Belgian roads," traveling under seal according to an intercontinental trucking agreement known as the TIR system. "Each Eastern European country has its Western target for such truck traffic, and Belgium has been assigned to Bulgaria," it said.

"The port of Antwerp has been Bulgaria's bridgehead for smuggling and illicit traffic. . . . The scenario is always the same. . . . Once the trucks reach Sofia, the drivers leave the keys to their cargo at the offices of Kintex. . . . On the return trip, one group of trucks heads for Switzerland and eastern France, a second for Munich and Frankfurt, a third for Trieste. . . .

"Eyewitness reports, by repentant truckers and customs officials, have revealed that [part of] this traffic is heroin. . . . In Trieste, it is taken over by the Henri Arsan network, in Munich and Frankfurt by Turkish dealers. . . . The same trucks carry arms, such as Belgian Herstals, back to the Middle East.

"What has surprised investigators the most is the constant presence of the extreme right in all the networks. In Sofia, as in Bekir Celenk's network, the Turkish contacts are mostly right-wing. In Munich and Frankfurt, they are the Gray Wolves, the friends of Ali Agca. In Switzerland and Alsace, they are former Nazis or young right-wing militants. In Lugano, Switzerland, a certain M.G. . . . is responsible for financing right-wing groups via the proceeds of the drugs. . . ."

There it was: the infrastructure, the channels for recruitment, the machinery in place to mount an operation in Rome that could never be traced to the East.

Some weeks later, a resourceful young Alsatian reporter named Jean-Marie Stoerkel brought the story full circle, in an account showing how nature can be so elegantly superior to art.

Stoerkel had stumbled on the story of a fifty-year-old French truck driver whom he called "Walter," who fell into the hands of Kintex and the Turkish Mafia "just at the time when the plot to murder the Pope was being hatched in Sofia. . . . In fact, Walter met Agca there."

"For Walter, everything started in June 1980, when his employer—a Swiss smuggler—asked him to take delivery of a truck and trailer in Munich," the story began, as enlarged upon by Fabrizio Calvi in the French socialist daily *Le Matin*.[31] "Walter was to go to an electrical-goods shop in front of the Munich railroad station, *the Vardar Company* [my italics]. . . . His journey started in an unusual way. A young man of about 30 answering to the name of 'Omer' was given to him as a guide. . . . Walter would soon find out that Omer would look after all the customs formalities during the journey.

"Walter was supposedly carrying 16 tons of cocoa to Saudi Arabia. Sofia was on the way, so Walter didn't mind when Omer suggested that they spend two nights at the Hotel Vitosha. Walter's nightmare was just beginning.

"In the Vitosha car park, Omer told Walter to leave the keys and the truck's registration papers in the glove compartment. An hour later, the truck had vanished. 'It's okay,' Omer told Walter. 'Our Bulgarian employer has taken it back.' Their Bulgarian employer was Kintex . . . which was footing all of Walter's bills.

"On June 14, 1980, Walter got his truck back from the Vitosha car park. Apparently, the customs seals affixed in Munich were intact, but his route sheet had been changed. The cocoa was now destined for Turkey. Escorted by Omer as far as the Turkish border, Walter and his truck were taken over the Kapikule border post by a member of the Turkish Mafia. . . .

"Since his stop at the Kintex warehouse in Sofia, Walter's truck seemed much heavier. . . . It turned out that the Kintex men had added 7.6 tons of goods to his truck. He thought it could only be weapons, and he was probably right.

". . . After Kapikule, Walter was completely taken care of by the Turkish Mafia, escorted from one TIR parking area to another by a mysterious black Mercedes. Sometimes he was given orders by uniformed policemen, at others by mysterious Turks always impeccably dressed."

Unaccountably, "in a car park about 100 kilometers from Ankara, three armed men confiscated Walter's truck," imprisoning him in an abandoned thermal resort for three weeks. Then he was sent back to Sofia with an extra 3,000 kilometers on the clock.

"Back at the Vitosha, Walter realized he was not the only truck driver employed by the Turkish Mafia. Half a dozen others waited in the hotel lounge, ready to go back to Western Europe" with what turned out to be shipments of heroin. Returning to Sofia, "they would give their trucks back to Kintex, and their passports to Turkish intermediaries. They never dealt directly with Bulgarian functionaries. . . ."

They didn't talk to the Mafia Godfathers either, "watching them from afar in the hotel bar or restaurant. . . . But they noticed the Godfathers' armed bodyguards and secret meetings when, surrounded by a large retinue, they shut themselves into their suites.

"One Friday night . . . Walter and two other drivers went on a bender at a Sofia nightclub. At about 2:00 A.M. there was a fight with a few Bulgarians over a stripper. The police, arriving in force, demanded their papers. 'Don't have any; we work for Kintex,' replied Walter. The police quickly sent them back to the Vitosha, saying 'Okay, no problem.' Walter thought he saw fear, and definitely respect, on the faces of the police, who beat a quick retreat."

Walter remained at the Vitosha until October 1980, as his passport shows. Back home, well over a year later, the enterprising Jean-Marie Stoerkel and Fabrizio Calvi found him. His story checked out, as I quickly learned for myself; and its last words brought to a remarkable end the two wearying years I had spent on this case.

In all the time he had spent at the Vitosha, Walter told the French reporters, he had really gotten to know only one Turk—"his guide-interpreter-foreman, Omer." Among the Bulgarians with whom Omer was in contact, "Walter knew only two names—Mr. Traikonov and Mr. Terzieff, who seemed to live in the Vitosha lobby and to work for Kintex. . . ."

So they did.

16

"Omer" was Omer Mersan—the only man named and identified accurately in Mehmet Ali Agca's earliest interrogation, Agca's sole proven link to Bulgaria, the first lead to the nature of the papal conspiracy.

"Mr. Terzieff" was a high-ranking agent of the Bulgarian Durjazna Sigurnost—responsible for all Kintex contraband deals in Sofia, accountable to the KGB in the DS First Department, the lead pursued to the end.[1]

Not a single Western authority made a purposeful effort to help the Italian judiciary pursue it to its logical, irrefutable conclusion.

Up to the last, the Italian police knew very little of Mersan's true occupation, and nothing at all of the connections taking him from a Turkish Mafia front company in Munich to the Godfather's stronghold in Sofia straight to the top of Kintex and the Bulgarian secret service. Neither did Judge Martella, until the final weeks of the second year of his investigation. Had others told him what they knew, the conspiracy might have been exposed long ago. They didn't tell him.

The information was scattered around half a dozen countries. It was in the proceedings of Ankara's Military Tribunal, the files of Interpol, the Bundeskriminalamt's data bank, the documents confiscated by German prison authorities from an ex-lieutenant of Abuzer

Ugurlu's named Suleyman Necati Topuz, the letters of a murdered gangster in Istanbul called Ibrahim Telemen, court records in Munich, confidential Swiss police reports, and the dossiers of four or five national anti-narcotics bureaus in the West.

Much of the material went unnoticed—filed and forgotten, buried unread, never matched against reports filed elsewhere for want of anyone inquisitive enough to run the thing through a computer. The invincible incuriosity prevailing among Western policemen and intelligence agents in regard to this case—their indifference to the problems of a single judge trying to investigate a crime crossing six or seven national frontiers, their vision of the crime as an Italian affair and no concern of theirs—has never ceased to amaze me.

But much was withheld deliberately, to protect an influential figure in the criminal underworld, or police informers, or bent cops, or politicians on the take, or banks laundering money for the mob— or for what might be held in certain Western circles to be reasons of state.

A normal amount of reticence was only to be expected in a crime of such international intricacy and portent. What I found, in my own pursuit of the single hard clue I had to start out with, went far beyond the normal bounds of reticence.

Omer Mersan's name inevitably had caught my attention when I read the Italian court documents of Agca's trial. He was unmistakably some kind of signal sent by Agca to his Italian interrogators, a signal they continued for months to miss.

Within days of his arrest, it will be recalled, Agca had spoken of this Turk living in Munich who worked for a Vardar Company there, whose phone numbers he had at his fingertips, and *who could prove Agca's stay in Bulgaria*.

He had said that a comrade in Turkey sent him to Mersan in Sofia, that Mersan was "a friend of people involved in the black market on a vast scale in Turkey . . . engaged in smuggling cigarettes, liquor, and, on occasion, arms." Agca claimed to have met Mersan several times, in Room 911 of the Hotel Vitosha, where Mersan introduced him to a "Mustafaeff," and offered to help procure his counterfeit Faruk Ozgun passport. He said he gave Mersan 60,000 Turkish lire (around $3,500) and four passport photos, to pass on to "friends in Turkey who could falsify a passport there." Mersan, Agca claimed, had said "it was easy for him to get to the Bulgarian-Turkish border."[2]

Such was the already indestructible image of Agca as the inveterate liar that it scarcely crossed anyone's mind that he might be telling the simple truth, if only for his own protection. It surely did not appear to cross the minds of the German authorities who questioned Omer Mersan, on Italy's request. Indeed, the counterimage they produced of Mersan the clean-cut, upright, much-put-upon victim of a lying Fascist hood would deflect Judge Martella's vision for many months—and go far to persuade the public that anything else Agca said was so much hogwash.

As we have seen, eight days after the attack on the Pope, the Italians asked Federal Germany's Bundeskriminalamt to check on Omer Mersan. A telex from DIGOS in Rome provided Mersan's whereabouts as described by Agca, and reported everything else Agca had said about this Turk in Munich.[3]

The BKA's answering telex on May 22 stated that Mersan admitted to having met Agca as "Metin" in Sofia. Only after seeing Agca's picture in the papers as the Pope's would-be assassin had he recognized Agca as Metin. Earlier that winter, he also admitted, Agca had phoned him at the Vardar Company "to inquire about his health." Mersan denied the passport episode and Mustafaeff story.[4]

The BKA telex entirely ignored the rest of the DIGOS message, the part about Mersan's friends engaged in a vast black market. No German authority on the case would ever refer to it from then on.

Had the German police asked Mersan about that, in the short time they held him for questioning? Had they inquired into the Vardar Company's employing him, or the line of work that had brought him to Sofia—this single living witness known to have been in contact with Agca there? The BKA did not say, then or later.

As we know, Mersan was released by the Munich police in twenty-four hours.

By the time my *Reader's Digest* article appeared, I had at least managed to find one connecting link that bore out Agca's story. From his West German prison cell in Bayreuth, the convicted Turkish dope smuggler Suleyman Necati Topuz had written to Turkish columnist Ugur Mumcu in Ankara, establishing the fact that Omer Mersan was a lieutenant of Abuzer Ugurlu, Godfather of the Turkish Mafia. My information stopped there.

In Turkey, Interior Ministry officials had told me only that Mersan was known to them as an army deserter. German authorities had refused their requests to interrogate him, and "as far as we know," were not even tapping his telephone.[5]

West Germany had been one long stonewall, as far as Mersan was concerned.

Barely two months after the papal shooting, the State Prosecutor's Office in Munich had formally and specifically cleared Mersan of all suspicions deriving from Agca's statements. "The proceedings have failed to substantiate in any way whatsoever claims made by the Pope's would-be assassin," the prosecutor ruled.[6] The case was closed.

Did this mean that the Munich State Prosecutor's Office had investigated the circumstances in Bulgaria and Turkey during the summer of 1980? That it could thus rule out any possibility whatsoever of the claims Agca made? That Mersan never took money and passport photos from Agca in Sofia and passed them on to "friends in Turkey who could falsify" the passport? That Mersan himself was not associated with a vast black market?

Not at all. What could not be substantiated, said the state prosecutor, was Agca's claim that "Mersan had falsified, in 1980, in Munich, the Turkish passport in the name of Faruk Ozgun . . . and had delivered this passport" to Agca in Sofia.[7]

As Agca had never claimed anything of the sort, the ruling was not only gratuitous but singularly irrelevant. It did much for Mersan's stainless reputation all the same.

At the BKA in Wiesbaden the next winter, two senior officers had told me that "Mersan was very cooperative. He answered all questions readily. We considered his information to be true and reliable. All the indications were that his meeting with Agca was a chance encounter. . . . Mersan had committed no crime in Germany. To all appearances, he was a respectable businessman, free to do as he pleased and entitled to his privacy" (meaning that the press was not entitled to his address).[8]

In Munich, as I have noted earlier, Mersan was not to be found at the address I managed to dig up anyway; and by the time I got to the Vardar Company in Bayerstrasse 43, the firm was hurriedly going out of business. At the city's Polizei Praesidium, the police president's press secretary was unusually costive even as such press secretaries go. Was the Vardar Company owned by a Turk named Selam Gultas engaged in contraband? "Many Turkish companies in Germany are involved in contraband. . . . Unless they break the German law, that is the last thing we think about here." Had the local police investigated Vardar? "We investigate many such companies. If there are no results, we stop. We're not the Gestapo, you know."[9]

I was willing to overlook the unfortunate implication that the Gestapo might have been more efficient. The fact was, though, that the Munich police had only to use normal democratic channels—a routine police telex to Ankara, in this case—to learn what it ought to know about the Vardar Company.

A telex of that elementary kind would have elicited the information that the proprietor of Vardar, Selam Gultas, had been wanted by the Turkish police, as a member of Abuzer Ugurlu's band, *for a full year* before my call on Munich's Polizei Praesidium.

Indeed, the search warrant for Selam Gultas had been issued by the First Army Command in Istanbul on April 17, 1981[10]—well over a month before Omer Mersan was brought in for questioning on the papal shooting. To my knowledge, the Munich police sent no telexed queries to Turkey at all, about Mersan, Gultas, or the Vardar Company, during or after the twenty-four hours they held him.

I learned about this (and more) on returning to Turkey in the autumn of 1982. Most of that visit was devoted to finding out about the whole Turkish Mafia, starting with Abuzer Ugurlu.

The Godfather and his clan had been powerful enough to escape the clutches of the law repeatedly, under a succession of civilian governments. When the armed forces took over in September 1980, they were determined to get Abuzer Ugurlu, and did.

The official Turkish announcement said that he had "surrendered" on March 21, 1981. The Bulgarians later insisted that they had "delivered" him voluntarily (an assertion causing the starchiest of Turkish generals to look amused). According to my most reliable source in Interpol, Ugurlu had actually been snatched on Bulgarian soil by Turkish agents, and whisked home to face the music.

Upon his arrest (whatever the circumstances), Ugurlu told the Turkish press that he was just "a simple businessman working for Kintex."[11]

Though the generals had him at last, their troubles had just begun.

At his first trial in Istanbul, he was found guilty of bribing a former minister of customs with 10 million Turkish lire (about half a million dollars at the time). The ex-minister, Tuncay Mataraci, was sentenced to forty-three years, and Abuzer Ugurlu to two.

There followed parallel open and secret trials before Istanbul's military tribunal: the open trial was concerned with smuggled cigarettes, transistor radios, and the like; the secret trial, with arms and drugs.

Almost at once, both trials developed such glaring peculiarities that Turkey's ruling generals ordered a full investigation. They found their own military judiciary in Istanbul under heavy sedation, induced by massive bribes from the Ugurlu clan. Among others fired summarily was the chief military prosecutor of Istanbul, Judge-Colonel Suleyman Takkeci[12]—the very judge-colonel who had reared up and fled, never to return, when I'd asked him about Agca's trial for the murder of Abdi Ipekci. (That certainly told me something about how rigged the Ipekci trial must have been.)

The parallel trials of Abuzer Ugurlu and fifteen of his accomplices were thereupon moved to Ankara.

By pulling strings and sounding desperate (I *was* desperate), I got a copy of the twenty-two page, single-spaced indictment for their open trial.[13] Abuzer and his brother Mustafa headed the list of defendants. Among those being tried *in absentia*—they were living it up in Munich at the time—were Selam Gultas of the Vardar Company and his brother Bekir.

Nearly all the charges had to do with contraband shipments by TIR truck, of cigarettes and other consumer goods mostly provided by Kintex from 1974 to 1980. Here are a random few:

1974–1975	Ten TIR truckloads of cigarettes supplied by Kintex, smuggled into Turkey.
1976–1977	Eighteen TIR truckloads of cigarettes supplied by Kintex, smuggled into Turkey.
1977	One TIR truckload of electronic goods smuggled from Munich into Turkey, with Selam Gultas and Bekir Gultas.
1980	Two TIR truckloads of electronic goods provided by Selam Gultas and the Vardar Company, smuggled into Turkey. The necessary foreign currency for the deal was also supplied by Gultas.

All those big TIR trucks coming in full would hardly be going out empty. In fact, according to Ahmet Altan, chief of Istanbul's Narcotics Brigade, *thirteen tons* of heroin had left Turkey, heading westward via Bulgaria, in the single year of 1982.[14] But that involved another, darker side of Abuzer Ugurlu's activities, under study in a secret trial and unlikely to be made public. (Were the facts of

Bulgaria's malevolent role in this traffic to come to light, Turkey would be hard put to respond suitably, short of going to war.)

Reading the indictment, though, what jumped out of the page at me was the 1980 Vardar shipment. Actually, it had been made in June 1980, shortly after Agca's arrival in Sofia. Was that what brought Omer Mersan to Sofia around the same time, taking care of Vardar's business? I felt in my bones it must be so, though "Walter's" story proving it was still months away.

Just around the time I was discovering all this in Ankara, two valiant young German television reporters, Silvia Matthies and Beatrice ("Trixie") Sonnheuter, were hot on Mersan's trail in Munich.

For one thing, they had discovered that Omer Mersan and Turkish Mafia boss Bekir Celenk knew each other well—so well that Celenk's business partner, Atalay Saral, would not talk to them before consulting Mersan first.

Somehow—they were resourceful reporters—they had also found that Mersan's uncle, Rafet Mersan, worked for a different department of the Turkish Mafia (gambling casinos). Expelled from Munich on May 27, 1979, Rafet had turned up again in May 1981, with false papers.[15] He was arrested in Munich on *May 14, 1981*—the day after the Pope was shot, and a week before his nephew Omer was brought in for police questioning in the same city. By the time Omer did get picked up because of the DIGOS telex, his uncle Rafet had already appeared before a Munich court, and been expelled from the country again.

Did the Munich police look into Mersan's family background during those twenty-four hours they held him?

That was among the awkward questions put to the Munich state prosecutor by the two reporters from Bavarian television. Before going on the air, they had asked if he might not, perhaps, have closed the Mersan case "prematurely and unjustifiably." I have a copy of his telexed answer of October 14, 1982,[16] which said:

"It is inexact to say that the proceedings pending against Omer Mersan were closed prematurely and unjustifiably. They were based on the suspicion . . . *that Mersan had falsified a passport in Germany . . . and delivered it to Agca* [my italics, here and below]." (Again! And this more than a year after the first time!)

"The investigation was closed after the necessary inquiries were made, *with help from the Italian authorities, and naturally after looking into the circles Mersan moved in.* These suspicions could not be confirmed in any way. Thus there were no motives for not closing the case, and there are none to reopen it now."

By October 1982, the prosecutor's reply was altogether incomprehensible, since Mersan's own lawyer had demolished the prosecutor's argument in a Munich Court.

The lawyer had appeared before the court on September 22,[17] to get a restraining order against all German press references to Mersan in this case. He had revealed in the courtroom that Mersan had been brought face to face with Agca in Rome the previous July, by Judge Martella. Agca had declared *"that the petitioner [Mersan] did not procure a passport for him. Rather, he gave Mersan 3,000 Deutschmarks, in order that another Turk . . . would procure such a passport."*

Nothing daunted, the Munich state prosecutor's same ruling was repeated for a third time, on the following November 8.[18]

The press was stirring, the worms were coming out of the woodwork, the legend of an upright and unfairly harassed young businessman was showing signs of wear and tear, but the State Prosecutor's Office in Munich held fast. Its ruling on Mersan still stands.

At a later courtroom hearing, Mersan's lawyer actually named Selam Gultas as Mersan's character witness[19]—this while Gultas was on trial *in absentia* in Turkey, as a gangster whose Turkish Mafia boss had helped to mount and direct the most colossal international criminal conspiracy uncovered in our time.

The Munich court did not question Selam Gultas's credentials as a character witness. He too was still accepted there as a respectable businessman who, having closed Vardar down, promptly reopened it at the same old address as Yugo-Import.

When I told Gultas on his Munich office phone that I knew he was a wanted man in Turkey, he roared with laughter. When two French reporters dropped in to ask questions, he threatened to call the police and have them thrown off the premises.[20] Selam Gultas knew his rights.

So did Omer Mersan, who was given prime television time on West Germany's second channel in May 1983 to present himself—unchallenged—as an aggrieved and innocent party in the whole affair.[21]

Throughout the affair, Omer Mersan was in the files of Munich's Narcotics Squad as a major distributor of heroin in West Germany—had indeed been in its files *before* the affair began.

This information had been supplied to the Germans by the Swiss Narcotics Brigade of Zug, near Basel, after intensive investigation of a huge Turkish drug ring operating in Switzerland and West Germany. I have excerpts of three reports drawn up by the Swiss Police Brigade between December 12, 1980, and March 24, 1981.[22] They state:

"A Turkish contraband ring operating in the Munich region has been introducing drugs into Germany and Switzerland since the spring of 1980. It uses the following methods:

"In Munich, trucking transport is arranged for various contraband goods (cigarettes, radios, TV sets, cocoa). These TIR trucks leave Munich under international seal (for Yugoslavia and Turkey). . . . But after reaching Bulgaria, the TIR carnet is canceled. The driver delivers his truck to others in the organization, and waits two or three days in a hotel, while the contraband is unloaded. . . . For the return trip, drugs are concealed in the truck . . . and the driver returns to Switzerland or Munich. The trip there and back always passes through Sofia. . . .

"The Vardar Company is the intermediary for contraband shipments to Turkey [along with Continentale Storage, also in the Gultas family]. . . . Those directing the operation are Chavit Gultas [reportedly Selam's son] and a certain Omer, whose telephone number is 00-49-89-6923689 [that was and is Omer Mersan's home number in Munich].

"The drivers bringing back the heroin know they are working for Mr. Gultas. . . . According to our witnesses, Chavit and Omer orchestrate all the drug traffic. Omer takes care of the distribution in particular. Both can be found through the Vardar Company. . . .

"The Narcotics Brigade in Zug is presently conducting a vast investigation in this direction. Its functionaries have gone to Munich to establish close liaison with the Narcotics Brigade there."

I know the identities of several truck drivers accepted as credible witnesses by the Swiss police. One was the "Walter" who told *L'Alsace* and *Le Matin* the amazing story of his journey with Omer Mersan from Vardar in Munich to the Hotel Vitosha in Sofia, all expenses paid by Kintex.

Interviewed by a *Reader's Digest* colleague of mine shortly after his story was published on March 17, 1983, "Walter" confirmed the whole account, showed the proper dates in his passport, and identified Omer Mersan's photograph.

I don't know whether the Munich Narcotics Brigade ever looked up Chavit and Omer, ever checked on the Vardar Company's TIR trucks passing through Munich customs, ever passed on the information from the Swiss police to Munich's Polizei Praesidium or the Federal Bundeskriminalamt—or ever gave a thought to the possibility that such information on a celebrated witness in the papal shooting case might have helped a judge whose search for the truth was of worldwide concern. (If they did give it a thought, they did not pass the word to the judge.)

Neither do I know whether the U.S. Drug Enforcement Administration (DEA) might have passed on related information of its own, either to its opposite numbers in Germany or to the Italian judge. But the DEA's information clinched the case on Mersan.

Omer Mersan had been known to the DEA in Washington since December 1981 as "a heroin-trafficker and associate of Ali Agca." It was also known to the DEA that Mersan had purchased 5.5 kilos of pure heroin in May 1982, which were subsequently seized in Istanbul on November 5, 1982. On a tip to that effect from a European source, I called the DEA on September 1, 1983, and put it to them in those words. Could they confirm or deny it? The answer was yes, they could confirm it.

One last link had still to be proved, in the interlocking chain leading, as I now knew, from Agca to Omer Mersan to Mr. Terzieff of Kintex and the Bulgarian secret service, by way of Mersan's boss in the Turkish Mafia—Abuzer Ugurlu. Could I be sure that Ugurlu himself was an enlisted agent of the Bulgarian secret service, as I'd learned from the file of that U.S. intelligence agency? After my last visit to Ankara, I could.

At the Martial Law Command in Ankara's Mamak Prison compound, a committee of amiable generals had spent a morning on my last visit telling me as little as possible about the Ugurlu trial (the Turks can be close with their information too). Before I left, though, they conceded that Abuzer had "very probably" been recruited into the Bulgarian DS in the early seventies. Enriched by Kintex since he'd moved to Sofia in the mid-sixties, they observed, he could hardly have done otherwise.

My most reliable source at Interpol did better. I put it to him that Ugurlu was said by a Western agency to have been recruited by the Bulgarian DS around 1974. Was it true? He laid a large hand over his heart. "You have my oath on it," he said. "It's true."

And Bekir Celenk? Did they sign him up as well? "Even before Ugurlu. Long before Ugurlu! It's true."

There ended my pursuit.

I'm sure Judge Martella got there his own way. But what a long and hard way it must have been! The Turks did not tell him everything they knew about the Turkish Mafia, Bekir Celenk, and Abuzer Ugurlu. The U.S. intelligence agency did not tell him about that file of theirs on the same subject. The German authorities never corrected the only image of Omer Mersan that Judge Martella had to go on—an image as shockingly wrongheaded as it was misleading and deceptive. The list could go on.

This was doubtless what that unnamed U.S. intelligence spokesman meant when he said that the investigation into the papal shooting was "an Italian matter, and it would be inappropriate for us to intrude."

"Inappropriate" was an odd word to use in that context. Might he not more appropriately have said "inexpedient," or perhaps "inconvenient"?

17

The ultimate enigma remains the posture of the Western world toward the conspiracy to murder Pope John Paul II. No adequate explanations have yet been found. Frankly, I doubt that they will be.

There is probably no single explanation. The simplest, I think, starts with the fact that Yuri Andropov came to power in Soviet Russia just when the Bulgarian Connection came to light in Rome.

As was only to be expected, there were those who refused to believe this could be a coincidence. "Why would the Bulgarian—meaning the Soviet—Connection take on renewed vigor after eighteen months of investigation?" demanded *Le Monde* a week after Judge Martella ordered the arrest of three Bulgarian suspects that November. "Could Andropov's succession to the Soviet leadership be considered extraneous to this affair?"[1]

Of course it was extraneous. The implication was that somebody had contrived to plant last-minute evidence on Judge Martella, roping him into a plot to bring about the new Soviet leader's downfall. But the judge had had the primary evidence in his hands since Agca began to confess on May 1, 1982, when Andropov still headed the KGB. Brezhnev was still alive, with Andropov about tenth in line to succeed him, while Judge Martella was preparing the Bulgarians' arrest warrants. He had asked the foreign minister about their diplomatic immunity on November 11, the day after Brezhnev died. Nobody could have rigged that whole judicial process in the expectation of making life hell for a man who hadn't yet made it to the Kremlin.

In spite of its strong bias, *Le Monde*'s effort to shield Andropov did him a world of good. To the freshly minted image of Andropov the art lover, jazz buff, swinger, innovator, and reformer, was now added the image of an Andropov fighting off his implacable enemies, the paleo-apparatchiks clinging to power since Stalin's day. In this guise, he appealed discreetly for Western understanding and forbearance.

At NATO's winter meeting in Brussels that December, an East European editor drew a veteran American reporter aside for a confidential chat. He revealed that Andropov considered the Russian economy to be in "catastrophic shape"; that he wanted to shift talented Soviet military personnel to the economy and give priority to settling the Afghanistan crisis; that he was "not yet strong enough to make any bold conciliatory gestures to the West"; and that he needed at least two years "to get all these things moving," during which he "hoped for a period of international calm."[2]

It was as self-serving a tale as might be expected from a man who had made an art of *Dezinformatsiya* during his fifteen years at the KGB. (He spoke of this art as "peaceful edification in a complex international situation.")[3] Yet even as the assembled NATO delegates professed themselves "skeptical," they longed to believe it. Two years of grace was all he asked to get a sure hold on his country—this promising innovator and reformer who might then sit down with the West at last to mend the tattered remnants of détente. Was that asking too much?

The old Andropov known to Western leaders in all those preceding years was somehow forgotten: the model of gray conformity who had not once in his life deviated from the party line; who had institutionalized state terrorism at home and nursed an international terror network abroad; who had set up a special KGB department— the Fifth Directorate—to silence dissidents, hound Jews, and persecute religious believers; who as head of the KGB had concentrated in his own hands all control over the espionage, counterespionage, and security police forces of the entire Soviet empire and built the most formidable secret police force the world has ever seen.

Whatever the old Andropov might have done—those "naughty

things" the KGB does that Vice-President Bush spoke of—it was the new Andropov who had to be saved.

Thus the papal conspiracy (not the fact, but its disclosure) spread consternation through inner Western circles. As a diplomatic and political imperative, Andropov must be *seen* to be innocent. But who, then, must be seen to be guilty?

A seeming profusion of choices really narrowed down to one.

True, some effort was made to put the blame on Bulgarian cowboys in the DS, playing a reckless game without telling their superiors. For a while, even Andropov seemed to lean toward this face-saving solution. By late May 1983, the Russians were reported to have shown "unusually visible signs of anger with the Bulgarians," when *Pravda* announced that a KGB mission headed by its new chief, Viktor Chebrikov, had descended upon Sofia for talks with its Bulgarian subalterns.

"Veteran diplomats," wrote the *Los Angeles Times*'s Robert Toth, ". . . could remember no Soviet news account in recent times that a KGB leader traveled abroad to confer with foreign officials. There was speculation in Washington that the visit was related to embarrassing ties found by Italian investigators between the Bulgarian intelligence service and Mehmet Ali Agca."[4]

Yet even as the Russians appeared to be conceding such ties, the United States was evidently ruling them out for good. It was in the same article of Toth's that the director of the CIA and the U.S. President's national security adviser both were quoted as saying that they no longer believed in the Bulgarian Connection.

That hardly left the Western public much choice.

If not even the Bulgarians, let alone the Russians, had conspired to murder the Pope, then the hit man in the plot was telling immensely complicated lies—lies that fit enough of the ascertainable facts to convince Italian judges, state prosecutors, several different courts, and the Ministry of Justice. That at once ruled out any of a dozen alternative theories on the plot, none of which could explain how Agca would know what to say.

The only plausible explanation was the one propagated all along by the East, in sentimental symbiosis with unnamed spokesmen for the West: that Agca was being coached in prison by the Italians, on behalf of or in connivance with the Americans, to frame the Bulgarians and, thus, the Russians.

The theory had its attractions for a multitude of Westerners who could not bring themselves to believe in the Russians' guilt. Evidently they could more easily bring themselves to believe in the Italians' and Americans' guilt. But where—into what impenetrable thickets of contradiction and confusion—would that lead them?

It was not impossible, theoretically, for the Italian secret services to get to Agca. In the summer of 1981, in the same maximum-security prison at Ascoli-Piceno, they had gotten to the king of Neapolitan gangland, Raffaele Cutolo of the New Camorra, and persuaded him to negotiate for the release of a Christian Democratic politician kidnapped by the Red Brigades.

In the spring of 1983, a neat example turned up showing how—in theory again—they might have done the same with Agca. Some eight hundred of Cutolo's men were rounded up at one fell swoop, among them the prison chaplain at Ascoli-Piceno, Father Mariano Santini, who turned out to be the gang's in-house messenger. Apart from Agca's prison guards in solitary confinement, Father Santini was the only man who visited his cell regularly, as he had every right to do. He was even said to have talked Agca into confessing, that May.

The chaplain may well have carried messages to Agca from Cutolo. Probably the boldest, slyest, and most resourceful figure in Italy's criminal underworld, Cutolo was notorious for his efforts to make his home his castle while in prison, achieving an ever higher standard of living there by one inventive means or another. By all reliable accounts (the most reliable was told to me in confidence by one of Italy's most widely respected judges) Cutolo had in fact tried to frighten the life out of Agca—precisely in order to make him confess *the truth*, on the assumption that a grateful government would thereupon fall on Cutolo's neck and ply him with favors. (It didn't. Cutolo was banished to Italy's bleakest island prison, Asinara, in April 1982, a good month before Agca uttered the first word of his confession.)

Though certainly not for want of trying, no proof of other mysterious visitors was ever found. Had there been the smallest sign of one—the slightest evidence that somebody was suborning the star witness—lawyers Consolo and Larussa would have had their client Sergei Antonov out of jail in a twinkle.

Supposing somebody did get in to see Agca regularly anyway. Just what would he be there for? To show Agca photos of the three Bulgarians, to make him memorize their unlisted phone numbers (one or two of which were in his pocket when he shot the Pope anyway), to jot down the measurements and decorations in their apartments (making a few mistakes here and there)? But that would barely be skimming the surface, compared to what Agca himself and others already knew.

A mass of information on the young man from Malatya had been gathered since he made his dramatic entrance in St. Peter's Square. He had not "come from nowhere," as Judge Santiapichi's court noted at the start. Witnesses had come forward, records were at hand, accomplices had been traced, all showing how he had made his way out of an Istanbul prison, had his false passports arranged by Abuzer Ugurlu, spent his summer in Sofia, met Omer Mersan and Bekir Celenk in Sofia, conferred with Musa Cerdar Celebi, Oral Celik, Omer Bagci, and others in Zurich and Milan, moved from one Gray Wolf safe house to another in Europe.

Every one of the people involved in getting him from Istanbul to Rome had operated in Bulgaria, as Judge Martella himself pointed out ("All those indicated as having participated in the criminal plan," was how he put it).[5]

Furthermore, there was now a wealth of evidence proving that Agca did not come to Rome with the single-minded purpose of shooting the Pope. He had come to be at the disposal of a Bulgarian spy ring that had been operating in Rome for years, a ring headed by Ivan Tomov Dontchev.

Two judges responsible respectively for investigating this Bulgarian spy ring and the papal conspiracy—Imposimato and Martella—had spent months examining the evidence that Agca was assigned by Dontchev to assassinate Lech Walesa in January 1981. The evidence was overwhelming. Agca's description of Dontchev dovetailed perfectly with that of Luigi Scricciolo, an agent on Dontchev's payroll for years. Agca had noticed house painters doing up some of the rooms at the Hotel Victoria before Walesa moved in there, something nobody else had noted, which turned out to be true. The account Agca gave to judges Imposimato and Martella of Walesa's hour-by-hour arrangements in Rome was more accurate' than the report on Walesa's visit prepared by SISMI itself.

And that connection to the Lech Walesa plot changed everything.

•   •

It had been clear from Agca's earliest interrogations in Rome that he was in fact a professional hit man, thoroughly familiar with the workings of a spy ring like Dontchev's. In its Statement of Motivation, Judge Santiapichi's court had written: "Agca had shown himself to possess an adequate knowledge of a composite phenomenon, of specific facts and intimate mechanisms, which he could not have had without somehow being involved in a criminal undertaking . . . on closely familiar terms with the interested parties."

Two years of investigation had now established that Agca had in fact come to Rome as a professional hit man, hired by a Bulgarian spy ring to serve as the occasion arose. Lech Walesa today, Pope John Paul tomorrow. The two cases were inseparable, the logic inescapable.

Yet Western leaders had implicitly decreed that it must not be so. The implications were tremendous. It was no longer enough to go along with the comfortable theory that a couple of right-wing Italian agents were giving the CIA a hand, by slipping Agca some lines to learn by heart. If the Bulgarians didn't hire Agca and send him to Rome—to kill both Lech Walesa and John Paul—who did? Who else, if not the Western agents suspected by unnamed European analysts (according to *The New York Times*) of planting "disinformation" on Judge Martella, to embarrass the Russians?

In that event, the CIA would have been not only feeding Agca his lines in prison, but running him from start to finish.

To do so, the CIA would have had to get Agca from Istanbul's Kartal-Maltepe prison to St. Peter's Square, inserting him meanwhile into a Bulgarian spy ring in Rome, *using all the personnel, facilities, and mechanisms controlled by the Bulgarian secret service.*

It would take another book to do justice to an intelligence service that could pull this off.

With all due respect, I don't think the CIA could have done it. Nor do I believe for a moment that it would have wanted to. I cannot imagine even the hawkish administration of President Reagan setting out to assassinate the head of the Roman Catholic Church— not to mention the head of Solidarity in Poland—merely to cause the Kremlin momentary discomfort. It is doubly difficult to see the CIA haring off on this adventure under President Carter, still in office when the Agca operation got under way in 1979.

It is altogether impossible to conceive of any Italian government I have reported on in the past quarter of a century having anything whatever to do with such a scheme.

The efforts of Western spokesmen to encourage just that public belief—for that is what it comes to—defy understanding. Not all the spokesmen were unnamed, and none could have gone on saying what they did for so long without clearance from above, in the United States particularly. By the time William Casey and William Clark stood up to be counted, this had to be national policy coming straight from the top.

I don't know how to account for that.

Perhaps Western leaders did think it was worth buying time for Yuri Andropov, although they might have done him a better turn by persuading the worldwide public that he could never have made the tremendous decision on his own. Only the late Leonid Brezhnev could have done that.

Maybe this was only part of the larger explanation that has grown so familiar over the last decade or so—the perpetual disinclination of Western leaders to confront the Russians with their darker sins. But even that did not seem to me a good enough reason for the concealment, evasion, inertia, and disinformation—unfortunately the only word for it—going into this monumental cover-up.

There was something here beyond the layman's comprehension, I felt, for which any number of exotic explanations have been offered. I include a few here, if only to suggest the climate of uncertainty and disbelief of official "statements" in which explanations of this sort are bound to flourish.

Some, for example, say that superpower intelligence agencies like the CIA and the KGB really do behave the way John Le Carré says they do, covering for each other in the implicit understanding that the favor will be returned someday.

Others feel that there must be some tie-in to the colossal arms-drug trade now known to be operating from Turkey and Bulgaria to all of Western Europe. Judicial investigations in both Italy and France have revealed that practically all intelligence services—Western and Eastern—have had shady dealings of some sort with this network: perhaps to secure weapons for covert operations unknown even to their own governments, or to pick up money for operations they cannot otherwise finance, or simply—for corrupt agents here and there—to make a fast buck. For any or all of these reasons, this explanation argues, the network must not be exposed.

Still others suggest that the CIA, possibly along with other West European secret services, might have been using the Turkish Mafia's arms-drug route to smuggle their own agents, couriers, and logistics supplies to and from Turkey and the Middle East. So, again, the network must not be exposed.

Several "in" people hint that maybe the Russians could have

latched on to such unspeakable American secrets that they have blackmailed Washington into silence, if not active compliance. (If this were true, however, it would hardly explain the similar silence amounting to complicity on the part of so many other Western states.)

Or else Andropov may simply have told the West that it could forget about nuclear disarmament and a Cruise/Pershing missile settlement unless and until its dogs were called off on the papal plot. (Not that doing so has made any discernible difference to East-West arms negotiations.)

My own feeling—and it has grown on me strongly toward the last—is that the likeliest explanation is the least sinister and the most depressingly bureaucratic: that the CIA was not instructed to follow the case, did not follow it, and in the beginning did not know what it was all about. Then it did not want to admit that it did not know what the case was all about, and felt the need to defend itself by insisting that other authorities in a position to know better had to be wrong.

•   •

Judge Martella is expected to close the investigation by the end of 1983. The *segreto istruttorio* will be lifted at last. His report to the Prosecutor-General's office will then be released to the public. It will contain everything he has been able to learn about the plot against the Pope—and against Lech Walesa as well—justifying the arrests he has made and the judicial decisions upholding them to the end.

Even so, and in spite of the judge's report, doubtless some will continue to defend their positions for years to come, no matter how much the evidence weighs against them: stories like this never end.

We can look forward confidently, and dishearteningly, to further outpourings of disinformation, distortion, and misinterpretation; to the curiously persistent reluctance of the West to accept the Bulgarian Connection; even to attempts to rescue from the dustheap of history the image of Agca the mad, fanatic, solitary would-be assassin.

Already there are signs of this next phase setting in. Just as I was completing this book, the Western press seized upon a minor judicial move by Judge Martella to announce that the Bulgarian Connection, if it ever lived, could now safely be pronounced dead.

The judge issued a judicial communication to Agca, indicating that Agca had libeled Sergei Antonov, the Bulgarian prisoner, in regard to a single and minor incident in this story. Martella's move, reported by the Italian news agency Ansa, became worldwide front-page news before any reporter took the trouble to ascertain the nature of Agca's libel. The thrust of these initial dispatches was that the entire case against Antonov had fallen apart.

On the following day, September 30, 1983, Italy's most authoritative daily, *Corriere della Sera*, drawing upon fact rather than rumor, brought the incident dramatically down in scale: "The judicial communication to Agca has created a lot of noise about very little. It had nothing to do with the investigation into the papal shooting. It regarded the investigation into the planned assassination of Lech Walesa. . . . The 'Antonov Case' remains unchanged. The Ministry of Justice has flatly denied 'the collapse of the Bulgarian Connection'. . . . Agca is said to have lied about a certain particular regarding Antonov in the Lech Walesa case. . . . This and nothing else is 'the specific episode' referred to.

"And the rest? The meetings, inspections of premises, topographical studies, choice of possible sites to kill Walesa? None of that has changed. . . . Generally speaking, nothing in the entire picture has changed."

•   •

Enigmas become the concern of soothsayers and oracles, and their contemporary counterparts, explaining the inexplicable. I have been content to write on a less exalted plane. The reporting, the deductions, the conclusions, the mistakes I may have made, are my own. I am willing to let the record gathered here speak for itself.

N O T E S

PROLOGUE: A WALL OF MIRRORS

CHAPTER 1

1. *Il Giornale Nuovo* (Milan), January 6, 1983, dispatch from London.
2. *The New York Times*, December 18, 1982.
3. As quoted in ibid., December 27, 1982, column by William Safire.
4. *Newsweek*, May 25, 1981.
5. *Washington Post*, May 19, 1981.
6. *Corriere della Sera* (Milan), July 23, 1981.
7. *The New York Times*, February 8, 1983.
8. The speech to the Swiss Guards is reported in *Il Giornale Nuovo*, July 31, 1981. For the warning from the French, see *Le Quotidien de Paris*, December 18, 1982; this report says that Count Alexandre de Marenche, then the head of SDECE, sent "a general and a colonel" to the Vatican on April 20, 1981, to warn the Pope of an impending attack.
9. *Osservatore Romano* (Rome), July 22, 1981.
10. As quoted in *Il Giornale Nuovo*, July 31, 1981.
11. *La Stampa* (Turin), August 1, 1981 (Cardinal Casaroli's speech was made at mass at St. Peter's and Paul's on June 29, 1981); *Il Giornale Nuovo*, July 31, 1981.
12. "In latere": a judge who sits at the side of the presiding judge in the trial and shares in judicial decisions.

13. Statement of Motivation, p. 44.
14. *Los Angeles Times,* January 31, 1982.
15. Statement of Motivation.

PART ONE: DISCOVERING THE PLOT

CHAPTER 2

1. Statement of Motivation, p. 32.
2. Ibid., p. 7.
3. Ibid., p. 33.
4. Ibid., p. 7.
5. Ibid., p. 11.
6. Ibid., p. 34.
7. Ibid., p. 13.
8. Ibid., p. 8. The Hotel Archimede's report to the police indicated that Agca had remained there only until January 11. Because of a widespread practice designed to dodge taxes, Roman hotels often cut off these dates, keeping guests on their own registers for longer periods. Judy Harris checked the Archimede's register personally, and saw that Agca had continued to stay there until January 17.
9. Statement of Motivation, p. 15.
10. Ibid., p. 13.
11. Ibid., p. 14.
12. Ibid., p. 4.
13. The estimate of $50,000 for traveling expenses was given to me by DIGOS.

CHAPTER 3

1. Manyan got the original Agca interrogations, spotted the importance of his Bulgarian summer, spoke of a big smuggling ring, and chased down Omer Mersan in Munich.
2. SISMI report no. 13569/1/04, May 25, 1981.
3. See chapter 15 in Claire Sterling, *The Terror Network* (New York: Holt, Rinehart and Winston, 1981); Colonel Stefan Sverdlev's interview in *Libération* (Paris), December 11–12, 1983; Colonel X.'s interview in *Le Quotidien de Paris*, January 24, 25, 26, 1983; and the SISMI report to the Parliamentary Moro Commission, published by *La Nazione* (Florence), May 22, 1983.
4. Document A, court records.
5. DIGOS report no. 051195/81, May 27, 1981.
6. DIGOS report signed by Chief Commissioner Lidano Marchionne, June 24, 1981.
7. I have a copy of this composite drawing; it was circulated by DIGOS on May 25, 1981, as a Rome circular to International Police.
8. DIGOS report signed by Chief Commissioner Lidano Marchionne, June 26, 1981.

9. Report by SISMI (date illegible on photocopy).
10. Statement of Motivation, pp. 8–9.
11. SISMI report no. 13569/1/04, May 25, 1981.
12. Ibid.
13. DIGOS to Bundeskriminalamt, May 21, 1981, telex no. HR 63/81, 24/16349/1 Div. "Mersal" was, of course, an error in the original.
14. BKA reply, "Urgentissimo," to DIGOS telex, May 22, 1981, telex no. TC/Z 120504/81/68.
15. Agca made no reference at any time to whoever actually delivered his Faruk Ozgun passport.

CHAPTER 4

1. *Hurriyet* (Istanbul), July 4, 1981. The official announcement was from the General Staff Headquarters Coordination Center, Turkish Army.
2. The Special Branch in Hamburg told me that the Interpol arrest warrant for Omer Ay was received in Wiesbaden on February 13, 1982. See also p. 65.
3. Cihan Aytul, editor of *Milliyet* (Istanbul), told me this; it was confirmed by Nahir Erman.
4. The name of the Gray Wolves comes from the legend of Bozkurt, a gray wolf who saved the original ancestors of modern Turkey during their migration from central Asia. The Turks were caught in an "iron mountain" when a gray wolf appeared with a burning torch clenched in its jaws. The Turks used the torch to melt the mount and escape, with Bozkurt supposedly leading them to safety in what is now Turkey. This account is given in the *Washington Post*, July 3, 1983.
5. Agca to Martial Law Court, October 12, 1979.
6. *Terçuman* (Istanbul), October 25, 1979.

CHAPTER 5

1. The first visit was January 5, 1982; the second, March 3, 1982.
2. As published in Ugur Mumcu's *Arms Smuggling and Terrorism*.
3. The warrant was issued by Interpol Paris, November 1979. Topuz is listed as an "accomplice" of Ugurlu's, subject of Red Notice 7961/79 A-275/1979. Abuzer Ugurlu's arrest warrant is numbered 1 GS 1905/79, issued July 19, 1979, by the authorities of Würzburg, Federal (West) Germany, for violation of drug laws.
4. I have a copy of this letter, originally published by Mumcu in his *Arms Smuggling and Terrorism*, pp. 50–60.
5. Turkish Embassy in Bonn, report for the last half of 1982.
6. Turkish Consular Services, Ankara.
7. His sentencing was on October 1, 1980, by the Martial Law Supreme Court.
8. See Chapter 16.
9. Special Branch, Hamburg.
10. Ibid.

11. *Milliyet* (Istanbul), June 19, 1982, citing the Konya Martial Law Court arrest order for Omer Ay.
12. I have a copy of this letter, which is dated May 10, 1982.

CHAPTER 6

1. The item was carried in *La Repubblica* (Rome), November 26, 1981. The letter, although it was a photocopy, and undated, pronounced authentic by the court, was introduced as "irrefutable proof of Agca's ties to Colonel Türkes."
2. *Corriere della Sera* (Milan), August 8, 1981, citing Baum's formal statement of August 7.
3. This document describes several meetings, in Damascus and Istanbul, between a certain Badatioglu of Dev-Sol and PLO representative Sayed Haliton. The first took place on May 2, 1979. A second meeting lasting ten days was held in Damascus in February 1980. A third meeting followed in December 1981.
4. Statement of the Martial Law Coordinator's Office, Turkish General Staff.
5. This witness was Hoca Koçyiğit, who gave lengthy testimony at the Türkes trial in the autumn of 1982. He claimed to have served as a MIT informer and provocateur in the Türkes National Action Party.
6. *Corriere della Sera*, May 16, 1981.
7. *Cumhuriyet* (Ankara), September 11, 1982, column by Ugur Mumcu.

CHAPTER 7

1. His letter was sent to Ugur Mumcu in 1979. Mumcu published it in *Cumhuriyet* (Ankara) March 2 and 3, 1982.
2. Ugur Mumcu told me this.
3. Mumcu describes the entire Topuz episode in his book *Arms Smuggling and Terrorism*, pp. 50–60.
4. *Avanti!* (Rome), January 20, 1983.
5. *Newsday*'s team was made up of Robert Greene, Knut Royce, and Les Paynes, who deserve warm praise for a terrific reporting job. See also *The Heroin Trail* (New York: Holt, Rinehart and Winston, 1975), pp. 51–61.
6. My source at Interpol in Ankara has proved repeatedly to be reliable.
7. *Hurriyet* (Istanbul), November 17, 1981.
8. Mumcu's *Cumhuriyet* story was reproduced in his book *Arms Smuggling and Terrorism*, p. 58.
9. *Anarchy and Terror in Turkey*, published by the Turkish General Staff, p. 77ff.
10. I was told this by my own police sources. The *Wall Street Journal*'s correspondent in Turkey, Metin Demirsan, reported similar information on December 20, 1982: "Mr. Celik is believed by the Turkish police to have been on the payrolls of both Mr. Celenk and a right-

wing terrorist organization. He is thought by police here to have helped Agca escape to Bulgaria from a Turkish prison."

11. Interview with NBC in preparation for Marvin Kalb's White Paper. I have the full text of this interview, only part of which appeared on the program.

PART TWO: PUBLISHING THE PLOT, DISTURBING THE PEACE

CHAPTER 8

1. Turkish Consulate, Rome.
2. The Hotel Vitosha–New Otani charges $100 a night. See *Corriere della Sera* (Milan), December 20, 1983; *Paris-Match*, January 14, 1983.
3. Ibid.
4. *Paris-Match*, January 14, 1983.
5. An Italian reporter returning from the Sofia press conference of December 17, 1982, told this to Judy Harris, who was on special assignment for NBC to cover the papal shooting story.
6. SISMI report on Grillmayer, May 25, 1981.
7. Interview with Mr. Celikov, Turkish Consular Services, Ankara.
8. Interview with Ilderen Türkmen, Ministry of Justice, Ankara.
9. Orsan Oymen's series appeared in *Milliyet* (Istanbul), July 11, 12, 13, 14, 1982.

CHAPTER 9

1. *Polimya*, March 1981.
2. *Soviet Analyst*, vol. 8, no. 13, June 28, 1979, p. 7.
3. *The New York Times*, March 23, 1983.
4. The CIA called this "third-rate hearsay" in *Newsweek*, April 4, 1983. On April 7, 1983, the *Washington Post* said: "Privately, U.S. intelligence officials put no credence in the source [Mantarov]."
5. Alex Alexiev, "The Kremlin and the Pope," April 1983 report for the Rand Corporation. Most of the Soviet sources quoted here are from this admirable report.
6. *Washington Post*, June 4, 1979.
7. Ibid., June 3, 1979.
8. *Soviet Analyst*, vol. 8, no. 13, June 28, 1979.
9. As quoted in *Avanti!* (Rome), December 30, 1982.
10. *Chronicle of the Lithuanian Catholic Church*, no. 44, July 30, 1980.
11. *L'Espresso* (Rome), May 8, 1983; *Corriere della Sera* (Milan), May 12, 1983.
12. *Komunist* (Vilnius), no. 11, November 1981.
13. *Die Presse* (Vienna), January 19, 1983.
14. As quoted in *Corriere della Sera* December 31, 1982; *La Repubblica* (Rome), December 30, 1982.

15. NBC White Paper, "The Man Who Shot the Pope," September 23, 1982.
16. *Time*, September 27, 1982.
17. The ABC documentary was broadcast on May 10, 1983.
18. In an Associated Press dispatch on December 12, 1982, Reverend Romeo Pancirolo is quoted as saying, "The Church did use diplomatic channels to let the Soviet Union know about the Holy See's 'firm determination' regarding increasing tensions . . . in Poland." He avoided mentioning a letter.
19. Neal Ascherson, *The Polish August* (New York: Viking Press, 1982), p. 223.
20. Press office of the *Polish Episcopal Bulletin*, no. 19/81/661, Warsaw, May 4–10, 1981. This source was supplied by Michael Ledeen, who probably has the only copy extant in the West.
21. *Newsweek*, June 20, 1983.
22. Ronald Segal, *Leon Trotsky* (New York: Pantheon, 1979), p. 402. As Jacques Mornard, alias Jacson—his true identity of Ramón Mercador was not discovered until 1950—he was "brought to trial [in Mexico] in the spring of 1942 and sentenced a year later to twenty years in jail. His mother, Caridad, received from Stalin the Order of Lenin for herself," and, on behalf of her absent son, the Order of "Hero of the Soviet Union."
23. *The Columbia Encyclopedia*, third ed. (New York: Columbia University Press, 1963).
24. John Barron, *KGB* (New York: Reader's Digest Press, 1974), p. 319.
25. John Barron, *KGB Today: The Hidden Hand* (New York: Reader's Digest Press, 1983), p. 15.
26. The Bulgarian ambassador's press conference was held in Washington, D.C., on July 6, 1983, at the Kennan Institute for Advanced Russian Studies of the Smithsonian Institution.
27. Ascherson, *The Polish August*, p. 262.
28. Ibid., p. 223.
29. Ibid., p. 225.
30. *Il Messaggero* (Rome), January 16, 1981.
31. Ibid., January 18, 1981.
32. NBC White Paper, "The Man Who Shot the Pope," September 23, 1982.
33. Ascherson, *The Polish August*, p. 264.
34. Ibid., p. 265.
35. *La Repubblica*, May 29, 1981; *Il Giornale Nuovo* (Milan), July 31, 1981; *La Stampa* (Turin), January 7, 1983.

CHAPTER **10**

1. As quoted in *The New York Times*, August 19, 1982.
2. *Dossier on the Anatomy of a Calumny*, pp. 12–13, Italian version. This was prepared by BTA, the Bulgarian state news agency, reviewing the early developments in the Bulgarian Connection.
3. Ibid., p. 17.

4. As quoted in *The New York Times*, September 23, 1982.
5. *Rabotnichesko Delo*, September 8, 1982, pp. 2, 4.
6. Assorted Bulgarian citations from *Covert Action Bulletin*, no. 18, Winter 1983, p. 13.
7. *Bulgaria*, state bulletin in English, December 14, 1982, pp. C1, C2.
8. Wilfred Burchett in *Otecestvo*, no. 3, 1983.
9. *Rabotnichesko Delo*, September 8, 1982, p. 4, as quoted in *Anatomy of a Calumny*.
10. *The New York Times*, December 18, 1982.
11. *Il Giornale Nuovo* (Milan), January 6, 1983, dispatch from London.
12. *The New York Times*, December 27, 1982, column by William Safire.
13. Defense Minister Lagorio told me this, in describing his meeting with the *New York Times* editors in New York, during his visit to the United States, January 14–24, 1983. Nicholas Gage confirmed to me that the *Times* had been informed of the CIA's view on this point by the CIA itself.
14. *Time*, September 27, 1982.
15. SISMI report to the Parliamentary Moro Commission, published in full by *La Nazione* (Florence), May 22, 1983.
16. Cited in Michael Ledeen, "The Bulgarian Connection and the Media," *Commentary*, June 1983; also cited by Geoffrey Hart, King Features Syndicate, July 17, 1983.

CHAPTER **11**

1. Combined reports from *Newsweek*, July 9, 1983; *The New York Times*, July 9, 1983; all Italian dailies; and my own viewing of RAI-TV (Italian television). By "Kolev," Agca was referring to Major Želio Kolev Vasilev.
2. All Italian papers, November 25, 1982.
3. Judge Carlo Palermo's warrant, December 22, 1982.
4. Quoted by Justice Minister Clelio Darida in the Parliamentary debate of December 20, 1982.
5. Ibid.
6. Scricciolo's earliest confession was reported in the Italian press in July 1982. I reported it in the *Wall Street Journal* that August.
7. Antonio Savasta, as reported in *La Repubblica* (Rome), May 19, 1982, *Corriere della Sera* (Milan), March 10, 1982. Savasta, who headed the Red Brigades team holding General Dozier, testified to this during his trial, as did his companion Emilia Libera. Minister of Interior Rognoni, speaking in the Parliamentary debate of December 20, 1982, spoke of "the Red Brigades possibly acting for purposes of espionage" in this connection.
8. *La Repubblica*, March 1, 1983; *Il Giornale Nuovo* (Milan), January 6, 1983. Scricciolo's lawyers have also said this in confidence to several reporters.
9. *La Repubblica*, December 16, 1982, and March 15, 1983.
10. See *n.* 8 to Chapter 2, above. See also *Il Giornale Nuovo*, January 5, 1983.

11. Judge Martella to *Il Messaggero* (Rome), December 16 and 17, 1982.
12. *Corriere della Sera*, November 26, 1982.
13. *Herald Tribune* (Paris), November 27, 1982; *Corriere della Sera*, November 28, 1982; and Ansa (Italian news agency), November 26, 1982.
14. *Corriere della Sera*, November 26, 1982.
15. Combined reports of *La Nazione* (Florence), December 3, 9, 1982; *La Repubblica*, November 27 and December 3, 1982; *Corriere della Sera*, November 26, 28, 1982; *L'Adige* (Trento), December 12, 1982; *Il Messaggero*, November 28 and December 5, 1982; Ansa, November 26, 1982; *Avanti!* (Rome), December 4, 1982; and *Il Giornale Nuovo*, January 20, 1983.
16. *L'Adige*, December 12, 1983.
17. *Corriere della Sera*, December 7, 1982, reported: "Agca claimed they settled the final details of the plan at Antonov's house, which he described in detail, including furniture, objects, and so on." *La Nazione*, December 9, 1982, reported: "Agca described the interiors of both the Aivazov and Antonov apartments."
18. *La Repubblica*, December 3, 1982, reported: "One of the numerous particulars provided by Agca that convinced Martella was the private and unlisted phone number of Antonov, which indeed exists."
19. Ibid., March 30, 1983, citing this ruling.
20. John Barron, *KGB Today: The Hidden Hand* (New York: Reader's Digest Press, 1983), p. 15. The name of the agent was Lieutenant Colonel Mikhail Talebov.
21. *Le Monde* (Paris), December 31, 1982; *Avanti!*, December 19, 1982.
22. BTA communique from Sofia, November 25, 1982, in *Dossier on the Anatomy of a Calumny*, pp. 28–29, Italian version.
23. *Bulgaria*, state bulletin in English, December 6, 1982, citing *Rabotnichesko Delo*, December 1, 1982, p. 8.
24. *Bulgaria*, December 6, 1982, p. C3.
25. Nicholas Gage in *The New York Times*, March 23, 1983.
26. Ibid.
27. *Washington Post*, December 26, 1982, "Outlook" section.
28. See *Wall Street Journal* editorial "The Spy Wars," April 8, 1983.

CHAPTER **12**

1. *Il Messaggero* (Rome), December 6, 1982.
2. *La Repubblica* (Rome), July 15, 1983.
3. Boyan Traikov's interview with BTA, February 22, 1983, Sofia; text distributed by the press office of the Bulgarian embassy in Rome.
4. *Corriere della Sera* (Milan), January 22, 1983.
5. Ibid., December 7, 1982.
6. Ibid., March 30, 1983.
7. *Dossier on the Anatomy of a Calumny*, p. 62, Italian version.
8. *Il Giornale Nuovo* (Milan), December 1, 1982; *Il Messaggero*, December 1, 1982; *The New York Times*, December 2, 1982. On December 5, *Corriere della Sera* said Foreign Minister Colombo explained

that this affair "cannot be discussed at a political level," and referred to Gostev's proposal as an "unacceptable proposal."

9. *The New York Times*, December 2, 1982; *La Nazione* (Florence), December 2, 1982. Both these papers cite the Italian ambassador's report to the foreign ministry on his conversation in Sofia with the Bulgarian foreign ministry.
10. Oral Celik was identified by fellow Gray Wolves in a TV documentary on West Germany's second channel, ZDF, in May 1983.
11. Official BTA transcript of press conference, p. 77, Italian version.
12. Ibid., p. 92.
13. Ibid.
14. Ibid., p. 89.
15. Foreign Minister Colombo to Parliament, December 20, 1982.
16. *La Repubblica*, March 4, 1982, dispatch from Sofia reporting on interview with Farsetti's brothers.
17. Foreign Minister Colombo to Parliament, December 20, 1982.
18. So he told the press conference in Sofia on December 17, 1982.
19. Paris Interpol confirmed this to me.
20. *The New York Times*, January 25, 1983.
21. Paris Interpol, text of Italian request no. 2793/81A, dated October 26, 1982.
22. *Corriere della Sera*, December 23, 1982; *La Repubblica*, December 23, 1982.
23. Official BTA transcript of press conference, pp. 94–95, Italian version.
24. Bekir Celenk in ibid., p. 104.
25. In all his company offices scattered around Europe, he was never bothered by the police.
26. *The New York Times*, December 18, 1982.
27. Michael Ledeen, "The Bulgarian Connection and the Media," *Commentary*, June 1983.

CHAPTER **13**

1. As reported by BTA's London correspondent V. Krimov in BTA's January 1983 bulletin.
2. Ibid.
3. *Otecestvo*, no. 3, 1983.
4. Kirill Chenkin, *Andropov: Portrait of a Tsar* (Milan: Rizzoli, 1983), pp. 223–24. He refers to an American ex–prisoner of war in Korea who testified that Burchett had told him that he *personally* could have this prisoner shot. There is also a reference to courses taught by Burchett for Vietnam propagandists. Chenkin writes: "The aviator Paul Kniss testified in a libel claim of Australian ex-senator John Kane that Burchett appeared among prisoners of war in Chinese uniform. The witness testified: 'I am absolutely persuaded that he is a big shot in organizing the propaganda about U.S. use of bacteriological warfare' in Korea (charges which proved entirely unfounded)."

5. *La Repubblica* (Rome), January 5, 1983.
6. Ibid.; also reported in *Corriere della Sera* (Milan), *La Stampa* (Turin), and *Il Messaggero* (Rome).
7. *La Repubblica*, January 6, 1983; RAI-TV news, January 6, 1983; *Avanti!* (Rome), January 6, 1983; *Corriere della Sera*, January 6, 1983. I have the official text from the Italian foreign ministry, dated January 5, 1983.
8. Official BTA transcript of December 17 press conference, p. 92, Italian version.
9. *Il Giornale Nuovo* (Milan), January 15, 1983.
10. *La Repubblica*, November 26, 1982; Agence France Presse, United Press International, Reuters, all November 25, 1982, cited in *Dossier on the Anatomy of a Calumny*, p. 27, Italian version.
11. According to a report in *Il Giornale Nuovo*, January 15, 1983.
12. BTA, "News from Bulgaria," January 1983.
13. *The Times* (London), January 5, 1983; *The Sunday Times* (London), April 24, 1983.
14. On January 11, 1983, *Corriere della Sera* stated that Agca was notified of his ineligibility for the benefits of the Penitents' Law as early as December 29, 1981, while this law was under Parliamentary consideration. On January 11, 1983, *Avanti!* stated: "Agca was informed by the investigating magistrates and his own lawyers, when the law was passed in May 1982." The same report appeared in *La Repubblica*, January 11, 1983.
15. *La Repubblica*, December 3, 1982.
16. *Time*, March 14, 1983; *The New York Times*, March 23, 1983.
17. Boyan Traikov in a BTA interview, February 22, 1983, issued by the press office of the Bulgarian embassy in Rome.
18. *La Stampa*, April 23, 1983.
19. Boyan Traikov in the same BTA interview cited above, February 22, 1983.
20. *Il Giornale Nuovo*, February 21, 1983, referring to a formal letter from Judge Martella on January 28, 1983.
21. Associated Press, March 4, 1983.
22. *The New York Times*, January 27, 1983.
23. As cited in *n*. 10 above.
24. See also *Corriere della Sera*, December 8, 1982.
25. At a press conference, at the Bulgarian embassy in Rome, March 29, 1983.
26. *La Repubblica*, April 22, 1983.
27. At a press conference, at the Bulgarian embassy in Rome, March 29, 1983.
28. *Corriere della Sera*, March 30, 1983.
29. Ibid., May 17, 1983; *Il Giornale Nuovo*, May 16, 1983.
30. *Corriere della Sera*, April 23, 1983.
31. Ibid., March 30, 1983.
32. *Il Giornale Nuovo*, February 4, 1983.

33. *La Repubblica*, April 21, 1983; *L'Espresso* (Rome), May 8, 1983; *Corriere della Sera*, March 30, 1983, citing Consolo himself.
34. *La Repubblica*, December 17, 1982.
35. *Corriere della Sera*, December 16, 1982. *La Stampa*, December 16, 1982, stated: "The Bulgarian Connection was confirmed by a summit of the secret services before Parliament."
36. *The New York Times*, January 27, 1983.
37. *La Stampa*, December 16, 1982.
38. Ibid.; also in *Il Messaggero*, December 16, 1982.
39. *Washington Post*, December 13, 1982.

CHAPTER **14**

1. The staffer was Angelo Codevilla. I have asked if he was willing for me to report this, and he agreed.
2. The denial was made by Enzo Perlot, chief of press affairs for the foreign ministry. His letter appeared in *La Repubblica* (Rome) on January 29, 1983.
3. Senator Alfonse D'Amato at a press conference in Rome, February 11, 1983.
4. Judge Palermo's investigation turned up dozens of Turks, Syrians, Lebanese, Italians, and Armenians acting as drug enforcers abroad. But he has stated specifically that he has not ordered the arrest of a single Bulgarian. And my own evidence on Kintex in Chapters 7 and 16 confirms that only foreigners were used in such a capacity abroad.
5. *The Times* (London), February 2, 1983.
6. Ibid.
7. *The New York Times*, February 4, 1983.
8. *Le Monde* (Paris), December 29, 1982; *La Repubblica*, April 6, 1983. *Il Messaggero* (Rome) added in its report that Ambassador Martinet said, "The problem for us as for you was to decide if France should break relations with the East, or just condemn these new acts of interference in the democratic life of our country."
9. Judge Martella's ruling is reported in *The New York Times* of May 17, 1983, based on a Reuters dispatch.
10. Casey's belief up to November was reported in the *Los Angeles Times*, January 31, 1983.
11. Marvin Kalb broadcast on NBC "Nightly News," February 7, 1983.
12. *The New York Times*, February 9, 1983, Philip Taubman's account from Rome.
13. See *n*. 1 above. Codevilla has confirmed this account to me, with added details.
14. *The New York Times*, February 9, 1983.
15. Ibid.
16. Judy Harris was present at this conversation. Her notes of the talk, dated February 8, 1983, quote Pennachini as adding: "I was stunned to see a U.S. film from which I learned a great deal unknown to our secret services. Now either the TV network made this up, or else it had information unavailable to us." (He was referring to the NBC

White Paper.) In fact, this information was not available to *us* either (Marvin Kalb and me) from U.S. sources. It was all gathered by our own reporting abroad.

17. *The New York Times*, February 8, 1983. Additional details from *Avanti!* (Rome), February 11, 1983.
18. *The New York Times*, February 8, 1983.
19. Judy Harris's notes of this lunch at the Girarrosto Toscana in Rome, February 5, 1983.
20. See *n*. 13 for chapter 10, above.
21. *The New York Times*, February 9, 1983.
22. I have checked that personally everywhere save in Sofia, where my requests for information from the U.S. Embassy went unanswered.
23. Several correspondents known to me have had such briefings. I am not legally permitted to name the CIA officer involved, and wouldn't want to anyway. Colleagues passing through Rome on this story will know who I mean.
24. *The New York Times*, February 19, 1983; the briefing took place February 18.
25. See chapter 7, particularly p. 96. A high-ranking SISMI general told me that neither he nor anyone in his agency had received the information in the U.S. intelligence agency dossier from the United States or any other source. The same goes for Judge Martella.
26. Personal conversation, April 23, 1983.
27. *Corriere della Sera* (Milan), February 20, 1983; *Il Giornale Nuovo* (Milan), February 20, 1983.
28. Kalb's report on the three CIA men was broadcast on March 24, 1983. He was quoted in *La Repubblica*, March 25, 1983.
29. *The New York Times*, March 28, 1983, Reuters dispatch. On April 8, 1983, *The New York Times* reported a Bulgarian spokesman as saying that Iordan Mantarov "worked in Paris as a maintenance mechanic for Agromachineimpeks, a Government agency that exports farm equipment."
30. *Newsweek*, April 4, 1983. In the *Washington Post* of April 7, 1983, Michael Getler reported that "U.S. officials privately put no credence in the source" (Mantarov), thus agreeing with the Bulgarian ambassador to the United States who said at a press conference on July 7, 1983, that Mantarov was "a criminal who had never been in the Bulgarian secret service."
31. *The New York Times*, March 28, 1983.
32. Mr. Brzezinski said this to me in Rome, during the 1983 Trilateral Conference.

PART THREE: ANSWERS AND ENIGMAS

CHAPTER 15

1. *AIM Report—Accuracy in Media*, January 1983.
2. *The New York Times*, December 18, 1982.

3. *Le Point*, December 20, 1982.
4. According to Enzo Bettiza in *Il Giornale Nuovo* (Milan), December 14, 1982.
5. Ibid.
6. *The Economist*, December 11, 1982.
7. *The New York Times*, March 23, 1983.
8. This was Colonel Sverdlev's estimate, at my meeting with him in Munich.
9. *The New York Times*, March 23, 1983.
10. *Le Quotidien de Paris*, January 24, 25, 26, 1983.
11. *Le Nouvel Observateur*, December 18, 1982.
12. *Libération* (Paris), December 11–12, 1982.
13. As quoted in *La Repubblica* (Rome), July 27, 1983.
14. Colonel X in *Le Quotidien de Paris*.
15. Judy Harris found the stewardess for Balkanair; her name must be withheld for obvious reasons.
16. This may explain why the identifying numbers were not filed off the Browning used to shoot the Pope, since it was easily traceable to a neo-Nazi gun dealer.
17. *Corriere della Sera* (Milan), August 4, 1983.
18. Ibid., July 27, 1983.
19. Ibid., July 28, 1983; *Avanti!* (Rome), July 28, 1983. *Avanti!* refers to the Red Brigade connection in its account, which *Corriere della Sera* does not.
20. *La Repubblica*, March 1, 1983.
21. This was told to me on the highest authority, but until the case is closed I cannot reveal the source.
22. *La Repubblica*, December 16, 1982, March 9 and April 21, 1983; *Corriere della Sera*, March 1 and July 28, 1983.
23. *La Repubblica*, March 1, 1983.
24. For the drugs, see Senator Joseph R. Biden, *The Sicilian Connection: Southwest Asian Heroin en Route to the United States*, report to the Senate Committees on Foreign Relations and Judiciary, September 1980. For the arms, see *The New York Times*, December 18, 1982.
25. *L'Europeo*, December 20, 1982, interview with Judge Palermo.
26. *Avanti!*, December 23, 1982.
27. Ibid., January 5, 1983.
28. *The New York Times*, March 23, 1983.
29. Ibid., January 25, 1983.
30. *Le Soir* (Brussels), January 12, 13, 1983.
31. *Le Matin* (Paris), March 17, 18, 22, 1983. This is an enlargement of Stoerkel's original story in *L'Alsace*.

CHAPTER **16**

1. Turkish Military Intelligence source.
2. See chapters 2 and 3.
3. Ibid.

4. Ibid.
5. Personal interviews at Interior Ministry, Ankara, and with policeman "Selim Bey."
6. District Court Munich 1, ruling in civil injunction suit, October 1, 1982, cites this ruling of State Prosecutor's Office on July 17, 1981.
7. Ibid.
8. See Chapter 4.
9. See Chapter 8, p. 106.
10. The Turkish Martial Law Court's indictment of Abuzer Ugurlu, May 4, 1982.
11. *Le Matin* (Paris), March 17, 1983.
12. Ibid., March 18, 1983.
13. The indictment is dated May 4, 1982.
14. *Le Matin*, March 18, 1983.
15. TV documentary on Bavarian network Bayerischer Rundfunk, October 19, 1982.
16. This telex is addressed to Dr. Guenther von Lojewski of the Bayerischer Rundfunk, in response to telexed queries by Silvia Matthies and Beatrice Sonheuter on October 14, 1982.
17. Petition for restraining order before State Court Munich 1, September 22, 1982, argued by Mersan's attorney, Dr. Klaus Boele.
18. Cited in ruling of District Court Munich 1, decision by Presiding Judge Dr. Steinbrecht and Judges Dr. Wagner and Dr. Markwardt.
19. Letter addressed to State Court Munich 1, Ninth Chamber, by Mersan's attorney, Dr. Klaus Boele, dated October 21, 1982.
20. Jean-Marie Stoerkel, who discovered "Walter," was one of the reporters calling on Gultas. He described the incident to me.
21. I have the transcript of his interview, in which not one question was put to Mersan regarding his alleged connections with the Turkish Mafia and Abuzer Ugurlu; the accusations made by Suleyman Necati Topuz; the Turkish indictment of Selam Gultas, Mersan's patron in Munich, as a member of Ugurlu's band; and the nature of the Vardar Company by which Mersan had claimed to be employed.
22. Excerpts of these confidential Swiss police reports were given to a French reporter investigating the international arms-drug traffic for some years. He has given me copies.

CHAPTER **17**

1. *Le Monde* (Paris), December 3, 1983.
2. *The New York Times*, December 13, 1983. Bernard Gwertzman was the reporter; his story was called "Here's a Tale of Two Tales of Andropov."
3. Kirill Chenkin, *Andropov: Portrait of a Tsar* (Milan: Rizzoli, 1983).
4. *Los Angeles Times*, May 28, 1983.
5. *La Repubblica* (Rome), December 11, 1982.

INDEX

Abate, Antonio, 9, 194
ABC, 122, 130
Accomplices, 161–62, 206, 231
   named by Agca, 32, 109–10, 140, 148–49, 179, 207, 209
Accomplices, alleged, 26–27, 32–33, 35, 44–45, 51, 62, 64, 100
   composite drawing, 32–33, 55, 66
   named by Martella, 145–47
Afghanistan, 133
Agca, Adnan (brother of Mehmet Agca), 41, 42, 43
Agca, Ahmed (father of Mehmet Agca), 40
Agca, Fatma (sister of Mehmet Agca), 41, 43
Agca, Mehmet Ali, 3, 6, 21, 31–32, 33, 52, 62, 79, 138
   as all-purpose hit man, 196, 204–5, 206, 210, 231–32
   anomalies in record as terrorist, 44–45, 51, 101, 210
   charge against, 3
   childhood, family background, 17–18, 39–43
   claimed offered 3 million DM to kill John Paul, 112
   contacts with accomplices, 147
   credibility, 4–5, 56–57, 149, 151, 160, 170–76, 217–18, 229
   did not want to be freed from Italian jail, 141
   drank alcohol, 42, 78
   escape from Turkish prison, 19, 23, 29, 36, 51, 60, 92, 93, 112, 148, 194, 231, 232, 240n10
   European itinerary, 20–22, 23, 25–26, 75, 109
   fear of being killed in prison, 207
   financing of, 19, 20, 23, 28, 49–50, 71, 79, 101, 102, 111, 147
   forged letter to Col. Türkes from, 69–70
   image of, in press, 6, 9–10, 39–40, 80–81, 234; see also Agca, persona as terrorist killer
   imminent transfer to ordinary prison, 181
   implicating Bulgarian secret service and KGB, 140–41
   information gathered re, 231
   information supplied by, 32, 73, 110, 113, 135, 179, 243nn17, 18
   information supplied re plan to assassinate Walesa, 143, 209–10

Agca, Mehmet Ali (*cont'd*)
  intention to eliminate following shoot-
    ing, 4, 196, 206
  and Ipekci murder, 20, 46, 49, 50–51,
    56, 62, 78–79
  key to papal plot lay in past of, 100–104,
    105, 106, 108–12
  libeled Antonov, 234–35
  links with Bulgarian secret service, 216,
    225
  persona as terrorist killer, 51, 64, 70, 80,
    102, 113, 126
  personal characteristics, 11–12, 25, 43,
    79
  picked as sleeper, 50, 58, 101–3
  political ideology of, 25, 36, 42, 43–44,
    47, 74–75, 78–79, 206
  sanity issue, 9–11, 79, 93–94, 100, 188,
    189–90, 197
  sending signal through testimony to his
    interrogators, 217–18
  solitariness, 41, 42, 45
  sponsors, 79–80
  statements re Mersan, 223
  statements to reporters, 140–41
  telephone numbers supplied by, 22, 148,
    160, 172
  tests of interrogations of, 11; *see also*
    Confessions, statements (Agca)
  theory that coached in prison, 229–31,
    232
  threat to kill John Paul, 19–20, 51, 187,
    188
  ties to Col. Türkes, 239n1
  as time bomb to Bulgarians, 206
  trial, sentence, 6–7, 8, 9, 37
  see also Accomplices; Gun (attack on
    John Paul); Passports, false; Plot to
    kill John Paul II
Agca, Muzeyyen (mother of Mehmet
  Agca), 40, 41–43
Agromachineimpeks, 247n29
Ahmed (Syrian "student"), 20
Aivazov, Todor Stoyanov (aka "Kolev"),
  146, 147, 148, 149, 156–57, 165, 172,
  174, 176, 178
  Agca's description of apartment of, 173,
    243n17
  lying, 166–67
  named by Agca, 140, 207, 209
  at press conference, 160–61
AKINCILAR, 18, 73

Alawis, 42
Alawites, 39
Alexander II, tsar, 202
Alexiev, Alex, 117
Alsace, 213
Alsace, L' (newspaper), 224
Altan, Ahmet, 221
Amato, Nicoló, 6
Amin, Hafizullah, 125, 150
"Anarchy, The," 72–74
Anarchy and Terror in Turkey, 90–93
Andreev, Aleksandur, 173
Andropov, Yuri, 124, 138, 145, 146, 153,
  182, 190, 233
  coincidence of coming to power at time
    Bulgarian Connection came to light,
    227–28
  image as new leader of USSR, 228–29
  possible role in papal plot, 201, 203–4
  and theories re papal plot, 229
  and Western cover-up, 234
Angleton, James Jesus, 134
Ankara, 38
  Military Tribunal, 216
Ankara University, 42, 43, 45
Ansa (Italian state news agency), 169,
  235
Antonov, Ani, 173
Antonov, Rosica, 159, 173, 174–76
Antonov, Sergei Ivanov, 140, 144–46, 147,
  148, 149, 163, 166, 173, 182, 196
  Agca libeled, 234–35
  Agca testimony re, 243n17
  alibi, 170, 171, 172, 173
  arrest, 150, 152
  belief in innocence of, 169–70
  Bulgarian press conference re innocence
    of, 156–61
  Bulgarian security agent, 205
  continuing detention of, 175–76, 185, 191,
    197, 230
  lies, 195
  named by Agca, 207, 209
  phone in Rome, 172, 174, 207, 243n18
  U.S. intelligence comments on, 193
Antwerp, 212
Armenian Secret Liberation Organization, 73
Arms smuggling, 34, 74–75, 80, 81, 82–83,
  86, 88, 89, 90–93, 210–11, 212
  intelligence services and, 233
  Left/Right exchanges in, 90–91

Arms Smuggling and Terrorism (Mumcu), 85–88
Arrest warrants, 6, 209
  accomplices, 32–33, 147, 161–62
  Ay, Omer, 44–45, 54–55, 65, 66, 67, 76
  Sener, Mehmet, 106
  Tore, Teslim, 92
Arrests, 4–5, 109–10
Arsan, Henri, 211, 212
ASALA, 109
Ascherson, Neal, 127
  Polish August, The, 123
Ascoli-Piceno (prison), 230
Assassination:
  as instrument of Soviet policy, 125–26
Ataturk, Kemal, 46
Avanti! (newspaper), 85, 150
Ay, Omer, 27, 32–33, 35, 52, 54–55, 76, 100, 107
  alibi, 66
  arrested in Hamburg, 62, 64–68
  extradition hearings, 67–68
  proof of collusion, 51
  wanted by Turkish martial-law court, 44–45
Aytul, Cihan, 70

Badatioglu (of Dev Sol), 239n3
Bagci, Omer, 109–10, 112, 145, 146, 147, 159, 231
Balgat, Turkey, 92
Balkanair, 144, 148, 171, 176, 205, 248n15
BalkanShip (company), 94
Balkan-Tourist (company), 94
Bank accounts (Agca), 49–50, 71, 78–79, 102
Barron, John, 125
Barry, Robert L., 212
Basil II, emperor, 165
Batcharov (Mr.), 167
Baum, Gerhard, 72
Belgium, 212
Bennaui, Ahmed, 108
Bertolucci, Bernardo, 30
"Bey, Selim," 44–46, 47, 66
BKA, *see* Bundeskriminalamt (BKA)
Black market, 35, 52, 74, 217, 219
  see also Smuggling
BND (West Germany), 136, 180
Boele, Klaus, 249n17
Bourguiba, Habib, 22, 36

Brandt, Willy, 67
Brezhnev, Leonid, 117, 125, 129, 153, 181, 203, 227–28, 233
  John Paul's letter to (alleged), 116, 122–23, 137
British government, 4–5, 164, 170, 185
  intelligence service, 135–36
  MI-6, 180
Browning 9-mm automatic, *see* Gun (attack on John Paul)
Brzezinski, Zbigniew, 116, 196, 198
Budapest, Hungary, 122
Bulgaria:
  Agca in: 20, 22, 23, 28, 36, 52, 58, 101, 148, 172, 173–74; *see also* Sofia, Agca in
  all participants in papal plot operated in, 231
  attempted swap of Italian prisoners for Antonov, 159, 161, 164, 196–97
  campaign to destroy Agca's credibility, 135
  denied charges in *Reader's Digest* article, 134–35
  did not run agents outside borders, 189
  embassy radio traffic, 136, 179, 193
  espionage ring, Rome, 142–43, 207–10, 231–32
  failed to cooperate in smuggling investigation, 142
  hit list, 152–53, 155
  home base of Turkish Mafia, 59–60, 81
  lack of motive to kill John Paul, 124
  linchpin of arms/drugs smuggling, 74–75, 82–83, 85–88, 211–15
  press conference claiming Antonov's innocence, 156–61, 167
  state news agency reaction to Agca confession, 150–51, 152
  surrogate for Soviet Union, 29, 202, 204
  theory that agents acted without official knowledge, 185, 187, 188, 197, 202, 210, 229
Bulgarian Chancellery, Rome, 148
Bulgarian Connection, 28–30, 134, 142–55, 163–64, 176–77, 178–79, 181–82, 201
  charge that created by CIA, 168
  manipulation of public opinion re, 183–84, 185, 186–93, 195–98
  rejected as theory by U.S., 229
  reluctance of West to accept, 234–35

Bulgarian Connection (*cont'd*)
  and timing of Andropov's coming to
    power, 227–28
Bulgarian consulate, Rome, 148
Bulgarian embassy, Rome, 144, 166–67
"Bulgarian Factor," 109
Bulgarian secret service (DS, Darzhavna
    Sigurnost), 3, 29, 59, 60, 76, 116, 148,
    150, 202–8, 216, 232
  Agca link to, 225
  controlled Turkish Mafia, 84–85, 86, 88
  Godfather's links to, 93, 103, 104, 194,
    225
  integration of, with KGB, 201–15
  Mantarov defected from, 195
  and plot to kill John Paul, 96, 100, 111,
    113, 138, 142, 145, 146, 149
  ran Kintex, 94
Bulgarian Telegraph Agency (BTA), 150–
    51, 165, 169
  attacked *New York Times* for Gage ar-
    ticle, 196
Bulgar-Tabac (company), 111
Bundeskriminalamt (BKA) (West Ger-
    man police), 8, 33, 34, 35, 53–57, 60,
    62, 64, 65, 225
  check on Mersan, 218, 219
  Sterling's interviews with, 53–57, 60–61
  and Turkish immigrants, 60–61
Burchett, Wilfred, 165–66, 244n4
Burgas, Bulgaria, 82, 94, 95
Bush, George, 138, 229
Büyük Ankara (hotel), 81
Byelorussia, 120

Café Berlin, Sofia, 211
Calvi, Fabrizio, 213–15
Carter, Jimmy, 116, 194–95, 232
Casaroli, Cardinal Agostino, 9
Casey, William, 191–92, 196–97, 233
Castro, Fidel, 150
Catholic Committee for the Defense of
    the Rights of Believers (Lithuania),
    118
Catli, Abdullah, 92–93, 106–7, 111–12
CBS "Morning News," 130–31
Celebi, Musa Cerdar, 32, 145, 147, 162,
    231
Celenk, Bekir, 89–90, 92, 104, 112, 145,
    147, 185, 222, 239n10
  agent, Bulgarian secret service, 226
  contacts with Agca, 102, 205, 231

liaison for drug traffic, 142, 211, 213
named by Agca, 135
and papal plot, 111
paymaster for Agca, 147, 148, 161
questions re, at Bulgarian press confer-
    ence, 159–60, 161–62
Celik, Oral, 32, 39, 92, 93, 106, 112, 231,
    239n10
  identified by Gray Wolves, 244n10
  identified in St. Peter's Square photo-
    graph, 160
Chebrikov, Viktor, 229
Christian Democratic Party (Italy), 177
Christie, Agatha:
  Murder on the Orient Express, 46
*Chronicle of the Lithuanian Catholic
    Church*, 118
Church of Silence, 118
CIA, 5, 11, 109, 116, 132, 133–34, 135,
    138, 153, 154, 155, 233, 242n13
  accused of implication in papal plot, 134,
    135, 164, 168, 183
  attacked *New York Times* for Gage ar-
    ticle, 196
  attempt to assassinate Castro, 150
  claim of involvement/noninvolvement in
    investigation of papal plot, 8, 180, 184,
    186, 188
  and cover-up of papal plot, 234
  denied Italian proof of Bulgarian Con-
    nection, 137–38, 181–82, 185, 187–90,
    191–93, 197–98
  lack of aid to Italy, 194
  in Rome, 195
  "running" Agca (theory), 232–33
Clark, William, 192, 195, 197, 233
Codevilla, Angelo, 246nn1, 13
Colombo, Emilio, 161, 178, 192, 196–97,
    243n8
Colonel X., 202, 203, 204–5
Communist Party:
  Poland, 121, 124, 127, 129
  USSR, 116
Confessions, statements (Agca), 4–5, 11,
    13, 17, 18, 22, 41, 42, 110–11, 112,
    151–52, 171, 179, 193, 195, 209, 227,
    230
  confirmation of, 22
  Bulgarian Connection, 136, 182
  Ipekci murder, 48–49, 52, 78, 80,
    101
  re Mersan, 35–36

naming accomplices, sponsors, 135, 136, 147–51
published in *Milliyet*, 148, 159, 207
Consolo, Giuseppe, 158, 172, 174–75, 176, 230
Conspiracy theory, 11, 24
 cover-up of evidence of, 5–6, 7–8, 138–39
 dangers of exposing, 5
 proof of, 3–4, 10, 11, 27, 28, 31, 45, 96, 100–101, 138, 145, 148
 see also Plot to kill John Paul II
Continentale Storage (company), 224
Corriere della Sera (newspaper), 144, 145, 147–48, 149, 175, 177, 183, 235
 Agca confession in, 171
Cosa Nostra, 142
 see also Mafia
Cotur, Saim, 47
Craxi, Bettino, 169
Criminalpol (Italy), 211
Cudillo, Ernesto, 162
Cumhuriyet (newspaper), 81, 85, 89
Cupperi, Giancarlo, 9–10
Currency smuggling, 83
Cutolo, Raffaele, 230
Czechoslovakia, 118, 119, 120, 126, 133

Dag, Youssef, 33, 52, 108–9
Daily American (newspaper), 170
Damascus, 19
D'Amato, Alfonse, 192–95
Darzhavna Sigurnost, *see* Bulgarian secret service
Darida, Clelio, 142, 242n4
Demirel, Suleyman, 47
Demirsan, Metin, 239n10
Destabilization, 86, 89, 90, 95, 204
Détente, 7, 113, 131, 133
Dev Genc (revolutionary movement), 88
Dev-Sol ("Revolutionary Youth"), 72, 77, 80, 88, 90, 95, 239n3
Dezinformatsiya, 164, 169, 228
 see also Disinformation
DIGOS, 6, 17, 44, 54, 55, 56, 59, 76, 110, 146, 174
 and arrest of Antonov, 144
 commissioners of, at arrest of Omer Ay, 62–64
 commissioners of, on conspiracy theory, 24–28, 29–30, 31, 32, 35, 44

documents re Agca case, 30–33, 34–35, 36–38
list of 17 "Suspect Turkish Citizens," 92, 106–7
message to BKA re Agca statements, 218
Dimitrov, Georgi, 134
Din, Wakkas Salah al-, 211
Diplomacy, international:
 fears for, if Bulgarian Connection proved, 190, 191
Disinformation, 5, 70, 163, 179, 183
 in cover-up by Western governments, 233, 234
 in press, 166–70
 theory that was planted on Martella, 197, 232
Diskaya, Nadim, 82
Dontchev, Ivan Tomov, 143, 208–9, 210, 231
Dossier on the Anatomy of a Calumny (Bulgarian communiqué), 135
Dozier, James Lee, 142, 143, 179, 209, 242n7
Drug smuggling, 59, 86–88, 89, 90–91, 210, 211–12, 214, 221, 223–25
 distribution from Bulgaria, 207–8, 212
 intelligence services and, 233
DS, *see* Bulgarian secret service

East Germany (German Democratic Republic), 118
Ecevit, Bulent, 47, 48, 65, 77, 91, 107
Edirne, Turkey, 63, 76, 82
Elazig, Turkey, 40
Elizabeth II, queen of England, 21
EMEGIN BIRLIGI, 18
Erman, Nahir, 47–48, 50
Erzerum, Turkey, 95

Fabrique Nationale Herstal, 33
Falangists, 73
Fanfani, Amintor, 176
Farsetti, Paolo, 159, 161
FBI, 195
Fidan, Hyseyin, 67
FIDEF, 61
Firas, Abu, 101
France:
 intelligence service (SDECE), 8, 116, 180, 196

France (cont'd)
  supported Italian claim of Bulgarian
    Connection, 191
Frankfurt, 60, 212, 213
Free Trade Union Committee, 121

Gage, Nicholas, 116, 195–96, 210, 211,
    242n13
Gallucci, Achille, 3
Gaziantep, Turkey, 18, 89
Gelman, Harry, 153
German Democratic Republic, see East
    Germany
German neo-Nazis, 72
Germany, Federal Republic of, see West
    Germany
Getler, Michael, 247n30
Ghenev, Stefan, 157, 173
Gierek, Edward, 118
Giornale Nuovo, Il (newspaper), 184–85
Girgin, Mehmet, 73
Godfather, see Ugurlu, Abuzer (God-
    father of Turkish Mafia)
Goldwater, Barry, 192
Görgülü, Fahri, 75–77
Gotsev, Liuben, 159
Gray Wolves (ÜLKÜCÜLER), 17, 18, 33,
    40, 46, 49, 51, 54, 58, 65, 71, 73, 145,
    146
  Omer Ay as member, 44, 68
  Agca's alleged association with, 6, 25,
    75, 231
  arms smuggling, 92–93
  Godfather's links to, 104
  involvement in smuggling networks, 213
  Ipekci murder links, 77
  name, 238n4
  National Action Party, Samsun, 90
  and papal plot, 60, 111, 113, 205
  Türkes patron of, 69, 70
  Turkish Federation, 61
Great Britain, see British government
Greece, 204
Greene, Robert, 239n5
Grillmayer, Horst, 28, 33–34, 59, 104, 105,
    112, 146
Gromyko, Andrei, 115
Guardian (newspaper), 165–66
Gultas, Bekir, 221
Gultas, Chavit, 224, 225
Gultas, Selam, 105, 219, 220, 224, 249n21
  tried in absentia, 221, 223

Gun (attack on John Paul), 20, 23, 28, 32,
    33, 34, 104, 105, 109, 112, 146, 149,
    248n16
Gunes, Hasan Fehmi, 46, 52, 77–81,
    84
Gunes, Kutlan, 77
Gunes, Nizamettin, 77
Gunes, Utkan, 77
Güvensoy, Celehattin, 82, 84
Gwertzman, Bernard, 185–87

Habash, George, 25, 72, 73, 101
Hadarpaşa, Turkey, 82, 83
Haliton, Sayed, 239n3
HALKIN KURTULUSU, 18
Hamburg:
  Special Branch, 65–68
  Supreme Court, 67
Hammamet, Tunisia, 22, 108
Harris, Judy, 152, 153, 192, 210, 237n8,
    240n5, 246n16, 248n15
Helms, Richard, 198
Heroin, see Drug smuggling
Heroin Trail, The, 86–88
Hotel Archimede (Rome), 143, 237n8
Hotel du Lac (Tunis), 22, 36
Hotel Flamboyan, 112
Hotel Torino (Rome), 33
Hotel Victoria (Rome), 231
Hotel Vitosha–New Otani (Sofia), 20, 22,
    34, 35, 56, 102, 103–4, 147, 148, 162,
    173
  Agca-Mersan meetings at, 217
  drivers of smuggled goods at, 213–15,
    224
  meeting place for international smug-
    glers, 142, 211, 212
  meeting place of Turkish Mafia in Sofia,
    59, 89
  as State Security's hotel, 204–5
Hungary, 126, 133
Hurriyet (newspaper), 56, 89

Idealists (Turkey), 40, 111
Imposimato, Ferdinando, 101, 142, 143,
    207, 209, 231
  briefed Senator D'Amato, 192
Infelisi, Luciano, 3, 6, 27, 100, 148
Initiative Group for the Defense of the
    Rights of the Church, 120, 225
Intercommerz (Bulgarian trade organiza-
    tion), 94

Interpol, 11, 32, 55, 59, 75, 89, 106, 144, 216, 220, 225
  Ankara office, 44, 211
  "Red Bulletins," 62, 65
  warrant for Celenk, 161
Interpred (Bulgarian trade organization), 94
Ipekci, Abdi, 23, 59
  Agca's confession to murder of, 41, 80
  Celik rumored to be killer of, 92
  murder investigation, 77–78
  murder of, 10, 19, 36, 45–51, 52, 56, 71, 106, 221
Ipekci, Sybil, 48
Ipsala, Turkey, 82
Iran, 20
Istanbul, 211
  Military Tribunal, 20, 220–21
  "patrons," 89
Istanbul University, 45, 72
Italian judiciary, 3, 9, 11, 153, 163, 177–78, 183
  and Agca's credibility, 229
  and evidence of conspiracy, 141–42
  Western governments cast doubt on efficiency and integrity of, 135–36
Italian Questúra, 93, 175
Italy:
  Agca's travels in, 20 21
  attempted swap of Antonov for Italian prisoners, 159, 161, 164, 196–97
  Court of Appeals, Investigative Divisions, 158
  Court of Assizes, Investigative Divisions, 158
  destabilization, 204
  Ministry of Justice, 172
  secret service, 163–64
  Socialist Party, 169
  staging area for heroin distribution from Bulgaria, 207–8
  State Prosecutor's Office, 158, 163
  upheld Martella's findings, decisions, 176–79
Izvestia, 183

John XXIII, pope, 117
John Paul II, pope:
  Agca's letter threatening attack on, 19–20
  attempt on life of, 4, 5, 129
  letter to Brezhnev (alleged), 116, 122–23, 137
  pilgrimage to Poland, 117–18
  Russians' view of, 115–16
  as threat to Kremlin, 115–21, 122–24, 127–28, 129, 137
  warned in advance of attempt on his life, 8
  see also Plot to Kill John Paul II
Justice Party (Turkey), 47

Kadem, Sedat Sirri, 18, 36, 39, 42, 43, 51–52, 71–72
Kalb, Marvin, 122–23, 136–37, 182, 191, 195, 247n16
  update on White Paper, 152, 153
Kalotina, Bulgaria, 63, 76
Kamm, Henry, 163, 184, 212
Kane, Sir John, 244n4
Kapikule, Turkey, 82, 111–12
Kapitan Andreevo, Bulgaria, 63, 76
Karl Hoffman band, 72
Kartal-Maltepe military prison, 19, 51, 112, 148, 232
KGB, 3, 7, 119, 125, 133, 137, 138, 145, 146, 184, 229, 233
  Andropov head of, 201, 203–4, 227, 228
  Bulgaria surrogate for, 29, 202, 204
  Fifth Directorate, 228
  integration of Bulgarian secret service with, 201–15, 216
  and plot to kill John Paul II, 100, 113, 140, 188, 195–96
Khomeini, Ayatollah, 109
Kintex (Bulgarian state company), 84–88, 90, 91, 93, 94–96, 179, 207, 216, 246n4
  and arms/drugs smuggling, 94–96, 208, 212–15, 221, 224
  branch of DS First Department, 208
  operatives in Hotel Vitosha, 104
  and papal plot, 111
  Ugurlu relation with, 220, 225
Kissinger, Henry, 198
Kissler, Herr, 106
Kniss, Paul, 244n4
Koçakerim, Fikri, 59, 84
Koçyiğit, Hoca, 239n5
Koppel, Ted, 130
Kotov, Vladimir, 203
Kraft, Joseph, 6
Krastev, Donka, 174, 175
Krastev, Kosta, 174, 175

Kurdish Communist Party (PKK), 73, 80, 91
Kurdish Democratic Front, 73

Labernas, Galip, 87
Lagorio, Lelio, 177, 178–79, 184, 193, 242n*13*
Larussa, Adolfo, 158, 172, 174–75, 176, 230
Latvia, 118, 120
Lazzarini, Alfredo, 6
Lebanon, 18
Le Carré, John, 111, 233
Ledeen, Michael, 241n*20*
Left/Right (Turkish terrorists), 18, 46, 47, 70, 71, 72, 74–75, 88
  exchange of smuggled arms, 90–91, 213
  PLO training, 72–75
Letizia (Italian nun), 4, 206
Lewis, Flora, 190–91
Libera, Emilia, 242n*7*
Libération (newspaper), 203, 204
Literaturnaya Gazieta, 183
Lithuania, 118–19, 120
Los Angeles Times, 11, 94, 188–89, 193, 196, 197, 229
Lubachivsky, Myroslav, 124
Lugano, Switzerland, 213
Lugaresi, Nino, 180

McCarthy, Joseph, 132–33
Mafia, 142, 183
  see also Turkish Mafia
Malatya, Turkey, 39, 40, 43, 89
  Teachers' College, 42
Mamak Prison, Ankara, 225
"Man Who Shot the Pope, The" (NBC White Paper), 122–23
Mantarov, Iordan, 116, 195–97, 247nn*29*, *30*
Manyan, Julian, 27
Marcevski (Mr.), 167
Marchionne, Lidano, 32
Marenche, Alexandre de, 236n*8*
Markov, Georgi, 153
Markwardt, Judge Dr., 249n*18*
Marlboro cigarettes, 111
Marmara Coffeehouse, 48
Martella, Ilario, 37, 134, 135, 136, 143, 152, 170, 178, 179, 186, 196, 205, 209, 223, 226, 231
  Agca's confession to, 110, 111, 112

and Aivazov, 157
on Antonov, 171
and arrest of accomplices, 143–46, 147
arrest warrants, 32, 161
asked help of Italian intelligence service, 180
briefed D'Amato, 192
BTA stated U.S. influenced, 151
CIA on, 187
detention, investigation of Antonov, 158, 162–63, 175–76, 191
disinformation planted on (theory), 183, 197, 227, 232
and FBI, 194
investigation by, 13, 23, 30, 64, 99, 100, 109–10, 141, 173–74
investigation enlarged, 185
judicial communication that Agca had libeled Antonov, 234–35
lack of knowledge re Mersan, 216, 218
questioning the Krastevs, 175
report of investigation to be released, 234
threats against, 207
to Trento (conference with Palermo), 210, 211
Walesa investigation, 143
Martinet (Ambassador), 246n*8*
Mataraci, Tuncay, 220
Matin, Le (newspaper), 213, 224
Mattei, Enrico, 183
Matthies, Silvia, 222, 249n*16*
Mersan, Omer, 52, 53, 108, 173, 213–15, 216, 217–19, 220, 222, 226
  admissions of, 35–36
  Agca's contacts with, 20, 21, 22, 62, 104, 231
  Agca's statements re, 36–37
  arrested by German police and released, 55–57, 222–23
  DIGOS telex re, 34–35
  on file as heroin distributor, 223–25
  known to DEA, 225
  link between Agca and Bulgarian Connection, 28, 225
  middleman in passport transaction, 45, 56, 76, 77
  named by Agca, 102
  in papal plot, 111
  smuggling connection, 56–60, 63, 84, 105, 224–25
Mersan, Rafet, 222

Mersin, Turkey, 82
Messaggero, Il (newspaper), 127–28, 174
Middle East:
  arming of, 204, 210, 212
  see also Arms smuggling
Milliyet (newspaper), 19, 47, 48, 51, 56, 58, 67, 69, 110, 135
  publishing Agca's confession, 148, 159, 207
Mintoff, Dom, 22, 36
MIT (Turkey's intelligence service), 36, 47, 77, 102, 180
MLAPU (Marxist-Leninist Armed Propaganda Unit), 95
Monde, Le (newspaper), 150, 170, 227
Moro, Aldo, 183
Moslem Brotherhood, 109
Mossad, 101, 109, 152
Motive (papal plot), 51, 63–64, 79, 114, 116–17
  Agca, 12, 23, 25; *see also* Statement of Motivation
  Soviet, 122, 123, 137, 138, 184, 187, 195–96
  Western denials of Bulgarian/Soviet Connection, 190, 191, 197–98, 217
Mumcu, Ugur, 89, 90, 102, 218
  Arms Smuggling and Terrorism, 85–88
Munich, 212, 213, 223–24
  Narcotics Brigade, 225
  State Prosecutor's Office, 219, 222–23
Murder on the Orient Express (Christie), 46
Mushin, Nadine, 130
Mustafaeff, 20, 23, 26, 56, 104, 108, 217
  contacts with Agca, alleged, 21–22, 35, 36
  confirmation of Agca's statements re, 24, 29
  director of Bulgar-Tabac, 111
Mystery of Folding Door, 170, 173, 174

National Action Party (Turkey), 90, 92, 95
National Security Council (U.S.), 164
NATO, 39, 126, 131, 137, 207
  winter meeting, Brussels, 228
Nazi-Soviet Pact of 1939, 119
NBC, 191, 192, 195, 210
  White Paper: "The Man Who Shot the Pope," 122–23, 136–37
  White Paper: update of, 152

Nese, Marco, 149
Nevsehir, Turkey, 44, 45, 54, 55, 62, 66, 68, 76, 92, 107
New Camorra, 230
New Republic, 133
New York Times, 4, 5, 6, 116, 132, 136, 163, 166, 170, 187, 192, 193, 201, 232, 242n*13*
  articles re papal plot, 176, 183–84, 185–87, 190–91, 195–96, 210, 211
  Safire article on Bulgarian Connection, 181–82
Newsday, 86, 87, 88, 89
Newsweek, 132, 185
Newton, Lowell, 27, 100, 160
"Nightline" (television program), 130
Nouvel Observateur, Le (newspaper), 203
Novo Hotel Europa (Sofia), 34

Oflu, Isamil, 92
Oktoberfest bombing (Munich), 72
Osmanli Bank, Istanbul, 63, 111
Osservatore Romano (newspaper), 8–9
Ostpolitik, 61
Otecestvo (Bulgarian review), 165
Ottoman Empire, 202
Oymen, Orsan, 58–60, 67
  Der Spiegel article on Omer Ay, 66
  story on Agca confession, 110–12
Ozgun, Faruk, 26, 44, 63

Pace e Guerra (newspaper), 168–69
Pacem in Terris (religious front group), 120
Paese-Sera (newspaper), 167–68
Palermo, Carlo, 142, 147, 161–62, 189, 207, 208, 246n*4*
  smuggling investigation, 211–12
Palestine Rejection Front (PFLP), 72
Palestinian training camps, 18, 19, 36, 72–74
  Agca at, 42, 43, 50, 51–52, 71–73, 101
Palma de Majorca, 21, 26, 112, 147, 148
Pancirolo, Rev. Romeo, 241n*18*
Panitza, John "Dimi," 99
Paris *Herald-Tribune*, 188
Park Hotel, 35
Parliamentary Oversight Committee (Italy), 177
Passport dates, questions re, 63, 76, 111–12

Passports, false, 23, 32, 34–35, 44–45, 51, 54–55, 56, 83, 107, 173, 231
  Agca: Faruk Ozgun, 20, 26, 28, 44, 76, 92, 100–101, 102, 104, 108, 111–12, 217, 219
  Agca: Yoginder Singh, 20, 103, 111
  provided by Omer Ay, 62–63, 65–66, 67
Paul VI, pope, 117
Paynes, Les, 239n5
Penitents' Law (Italy), 170, 185
Pennachini, Erminio, 192–93
Pensione Hiberia (Rome), 143
Pensione Isa (Rome), 31–32, 100, 143, 147
Pera Palas Hotel, Istanbul, 46, 51
Peretz, Marty, 133
Perlot, Enzo, 246n2
Photographs (attempt on life of John Paul), 27, 55, 66, 160
Pliska Hotel, 94
PLO, 72, 109
Plot to kill John Paul II, 7, 31, 64, 79, 80–81, 86, 96, 100, 110, 113–14, 122–23, 138–39, 142, 145, 146, 205–7
  as act of destabilization, 177–79
  blame in, 229–30
  connection to Lech Walesa plot, 231, 232
  cover for, 89
  enigma re, 227–35
  Godfather's role in, 107, 111, 112
  key to, in Agca's past, 100–108
  manipulation of public opinion re, 183–98
  nature of, 216
  questions in, 10
  as revealed in Agca's confessions, 110–12
  theories re, 30, 57, 101, 109, 185, 186–90, 192, 201, 202, 229–30, 232
  theory that killers acted on their own, 185, 187, 188, 197, 202, 210, 229
  Turkish Mafia in, 74–75
  see also Conspiracy theory; Western governments; Western intelligence services
Poland, 79, 121–24, 126–27, 129, 133, 196
  John Paul's pilgrimage to, 115, 117–18
  see also Solidarity
Pol-Bir (Turkish police union), 47
Pol-Der (Turkish police union), 47
Police reports, foreign, 11, 17, 21, 33
Polimya (journal), 115

Polish August, The (Ascherson), 123
Polititcheskoye Samoobrazovanie, 120–21
Popov, Jivkov, 150
Potter, Tony, 136, 152
Prague, 86, 122
Pravda, 168, 229
Press:
  coverage of action re attempt on life of John Paul, 4, 5, 27–28, 144–45, 147–48
  coverage of Agca's confessions, 144–45, 146–48, 150
  disinformation in, 165–70
  international, 70, 100, 158, 210, 234–35
  portrayal of Agca in, 39–40
  reaction of U.S. to Sterling Reader's Digest article, 131–35
Priore, Rosario, 143, 209
Public, Western:
  deceived by leaders re conspiracy, 3–4
  ignorance of documented proof of conspiracy, 10, 11
Public opinion:
  manipulation of, 183–98, 201

Qaddafi, Muammar al-, 109
Quotidien de Paris, Le (newspaper), 203

Rabb, Maxwell, 168, 192
Radio Vatican, 117
RAI-TV (Rome), 166–67
Rand Corporation, 117
Reader's Digest, 4, 93, 99, 109, 110, 113, 224
  journalistic reaction to publication of Sterling article, 131–34
  Sterling article, 136, 151–52, 160, 168, 185, 218
Reagan, Ronald, 190, 191, 232
Reagan administration, 177, 179, 183, 185, 190, 195
  see also U.S. government
Red Brigades, 26, 153, 230, 248n18
  collaboration with Bulgarian secret service, 209
  kidnapping of James Lee Dozier, 142–43, 242n7
  penetration of, by Bulgarian spy ring, 207
"Red Bulletins," 44, 62, 65
Repubblica, La (newspaper), 166, 174, 175, 185, 209

Right (the), *see* Left/Right (Turkish terrorists)

Rognoni, Virgilio, 178, 181, 182, 192, 242n7

Rome:
Bulgarian espionage ring in, 207

Rosenfeld, Steve, 132

Royce, Knut, 239n5

Rumania, 119

Rural Solidarity, 127, 129

Sadlowski, Father, 127

Safire, William, 181–82, 192

Saipem (firm), 33

Samsun, Turkey, 90, 95

Santiapichi, Severino, 9, 13, 23, 24, 27, 37, 100, 101, 194, 231

Santini, Father Mariano, 230

Santovito, Giuseppe, 33

Saral, Atalay, 211, 222

Savasta, Antonio, 242n7

Savov, Dimiter, 195

Scheer, Mathias, 67–68

Schmidt, Helmut, 61

Scricciolo, Luigi, 142–43, 179, 189, 195, 208–9, 210, 231

Scricciolo, Paola, 208

SDECE, *see* France, intelligence service

Segreto istruttorio, 30, 64, 110, 144, 158, 234

Sener, Mehmet, 49, 106–7, 111, 112

Sengil, Muzaffer, 95

Serangah, Haydar, 20

Sever, Tayyar, 71, 72

Singh, Yoginder, 172

SISDE, 174, 178, 179

SISMI (Italian military intelligence service), 17, 30, 55, 105, 136, 154–55, 168, 174, 178, 179, 193, 194
report re Soviet role in international terrorism, 137
reports, 33–34
visit to Agca in prison, 179–80
and Walesa plot, 210, 231

Smugglers:
terrorists reliance on, 73–74

Smuggling, 56, 59–60, 80, 84–85, 86–91, 106, 110, 217
arrests ordered, 142
Bulgaria linchpin of, 74–75, 82–83, 85–88, 211–15
Kintex, 94–96, 208, 212–15, 221, 224

Mersan's connection with, 34, 35, 56–60
see also Arms smuggling; Drug smuggling

Social Democrats (West Germany), 61, 62

Socialist Republican Party (Turkey), 47

Sofia, 34, 211
Agca in, 20, 22, 28–29, 56, 89, 102, 103, 104, 111, 231
center of smuggling, 59, 213, 224

Sofia Grand Hotel, 34

Soir, Le (newspaper), 212–13

Solidarity (*Solidarnosc*), 79, 116, 118, 121–24, 127–29, 137, 143, 177, 187, 196, 209

Sonnheuter, Beatrice "Trixie," 222, 249n16

Soviet Union, 4, 62, 153
advisers to Kintex from, 96
assassination as instrument of state policy of, 125–26, 150
and Bulgarian spy ring in Rome, 207
Bulgaria surrogate for, 29, 202, 204
master plan to force collapse of Turkey's democratic order, 86, 91
press treatment in U.S., 131, 132–34
reaction to free trade union movement in Poland, 122–25, 126–27, 129
role in international terrorism, 7, 137
role in papal plot, 100, 113, 115–16, 131, 138–39, 142, 145, 153–54, 188, 190–91; *see also* Motive, Soviet
view of John Paul, 120–21
Western governments denied evidence of involvement in papal plot, 183, 184–85
see also KGB

Spadolini, Giovanni, 180

Speakes, Larry, 201

Spiegel, Der, 66

Stalin, Joseph, 117

Stampa, La (newspaper), 3, 6

State Farm Ataturk Orman Çiftiliği, 69

Statement of Motivation, 9–10, 11, 13, 17–23, 24, 54, 189, 194, 231–32
questions raised by, 23

Steinbrecht, Judge Dr., 249n18

Stepanovicius, Bishop, 119

Sterling, Claire:
accused by Bulgarians of creating plot, 134, 151, 152, 154

Sterling, Claire (*cont'd*)
  allegedly on Bulgarian hit list, 152–53, 155
  attacks on, 165
  Reader's Digest article, 131–34, 136, 151, 160, 168, 185, 218
  Terror Network, The, 29, 38–39, 54, 85, 137
Sterling, Tom, 62
Stoerkel, Jean-Marie, 213, 214, 249n*20*
"Strategic Directorate," 147
Strikes (Polish), 121, 128, 129
Sulzberger, Cyrus, 204
Sunnites, 39
Svarinskas, Alfonsas, 118
Sverdlev, Stefan, 202–3, 204, 205–7, 208
Swiss Narcotics Brigade, Zug, 224
Switzerland, 212, 213
  police reports, 217

Takkeci, Judge-Colonel Suleyman, 47, 48, 50, 221
Tap-Ek (company), 94
Taskin, Hasan, 33, 54
Taskin, Pehlnel, 54
Tass, 118, 120, 129, 183
  response to *Reader's Digest* article, 133–34
Taubman, Philip, 192, 193–94
Tek, Haydar, 45
Telemen, Ibrahim, 82–84, 112, 217
Television:
  coverage of Sterling *Reader's Digest* article, 131–32
  documentaries re papal shooting, 27–28
Terror Network, The (Sterling), 29, 38–39, 54, 85, 137
Terrorism, international, 7, 12, 133
  Bulgarian role in, 29, 204
  contraband weapons in, 34; *see also* Arms smuggling
  Soviet role in, 7, 137
Terrorists, Turkish:
  in West Germany, 61–62
  see also Left/Right (Turkish terrorists)
Terzieff, Mr., 215, 216, 225
Thames Television, 27–28
Time, 122, 132, 137
Times (London), 170, 190
Tintner, Otto, 33
TIR truck system (Transports Internation-

aux Routiers), 64, 67, 82, 83, 91, 94, 103, 105, 212, 214, 221, 224–25
TKP (Turkish Communist party), 77
Topuz, Suleyman Necati, 59, 60, 84–85, 217, 218, 249n*21*
Tore, Teslim, 19, 36, 38–39, 43, 52, 77, 101
  gunrunning, 91–92
  Turkish People's Liberation Movement, 72
Torre, Pio La, 183
Torrebruno, Giuliano, 210
Toth, Robert, 188–90, 191–92, 229
Trabzon, Turkey, 86, 95
Traikov, Boyan, 157–58, 159–60, 161, 162, 165, 167, 171–72, 197
  list of Agca's "lies," 172–76
Traikonov, Mr., 215
Trevisin, Gabriella, 159, 161
Tribunal of Liberty, 148, 158, 163, 170, 208
Trieste, 212
Trotsky, Leon, 125
Tunis:
  Agca in, 108
Tunis Air, 33
Tunisia, 26, 108
Tunisia Welcome Service (travel agency), 108
Turker, Mustafa, 39
Türkes, Col. Alpaslan, 49, 69–70, 239nn*1*, 5
  trial, 77–78
Turkey, 6, 29, 126, 161
  army takeover, 29, 34, 39, 46, 61, 70, 73–74, 220
  Big Fright, 47
  black market, 217, 219
  Customs Ministry, 82
  plot to destroy democratic order in, 86, 89, 90, 91, 95, 204
  terrorism, 18–19, 23, 38–39, 45, 70–71, 74–75, 86, 88, 90
  terrorist kill-rate, 38, 39, 74
  see also Left/Right (Turkish terrorists)
Turkish Federation, 54, 61
Turkish General Staff, 44
  Anarchy and Terror in Turkey, 90–93
Turkish immigrant workers (*Gastarbeiter*) (West Germany), 21, 54, 56, 60–62
  claimed to have been smuggled by TIR, 67
Turkish Journalists' Union, 48

Turkish Mafia, 59–60, 64, 74–77, 79–80, 81, 82–96, 104, 107, 135, 142, 146, 194, 220–22, 225–26, 249n21
agent of Kintex, 208
co-Godfathers, 111, 135, 143, 145, 214
dealt with Gray Wolves in papal plot, 205
gambling casinos, 222
Omer Mersan's ties to, 63
political uses of, 86–91
role in papal plot, 110–11, 113
running Agca, 102
smuggling activities, 214
Turkish People's Liberation Army (THKPC), 18, 91
Turkish People's Liberation Movement (THKO), 18, 19, 72
Turkiye Is Bankasi, 49
Turkkoglu, Gihat, 33
Turkmen, Ilderen, 47

Ugurlu, Abuzer (Godfather of Turkish Mafia), 59, 60, 63, 64, 76, 77, 79–80, 89, 92, 102, 106, 107, 220, 231, 249n21
and Agca's stay in Sofia, 102–3
agent of Bulgarian secret service, 96, 103, 104, 194, 225–26
arrest, trial of, 77, 220–21
debut as Godfather, 86
links to Gray Wolves, 104
"loaned" Agca to Bulgarian secret service, 146
named by Agca, 135
Omer Mersan lieutenant of, 218
organizer of arms/drugs smuggling, 82–83, 211
questioned by Martella, 110
role in papal plot, 107, 111, 112
Ugurlu, Ahmet, 82
Ugurlu, Mustafa, 82, 89, 221
Ugurlu, Sabri, 82
Ugurlu brothers (family), 59, 79, 84
Ukraine, 118, 119–20
ÜLKÜCÜLER, see Gray Wolves
Uniate Church (Ukraine), 119–20
Union of Soviet Socialist Republics, see Soviet Union
United Kingdom, see British government
U.S. Congress, Senate Intelligence Committee, 181, 182, 194
U.S. Department of State, 88, 164

U.S. Drug Enforcement Administration, 225
U.S. embassy:
Rome, 155, 193
Sofia, 88
Ankara, 75
U.S. Freedom of Information Act, 137–38
U.S. government:
position on papal plot, 153, 154, 182–83, 184, 186, 191, 193–95, 197–98, 229
see also Reagan administration
U.S. intelligence analysts, 137
lack of cooperation with Italy, 225–26
stand on Bulgarian Connection, 183–84
theories re papal plot, 186–88, 192, 197

Vaivods, Bishop, 120
Van den Dreschd, Jacques, 125
Vardar Export-Import Company, 22, 35, 56–57, 59–60, 105, 106, 213, 217, 218, 249n21
closed and reopened, 219, 223
involvement in smuggling, 221, 222, 224–25
not investigated by German police, 220
Varna, Bulgaria, 59, 82, 86, 92, 94, 95, 211
Vasilev, Želio (aka "Petrov"), 140, 146, 147, 148, 156–57, 173, 174, 176
named by Agca, 207, 209
at press conference, 159, 160
Vassoula (ship), 80
Vatican (the), 117, 122
silence of, 8–9
"subversive" activities of, 120–21
Villiers, Gérard de, 103
Von Lojewski, Guenther, 249n16
Vreeland, Frederick "Frecky," 152–53, 154–55

Wagner, Judge Dr., 249n18
Walesa, Lech, 121, 123, 129, 143
plot to kill, 177, 189, 209–10, 234, 235
plot to kill/papal plot connection, 231, 232
received by John Paul in Rome, 127–28
Wall Street Journal, 132, 180, 211–12
Wallner, Özay, 105
Walter (truck driver), 213–15, 222, 224

Warsaw Pact, 177, 208
  army maneuvers "Soyuz '81," 129
  heroin smuggling as policy of, 208
Washington Post, 6, 132, 153, 180, 240n4,
  247n30
Weil, Simone, 21
West, the:
  attitude toward plot to kill John Paul II,
    227–35
  degradation of, 204
  see also Western governments
West Berlin, 60
West Germany (Germany, Federal Republic of):
  Criminal police, *see* Bundeskriminalamt
    (BKA)
  Gray Wolves' Federation, 145
  intelligence service, 135–36, 163, 185
  issue of Agca in, 21, 25, 53, 54–55,
    75
  secret service, 5
  Turkish immigrant workers, 21, 54, 56,
    60–62
  Turkish terrorists in, 21, 61–62
Western governments:
  covering up for USSR, 7, 131
  disinclined to confront Russians, 233
  lack of cooperation with Italy, 26, 107–8,
    216–17

"leaks" to media, in manipulation of
  public opinion, 183–98
suppression of conspiracy information,
  4, 11, 24, 37, 45, 86, 131, 135–39, 146,
  153–54, 163–64, 172, 182, 183, 190–
  91, 217, 233–34
Western intelligence services, 5, 135–36,
  137, 180
  arms/drug smuggling and, 233
  cover-up, 233–34
  lack of cooperation with Italy, 194, 225
  suspected of planting disinformation on
    Martella, 229–30, 232–33
"Wet work," 204, 205
Wiesenthal, Simon, 104–5
Witnesses, 27, 32
Wojtyla, Karol, *see* John Paul II, pope
Wyszynski, Stefan Cardinal, 123, 127, 129

Yapi ve Kredi Bankasi, 49
Yesiltepe, Turkey, 39
Yilmaz, Galip, 44, 55, 67
  forged passport, 65–66
Yugo-Import (company), 223
Yugoslavia, 204
Yurtaslan, Ali, 92–93

Zagladin, Vadim, 123
Zhivkov, Todor, 202, 204